CONSUMER BEHAVIOUR AND ECONOMIC GROWTH IN THE MODERN ECONOMY

Consumer Behaviour and Economic Growth in the Modern Economy

Edited by Henri Baudet
and Henk van der Meulen

CROOM HELM
London & Canberra

© 1982 Henri Baudet and Henk van der Meulen
Croom Helm Ltd, 2-10 St John's Road, London SW11

British Library Cataloguing in Publication Data

Consumer behaviour and economic growth
   in the modern economy.
   1. Consumption (Economic)—History—
   Congresses
   I. Baudet, Henri   II. Meulen, Henk van der
   339.4'7   HB801

ISBN 0-7099-0646-3

Printed and bound in Great Britain by
Biddles Ltd, Guildford and King's Lynn

2204129

CONTENTS

FOREWORD

Towards the end of the spring 1981, an International Conference on *Consumer Behaviour and Economic Growth in the Modern Economy* was held at the State University of Groningen (Netherlands).

The Department of Socio-Economic History, which organized the Conference, was particularly motivated in this work because of its specialist involvement in the forthcoming Eighth International Congress on Economic History, due to take place in Budapest in 1982.

In view of the necessarily tight restrictions on discussion time and publishing space, provided by the Congress, a separate, preliminary conference seemed to be an obvious opportunity for a more satisfactory, in-depth treatment of this important and topical subject. This book forms a permanent record of the Transactions of the Groningen Conference.

For the publication of the book in the technical sense, thanks are due to the Publishing House of Croom Helm, who were very willing to undertake to publish the Transactions in book form. Thanks are also due for the translations and textual corrections particularly to Fred Gemmell, who was most willing - and not for the first time - to put his excellent abilities as a translator at our service. Last, but certainly not least, our thanks for the layout and typescript, which were required by the printing method adopted for the production of this book, go to Cathy Drenth, who has attended to both with a personal involvement and dedication peculiarly her own.

May this book find its way into the wide and rapidly expanding circle of those interested in problems of consumption and economic growth.

CONTRIBUTORS AND COMMENTATORS

Contributors

Maurice Aymard	: Professor of economic history, Institut des Sciences de l'Homme, Paris, France.
Henri Baudet	: Professor of economic and social history, State University of Groningen, Netherlands.
David Felix	: Professor of economic history, Washington University, St. Louis, United States.
Henk van der Meulen	: Lecturer in economic and social history, State University of Groningen, Netherlands.
Walter Minchinton	: Professor of economic history, University of Exeter, United Kingdom.
Peter Scholliers	: Lecturer in contemporary history, Free University of Brussels, Belgium.
Hans J. Teuteberg	: Professor of history, Wilhelms University, Münster, F.R.Germany.

Chris Vandenbroeke   : Lecturer in social
                             history, University of
                             Ghent, Belgium.

Mine Yasuzawa   : Professor of economic
                             history, Kobe College,
                             Nishinomiya, Japan.

Commentators

Leonard Blussé   : State University Leyden
                             Leyden, Netherlands.

Jos Delbeke   : University of Louvain,
                             Belgium.

Jan Willem Drukker   : State University of
                             Groningen, Netherlands.

Patricia van den Eeckhout : Free University of
                             Brussels, Belgium.

Richard Griffiths   : Free University of
                             Amsterdam, Netherlands.

Frits van Holthoon   : State University of
                             Groningen, Netherlands.

Peter Klein   : Erasmus University,
                             Rotterdam, Netherlands.

Paul Klep   : University of Nijmegen,
                             Netherlands.

Angus Maddison   : State University of
                             Groningen, Netherlands.

Gé Prince   : State University of
                             Groningen, Netherlands.

François Souty   : State University of
                             Groningen, Netherlands.

Chapter 1
INTRODUCTION

Henri Baudet and Henk van der Meulen

Chapter 1

INTRODUCTION

Henri Baudet and Henk van der Meulen

GENERAL

"How did 19th and 20th century economic growth
change consumer behaviour and consumption patterns
in Europe, Asia and the New World?"
    This question is the concern of the seven
papers in this book. They are contributions dealing with vastly different geographical units. In
point of fact, as far as dating is concerned, the
contributions range, for the most part, over the
history of consumption in the 19th and 20th centuries and rely heavily on empirical research. Consumption is described and analysed with the help of
its manifestations which we now know: *mostly* statistical material dealing with quantities, prices
and incomes, supplemented by sources of a more
qualitative character. In the case of such research, the formulation of questions and the quality of the statistical material used determine, to
a great extent, the ultimate result. Besides, it
is almost inevitable that different research
workers differ greatly in the matter of approach,
analysis and results. This book is no exception.
This introduction is consequently intended to make
an attempt to place the seven papers more or less
in a framework of a theoretical kind for which,
naturally, the editors of this volume are solely
responsible, as they are for the placing of the
papers in the framework.
    The starting point for this collection of
papers is the pursuit of modern, historical consumer research. The extent to which the demand
side of the economic process interests economists
and historians, and the manner in which it interests them, have been rather subject to change, in
the course of the past 70 years or so; not least
influenced by the expanding social sciences and the

3

mainly post-war developments in economic theory. There are, in any case, clearly two trends: the interest in consumption as a subject of research is increasing and the nature of the interest is changing - from the traditional "standard of living debate" to a rather large number of different aspects.

In this introduction, we shall be dealing with three different lines of approach to consumption in the past which each demand their own methodology and, all three, in a sense even their own discipline (theoretical framework).

Firstly, there is the historical development of the standard of living, involving particularly that of the working class. This is the "traditional" historical approach, which, in no way, means that it is out of date. The main concern here is the development of (frequently improvement in) the "shopping basket", both quantitatively and qualitatively. The growing purchasing power of the masses brings with it social progress as well as a sharply improving general state of public health. The shifts among various groups of consumer goods which emerge from budgetary researches over a period of time, have engaged the attention of many research workers ever since the work of Ernst Engel and his well-known law (of 1857).

Secondly, there is (collective) consumer behaviour. How do consumers adapt to changes in their material environment, changes which occur gradually, but also frequently by fits and starts, in a revolutionary way? The range of consumer goods *and* the means many people have to acquire them (see the first aspect) change dramatically in the 19th and 20th centuries. Life style and markets change rapidly and consumers adapt to them. "The power to become habituated to his surroundings is a marked characteristic of mankind".[1]

This approach to consumption brings us face to face with the phenomenon of adjustment: the adjustment of demand to supply, possibly promoted by a positive inclination on the part of societies to accept new products (innovations).

This phenomenon, as well as the interaction between the demand and supply sides of the market, which is called into being by this innovative behaviour, is considered by us to be part of historical processes of a socio-psychological character.

Thirdly and finally, there is the connexion between business cycles and consumption. This approach

4

currently enjoys a growing interest on the part of writers concerned with the history of consumption, and this volume also bears witness to this fact.

This aspect certainly includes a modern standard of living debate based on macro-economics. During the Groningen Conference there was in fact some talk by one of the commentators of a "standard of living debate in disguise". Yet this does not do justice to recent profound questioning and much modern research in this field. Besides, it is mainly concerned with the relationship between business cycles and consumption and not solely with increasing purchasing power and patterns of consumption. We have merely to think of the immense field of research presented by the problem of changing income distribution. In this respect, the working class is naturally no longer the only group being considered.

However, business cycle research can also be focused on the connexion between the various cyclical stages and the innovative behaviour of both consumer and producer. It is obvious, in this connexion, that particularly the periods of depression and the lowest points reached before the upturn are of interest. The tendency which can be observed in consumers to react innovatively, precisely at these periods, forms, as it were, a parallel to Schumpeter's economic theory, whose starting point, as is well known, was the innovative behaviour of the entrepreneur.

It will be abundantly clear from the above remarks that the three lines of approach mentioned are not in any way mutually exclusive. In the end, it is a matter of various ways of looking at one single phenomenon, i.e. human consumption, however many forms it may take.

THE FIRST ASPECT : STANDARD OF LIVING

No argument is needed for the fact that the interest of historians in consumption grew very slowly and is now scarcely a hundred years old and that publications of good quality began to be produced about the turn of the century. Nor it is necessary to argue that interest, at that time, was mainly focused on the working-class standard of living which, following a lengthy period of immobility, began relatively late to move (upwards), and, finally, that emotional involvement with social abuses was the strongest incentive to all this.

5

In later years, these specialist researches were mainly slotted into dissertations on the Industrial Revolution. We shall revert to this later. Nevertheless, research purely into living standard remained a subject apart. Gradually, other than purely workers' budgets began to figure in it. Particularly after the Second World War, a link developed between this type of consumer research and studies of economic growth. At this moment, great attention is being paid particularly to the connexion between the standard of living and the level of economic activity, and this is understandable, in view of the depression of the 80's which seems to lie ahead of us. Our third line of approach will concentrate on this.

The quantitative material for research into the standard of living was provided by the surveys instituted in the 19th century, of the well-being and (particularly) the afflictions of the working class. These surveys were the outcome of the "Social Question" and the cautious beginning of social legislation. They were concerned with working and living conditions, workers' budgets and incomes. The beginning is naturally very important, but reviewed over longish periods, the information would seem indeed to be of secondary importance. There is a lack of usable statistics of family consumption in most countries until (well into) the period between the two World Wars. Consequently we are dependent, for the 19th century and a considerable part of the 20th, on case studies, having some normative validity, and on a great deal of indirect and sometimes fortuitous information, and for the rest, on the resourcefulness of the researcher himself in deducing data from material collected primarily, or even entirely, for other purposes.

Usable data are, for example, those of a fiscal nature derived from official statistics, especially those from the Excise, of course. This kind of data, however, serves, at best, to provide an insight into averages of per capita income and consumption and usually provides few starting points for disaggregation. Data on the 'macro'-composition of the shopping basket are of the same kind. Statistics of production, imports, goods in transit and exports can be helpful, provided they have reliability which, in a number of cases, however, cannot fail to be described as slight.

Finally, in this connexion, mention may be made of the research being carried out in Belgium, at the Universities of Ghent and Bruges, on anthropo-

metric characteristics. This comes down to the
analysis and exploitation of test reports on recruits for the Belgian armed forces. All kinds of
data from these reports, especially shifts in height
and weight, are being correlated, in this research,
with developments in the dietary pattern.

If, certainly for the first period, attention
was focused on diet and, above all, the standard of
living was, in principle, measured against it, the
announcement that the field of vision had gradually
opened out does not, of course, report anything new.
With economic development and social emancipation,
the share of expenditure on food in the budget has
been reduced, a fact which is in complete conformity
with Engel's Law (1857). With the gradual rise in
the standard of living and, ultimately, the increase
in so-called discretionary purchasing power (that is
the amount which is left when personal income is reduced by the basic costs of subsistence, taxation
and savings), the consumers' ordering of preferences
has become a more and more important, widely varying
element in what is taking place in the field of consumption.

The development of the standard of living (initially that of the working class, but subsequently
more widely understood; measured, in the first instance, against the level of supply with respect to
the prime necessities of life, and subsequently expanded to a much wider range of consumer goods) is
no longer central - in any case, no longer exclusi-
vely central - to the study of the history of consumption. There, the problems posed by the ordering of preferences have come to occupy a considerable amount of space. What is more, as already
stated, all sectors of consumption have come under
review, and the whole of the theory of utility and
value (and, incidentally, a good slice of economic
theory) has been brought in. In this way, a historically speaking new type of question, deviating
entirely from tradition, is being asked; if we want
to trot out an old formulation and give it a new
content, we can say that it is now more a question
of way of life, of life style than of mere standard
of living.

To enquiries about "what", numerous enquiries about
"how" and "why" have been added: how the ordering
of preferences works exactly, how this ordering
comes about, and why, in a historical context, preferences have arisen in a definite period and within
a given market in the way in which they have arisen,
why consumers have decided on their choices: certain

7

goods have caught on and others have been non-starters as far as consumers' shopping baskets are concerned. In short: what has been going on in human beings.

Six of the seven papers in this volume more or less fit into the pattern described above. Attention is paid to the traditional standard of living concept but, in no single case, is it an objective in itself.

- Peter Scholliers and Chris Vandenbroeke regard the development of food consumption patterns as being influenced, inter alia, by the process of industrialization and especially by the disciplinary effect of work which appeared with industrialization; the suppression of a distinct leisure preference which they see in the Ancien Régime. We shall revert to this in our concluding review.
- Henri Baudet and Henk van der Meulen use (food) consumption patterns, as deduced from (principally workers') budgets and food production statistics, on the one hand for discussions about more or less individual behaviour and a reconsideration of Engel's Law, and on the other hand, long-term collective developments are mirrored in other macro-economic developments.
- Maurice Aymard's paper goes into primarily physical changes in food consumption in France and Italy after 1500. Here, welfare development means pretty well literally the development of (physical) well-being. We count ourselves as being happy to see in this contribution a representative of the typical French 'ultra long-wave' (longue durée) approach.
- Mine Yasuzawa involves in her, geographically highly differentiated review of the living standard of the 'ordinary' Japanese, above all socio-cultural backgrounds, as well as the socio-political watershed of 1868, the end of the Tokugawa period.
- The paper by David Felix is concerned with an area (Latin America) which, put guardedly, can be counted among the less developed economies, having, for that reason, a number of special problems. Concepts such as standard of living and social emancipation play a somewhat different part here,

especially in their mutual relationship.
- The contribution by Walter Minchinton largely falls outside this aspect. We shall discuss it in our consideration of the second method of approach.
- Hans Teuteberg finally offers us a careful review of German food consumption after 1850. As with Maurice Aymard's contribution, this involves time series with respect to *consumed* quantities of a large number of foodstuffs. Teuteberg then provides a valuable contribution to the discussion revolving round specific methodological problems connected with this kind of research.

THE SECOND ASPECT : CONSUMPTION AND LIFE STYLE

In the 19th and 20th centuries, the Western World presents a picture of a stronger-than-ever model of product development and innovation. Changes in person-product relations have never, in the past, particularly attracted the attention of economic historians. It was a considerable number of years after the Second World War before people realized that the whole problem of product development and innovation, consumer behaviour and consumption in a developing industrial society, represented an important field of research in economic history. It is true that elements of the problem had already been previously discussed, but more often than not in isolation or, at any rate, not in the complex context in which the problem is now seen.
    This situation can be explained from at least three angles:

Firstly, we obviously did not see how promising a comprehensive formulation of the problem, in the above-mentioned sense, could be. Consequently, there was no necessity for research into the many kinds of relations which figure in this field.

Secondly, there was no economic theory explicitly occupied with the influence of the demand side on the market process (i.e. otherwise than in an absolutely general sense), on the structure of production and on the direction in which production could develop.

And thirdly, multi- or pluri-disciplinary research, indispensable for the handling of consumer behaviour problems, was scarcely developed some 20

9

years ago. The use by historians of not only economic theory but also sociology, social psychology
and other behavioural sciences does not go back any
further than the 60's. Only then did it gradually
become possible to study processes such as industrial development and product innovation, explicitly
from such a (consumer) behaviour standpoint.

The Industrial Revolution and industrialization
in a more general sense were, historically speaking,
successively looked at from a 'heroic' standpoint
(the triumph of technology), a 'sociological' standpoint (the emancipation of the working class) and an
'economic' angle. Starting from this last aspect,
it is possible to undertake special research into
the demand side of the economic process, which is a
collective consequence of individual *behaviour*. For
the rest, this does not mean to say that, in the
first two cases, no attention was given to consumption. But the point at issue was either an objective datum - in the first case - or purely the
workers' standard of living - in the second case.

Changes in habits and needs, changes in systems
of preference in a situation of increasing prosperity were likewise not subjects which economists were
primarily interested in.

Consumer preferences were, in theory, ultimately definitive for the composition of the production
package, but how these preferences originated and
developed, long remained in the 'black box'. Relative prices supplied, in any case, the 'most desirable' way out. If we understand him correctly,
Rostow went a step further by recognizing the connexion between the growth of the economy and the
consumers' willingness to accept innovations.

The readiness to innovate as a *collective* attribute
of consumers originates from two mutually connected
developments:
On the one hand, with increasing prosperity, an
ever-increasing number of consumers with purchasing
power available for innovations (i.e. discretionary
purchasing power) and, on the other hand, standard-
ized production of uniform consumer goods leading
to mass production.

While the number of products, manufactured in
massive, uniform series, increases, this process is
simultaneously stimulated, from the demand side, by
a large number of circumstances. Transport facilities, an increasing number of communication media
(in which publicity and advertizing can be included),
the availability of energy in new forms (gas, electricity) and many other infrastructural provisions

(also those connected with public administration), all these factors have promoted uniformity in consumption *and* in consumers' aspirations.

This can be seen as a characterisitic of the era of mass production and mass consumption in which we live. The process of industrialization involved a process of homogenization which, in the course of a century or so, was to permeate every part of society. Developments in the political or institutional field (e.g. with respect to credit facilities) will not be pursued here, but they were naturally no less important.

Throughout the ages, highly innovative periods have alternated with periods which, in this respect, showed a certain stability. Again and again, there seem to have been periods of relative 'equilibrium' when there was, so to speak, talk of a certain harmony between man and his environment, the backdrop against which society develops. We can call this harmony 'identity'. But this identity is constantly being threatened by all kinds of factors including the propensity to innovate, which engages our special attention here.

This propensity to innovation is, on the one hand, always present (as a fundamental human characteristic), but, on the other hand, seems to vary pretty much in intensity. For this reason, some periods are more strongly and more deeply affected by innovations, resulting in the latter evoking in us an illusion of stagnation, a stagnation which is, naturally, seen from the standpoint of innovation. In this connexion, we should of course, refer to Schumpeter's (exogenous) cyclical theory. In our opinion, however, one can just as well refer to even longer waves (of the Kondratieff type) or even to the secular trend (the ultra long wave - 'longue durée' - if you like.

Innovations, by their very nature, disturb existing forms of equilibrium, destroy established social relationships and threaten, as already stated, the identity of a society. Against the creativity of potential innovators - and we ought to have a look at who they are precisely - society must set another kind of creativity, if it wishes to hold its own against the 'threatening' character of processes of change, and not perish. This creativity (that is the creativity of people who have to live and work with the new 'products', whatever they are) can be described as *mental flexibility*, the capacity for creating one's own personal, dependable world again and again in changed circumstances, making identification possible all over

11

again.

In contemporary industrial society, the question of consumption, as an expression of the process of reaction described above, has had a positive and fundamental influence on the economic process. As far as this is concerned, the supply side still lags behind, but the arrears are being reduced reasonably quickly. Developments in consumer behaviour are increasingly leading to adjustments on the production side, which, eventually has to focus on demand. The effects which these adjustments entail are perceptible in all sectors of economic life. Moreover, there is a distinct possibility that the same part was played by consumers throughout past ages. However, the clues that lead to such a hypothesis, unfortunately become blurred all too quickly. Anyhow, the cardinal importance that shoudl be ascribed to consumer *behaviour*, i.e. to the demand side of the market process, is now clear to us.

Hitherto, the vast majority of economists ignored these behavioural factors, and most economic historians had just as little interest in this field. It is the behavioural sciences which have occupied themselves in recent years with theories concerning consumer behaviour, among other things: behavioural sciences, with which mainstream economics did not so much as want any dealings. Nevertheless, economic science could not go on ignoring knowledge acquired in this way: for example, the insight into the stimulating influence which consumers, as a movement, may have on economic development and the insight into the complexity of the mechanisms of choice and decision which play a part here.

Psycho-economics has consequently developed, in a relatively short time, into an important branch of the old, somewhat obstinate tree, or, to use another metaphor, the proverbial ugly duckling has turned into a swan, with positive authority, which can no longer be dismissed from one's thoughts. Suffice it here to name the work of Katona, which strikes the reader now as somewhat dated, but which, thirty years ago, was basic to the new field of study.

Economic history, in its turn, had every reason to pursue this exciting development. Because historical research into economic behaviour does not, in any way, have to be limited to the modern industrial period, the comparison of behaviour at various periods can lead to a better understanding of differences in types of behaviour

12

in one and the same period (e.g. today).

Such research may perhaps lead to a general insight into the part played by collective behaviour patterns in economic activity. It is true that, up to now, sources are available to an inadequate extent only, i.e. as inadequately accessible and usable data. It is, in our opinion, a question of better research strategy, possibly of a reformulation of the objectives of this research, so as to produce an adequate amount of desirable data. We have no doubt that there *are* sources. Think, for example, both for the pre-industrial and the industrial period, of texts, literature (also belles-lettres, fiction), pictures, advertisements, statistics of consumption, catalogues (inter alia, from mail order firms), notarial archives, auction catalogues, inventories and films.

The historical problem which ought, in any case, to be studied, can be defined in general terms as follows: What induces or constrains people constantly to change their pattern of choice (in consumption)? Why do they accept these changes and how do they therefore become consumers of an enormous variety of new products, which are the result of continual developments on the supply side? Why do they buy the new products, or, in any case, admit them into their private world, so that they are able, in a certain sense, to identify with them gradually, but do this time and again? How do people continually adapt to the new circumstances and, vice-versa, what influence in its turn, has the development of taste, style and habits on the part of the consuming public on the structure and policy of production (of the decisions of producers)?

Such a comprehensive formulation means neither more nor less than the whole problem area of cultural modernization. The social sciences, economic science and several brilliant examples taken from cultural sociology have devoted their attention to this field of study, but have gradually restricted themselves to several very special aspects so that the original problem has largely disappeared. The analysis of processes of change in their totality was never the favourite pursuit of the social sciences, and, in the opinion, for example, of Norbert Elias, it still isn't.[2] The introduction of quantitative methods of analysis based on models, the widespread use of ceteris paribus provisos have likewise made it possible succesfully to isolate and investigate various constituent problems. Economic research into consumer behaviour, in particular, has become possible.

This development is of great importance to economic history which is able to make profitable use of many of the insights provided by such new methods of research. Norbert Elias found that, in the social sciences, more often than not, neither the questions to be asked, nor the methods and techniques, nor the necessary information were on hand for undertaking an analysis of *genetic processes*. This meant processes of genesis and change. (Put in simple terms: the questions of 'how' and 'why'). The assembling of information, all too frequently without too much understanding of analytical techniques and (technical) possibilities, is a typically historical specialization. We are indebted to it for a large number of case studies wich are sometimes of a high, scientific standard. But economic history must, like economics, now develop in this field a set of tools, perhaps the one envisaged by Elias.

At this stage it is useful to mention four points:

<u>Firstly</u>, with regard to pre-industrial innovations – which do not especially occupy our attention in this volume – we consider that, however many obvious differences can be cited, the same statement of the problem can be used as for the modern period. The wheel, the plough, the clock, spectacles, the gun and, later on, candles, stoves, chairs, knives, forks and spoons, handkerchiefs, soap, perfume, tobacco and many innovations in food and clothing – this list is thoroughly arbitrary – can be considered in essentially the same way as the products introduced in the 19th and 20th centuries, such as matches, sewing machines, bicycles, vacuum cleaners, aspirin, motor-cars, radio and television, central heating, aeroplanes, refrigerators or ballpoint pens. This list could also include all kinds of new versions of existing products, especially through the use of new materials such as plastic, artificial fibres, etc. The techniques of research in certain periods could very well correlate with developments in the field of available raw materials. (The opposite, however, is likely to have arisen too).

<u>Secondly</u>, it is not only production, whether industrial or not (cottage industries), which brings society face to face with innovations. This may very well be brought about by trade too; the

14

(geographical) diffusion of innovations was and is achieved mostly by trade. In this connexion, it is of interest to note that wars have (in a way) been a powerful stimulus to commerce and, in that way, have brought about considerable changes in the western consumption package, as well as in the materials and techniques employed. It is superfluous to add that this occurred not only through the opening up of new markets etc. but also through product innovation and/or the introduction of new production methods even as a product of war. This connexion between wars and product innovation is, in itself, worth thorough investigation. A number of different starting points are available for such studies, but most of them lie outside the specific parview of person/product relationships, as we view them here.

Thirdly, theory should also do justice to the braking forces on the consumption side. What is the nature, the strength of this 'countervailing power', which Galbraith talks about in another connexion? Is it, *on the one hand*, that people have adapted more and more easily during the last few decades to the torrent of new goods on offer – and this rush is, in itself curious enough – however much this readiness to adapt also constitutes a necessary extension of the dynamic in modern production, and *on the other hand*, considerable resistance is being offered. Consumers have resisted a considerable number of the many post-war innovations. There is no reason to assume that such resistence is a typical present-day phenomenon. A large number of anti-innovative figures from the literary past are characteristic witnesses to this fact. And it was not just Galsworthy's Soames Forsyte and Dickens' Mrs. Skewton who refused to have anything to do with changing times. This kind of resistance, however, can be measured nowadays and that is, naturally, a new datum.

The above is not intended, in any way, to say that literature – and above all the novel, for obvious reasons – is of little importance as a source for our type of research. In a way, pretty well everything lends itself, of course, to being a possible source of the history of people and things. But, above all, the analysis of literature is a source of information about opinions, emotions, behaviour and sometimes colourful details which are, more often than not, hard to come by or completely unobtainable from other sources.

Acceptance or rejection? Consumer behaviour at, and especially between these extreme points, can be usefully considered against the background of the stages which make up the career of a product. If, in this scheme, acceptance is mentioned, it is, in the first instance, only provisional. Even during the subsequent diffusion stages, anything may go wrong. An excellent study in this special field is, for example, one by *Hägerstrand* who uses an interesting honeycomb model. It is true that the use of such a model is limited, but there are promising possibilities of improvement by way of extensions. A model of consumer behaviour, such as *Lancaster's*, appears to be eminently useful, at a certain level, for studying historic diffusion processes. The Research Group in Socio-Economic History of the University of Groningen presented three examples of such an application at the Sixth International Conference on Economic History at Copenhagen in 1974. In this kind of research, much can be gained from using data which are to be found, sometimes remarkably well preserved, in company records.

During the adoption stage, full acceptance can eventually be said to occur: practically the whole of the potential market has been penetrated. But, between 10% and 100% penetration, certain products may very well (relatively speaking) fail. Finally, we find problems of a completely different kind at the assimilation stage. We use this term to describe the 'counter-offensive' of fully accepted innovations, which, having been left to the capricious taste and arbitrary choice of the consumers in the previous stages, eventually exercise an almost autonomous authority over the habits and life style of a society. Typical examples from the recent past are the car and television, both products with an extremely high acceptance score, which have an ever-increasing influence on the forming of habits. The assimilation process has, in itself, considerable side effects which, in their turn, sometimes give rise to further innovations.

Fourthly, there is the question whether consumer goods of all kinds can all be treated alike and therefore studied by the same method. Engel's Law, which points to relatively declining spending on food with rising personal income, unintentionally implies that classification can be useful. Without complementary research, it is not clear whether innovations in the field of nutrition, clothing and housing, communication (roads, newspapers, tele-

16

phone, etc.), hygiene, pharmaceuticals, non-essential luxuries or whatever, can be treated in the same way. A second criterion for classification can be the question whether goods are wasted (directly) in the consumption process, or not (and are, consequently, often relatively cheap or dear): goods which are *consumed* against goods which are *used*. Here too, there is an obvious distinction in the method of analysis.

Furthermore, it is possible to link classification, not to the goods (or services) themselves, but to the functions which are fulfilled by goods or combinations of goods. These functions can be widely different for one and the same item. Two examples to clarify this: Food can serve to appease hunger, to keep up physical strength, but also as a means of communication (the dinner, the business lunch), and as a religious symbol too (the host, bread and wine, (holy) water). Water is, for that matter, pretty well the most impressive example imaginable of multiple applicability.
Most books are for reading or decorating your bookshelves. Or, as the Dutch literary critic, Lodewijk van Deyssel, once wrote in an article about the work of the previous generation of writers to his own, "They provide a handy supply of paper for cleaning combs or using in the lavatory".[3] That was a way-out example of alternative use for consumer goods.

What functions are fulfilled by products depends, in this view, on how the consumer thinks he can use them, how he looks at certain goods. Products which fail or 'fizzle out' in the function at cerentrepreneur intended for them, are sometimes accepted (again) in a completely different capacity. The best - Dutch - example of this is still, we think, the bicycle, very much back with us as a keep-fit aid.

Such a 'functional' method of investigating consumption takes us away from the products themselves - and, incidentally, largely from the producer-suppliers too - and brings us nearer to the consumer-enquirers and their behaviour. *Kelvin Lancaster* made it quite clear that the more or less traditional tools of economic theory are not completely wasted when this happens. Consumption, as an activity, can be seen as a mirror image of production: with combination of consumer goods as the input, after processing, supplying certain, desirable functions as the output. Such an approach also

17

offers scope for innovations, both as inputs for
the consumption process (a 'traditional' form of
innovation) and also as new processing methods - we
should almost say 'new combinations' - and new outputs (functions). Analytically speaking, it is a
question here of a certain number of functions at a
certain moment of time, which can be fulfilled by
an essentially unlimited quantity of goods.

We have investigated very extensively the second
aspect, consumer behaviour, especially with regard
to innovations; firstly, because this aspect has
been occupying our attention for a very long time.
Secondly, although it frequently came up for discussion at the Groningen Conference, it did so to
a lesser extent than the first and third aspects -
in our own contribution too.
    Actually only one paper, the one by Walter
Minchinton, comes wholly within this scope. It is
comprehensive rather than analytical. A subject
such as 'Convention, Fashion and Consumption' takes
us, however, in any case direct to the heart of the
complex of problems which we have previously attempted to explain.
    Mine Yasuzawa discusses 'Life Styles' in a
wider presentation of historical Japanese patterns
of consumption. She sees the life style - quite
rightly - mirrored in the consumption package.
    David Felix highlights aspects of behaviour in
pointing to the distinct preference of Latin-
American societies for European and North American
products. Veblen's demonstration effect plays an
important part here. What is one doing, for example, with a refrigerator with no food to put in
it or - worse still - no electricity supply to con-
nect it to?
    Peter Scholliers and Chris Vandenbroeke talk
about leisure preference and the glorious past -
at least as far as leisure is concerned. They are
concerned here, however, more with the control of
consumer behaviour (by the producers) than with
behaviour itself.
    Finally, Maurice Aymard, Hans Teuteberg, Henri
Baudet and Henk van der Meulen, in their contributions, range only incidentally over the field of
consumer behaviour and innovations. They provide
here a survey of available data, on various levels
of aggregation, and a provisional evaluation of
this data on the part of the last two contributors,
linked to the ideas propounded by Engel.

THE THIRD ASPECT : CONSUMPTION AND BUSINESS CYCLES

Having said all this, we can be brief about the
third and last aspect which we distinguish: a macro-
economic look at consumption and economic development, that is to say, the relationship between the
business cycles and consumer demand. Here we distinguish two problems areas.

The *first*, of a broader character than the
second, is the problem of the general connexion between consumer behaviour, cyclic movements in the
economy and economic growth. A start was made,
after the Second World War, with the study of behaviour with respect to the economic cycle because
of the need for some prognostic insight to use for
a highly desirable control of the business cycle
phenomenon. It is obvious that an investigation
should be made into how far theory and empiricism
interlock. At first, the theoretical beginnings
had reason to borrow from *Keynes*, *Chamberlain*,
Joan Robinson and the later (neo-)Keynesians; but
we need not discuss them further here. The period
between the two World Wars was empirical, naturally
an . ideal hunting ground for tracking down the connexion between consumption and crisis. Thereafter,
during the post-war years, research was carried out
to discover a possible periodicity in behaviour
with the help of consumer opinion polls. The results of these polls could be compared with, on the
one hand, discernable purchasing behaviour and, on
the other hand, the business trend. Such research
inspired economic historians to undertake further
study of consumption and consumer behaviour in
(mutatis mutandis) comparable pre-war years, in the
first place, naturally, the depression of the 30's
and, later, the whole period between the two World
Wars. Gradually, this type of research was taken
up in many places in Europe and outside. Very soon,
it was no longer restricted to the period 1920-1940
but began to cover the whole of the 19th century
and also what is called the pre-industrial period.
Pre-industrial should, in our opinion, be understood, in this context, to mean the period preceding
any mention of mass production and mass consumption.
But let us disregard the latter.

More important is the fact that, in this research
into the pre-industrial period, use is being made
of cliometric methods in addition to, in American
parlance, pre-cliometric or 'traditional' methods.
The two are, however, hard to bring into line with
each other.

The cliometrists or scientific historians, as they are pleased to call themselves, occupy themselves with the testing and refining of theoretical concepts. Incidentally, they make use of econometric models, which they make themselves, if necessary. Their aim is on-going theory formulating and, as a rule, seeing how their theories work out in political and social practice. The traditionalists' more autonomous historical approach doubtless will not, and can not, manage it without a theoretical economic basis, but it is not primarily aimed at the development of paradigms, capable of explaining the past and predicting the future. Against the certainty of the cliometrists, the more traditionally orientated historians oppose their characteristic scepticism and pronounced feeling for relativity. For this reason, it is not easy to see on what common denominator the who schools of thought could ultimately united.

Yet, among the New Economic Historians, a pronounced tendency is developing in this direction.

"The genuine differences between scientific and traditional historians over subject, matter, methods, and style should not obscure their more numerous and more fundamental affinities and complementaries.
... while scientific and traditional history are different and, in some respects, competing modes of research, they are neither mutually exclusive nor intrinsically antagonistic. Quite on the contrary, precisely because each mode has a comparative advantage in certain domains of research; they supplement and enrich each other".

This quotation has been taken from Robert William Fogel. We know no statement with which we could agree more.

The second problem in this aspect, that of the consumer and innovation, leads to several further remarks with regard to the cliometrics (or the New Economic History).

Schumpeter has already been mentioned by us. He denied wellnigh all creativity, every initiative on the consumption side of the economic process and looked upon (product)innovation as pretty well the exclusive activity of entrepreneurs. The slight reservation which we slip into this observation ('wellnigh' and 'pretty well') does full justice to

Schumpeter, we think. Anyhow, he was never quite
so biased. Yet his ideas in other situations were
hardly capable of shades of meaning: it is exclu-
sively the innovating entrepreneur who keeps the
cycle and trend moving and consequently is able to
pull a stagnating economy out of the depths again.
Initiatives on the part of the consumer are negligible from this point of view.

This rigour in neo-classical economic thinking also
clearly dominates the work of cliometrists in
regard to the influence of preference schemes i.e.
of changes in taste, aspirations and life style and
of the way of thinking (for it does indeed, come
down to this) on business cycles and economic
growth. More econometric approaches involve matter
like technology, labour (size and composition of
the population), capital, categorial and personal
distribution of incomes and, sometimes, institutional backgrounds. The exchange of ideas between
cliometrists and more traditionally orientated
historians is complicated here, not primarily in
the area of methodology, but by the problem of
definition. Neither business conditions nor growth
create problems in this area, but the question of
what is understood by change certainly does.

After the Second World War and, undoubtedly under
the influence of the complex of problems posed by
the developing countries, economic science showed
an increasing readiness to throw open to debate
many and various exogenous variables within the
theory, something for which it had originally felt
little attraction (the so-called 'data'): political
and socio-political factors, the system of justice,
religion and social structures, family relationships, psychic aspects, behavioural components, and
others too, and to recognize them, consequently, as
a source of explanation - other than 'datum',
'black box' or 'ceteris paribus provisos'. In some
cases, several of these factors themselves became
endogenous - we are thinking here, naturally, of
facets of consumer behaviour. An identical readiness must be demanded of cliometrists with regard
to the complex of problems posed by consumer behaviour, a readiness which, witness the important
contribution of David Felix in this volume, is
gradually increasing. There is a clear demonstration here how a deliberately econometric-historic
research project can have a broad view: on the one
hand, of a number of behavioural aspects of the
Latin-American consumption problem, and on the

21

other hand, of a number of exogenous factors which
we have already mentioned in the political and
social fields.

If, with Felix, interest in economic growth and
development problems of the lesser developed countries leads to a different view of consumer behaviour and politics, the other writers in this
volume take the same path, but in the opposite
direction. Researches into consumption and consumer behaviour lead more or less to problems revolving round distribution, growth and business
cycles. So we think, the complementarity which
Fogel speaks of was touched upon in Groningen.

Three views of consumption are proposed here in
order to bring unity to seven separate papers
written by nine authors of differing scientific
backgrounds, again from seven different countries.
(We could also day they come from three different
continents.) Finally, let us emphasize that our
being able to make the above enumeration at this
point indicates a project that is based on large-
scale, international co-operation, which we hope
will not be restricted to this book and the
Congress in Budapest in 1982.

NOTES

1. J.M. Keynes, The Economic Consequences of
the Peace, London, 1919.
2. Norbert Elias, Ueber dem Prozess der Zivi-
lisation, Bern/München, 1969; Einleitung (Introduction to this new edition).
3. "Hun boeken komen ons werkelijk van pas
als kammenschoonmaakpapier en op onze plee's".
Van Deyssel was famous (and feared) for his in-
sulting literary critiques. These keep being re-
printed, perhaps as a warning to writers of all
times.

Chapter 2

THE TRANSITION FROM TRADITIONAL TO MODERN PATTERNS OF DEMAND IN BELGIUM

Peter Scholliers and Chris Vandenbroeke

Chapter 2

THE TRANSITION FROM TRADITIONAL TO MODERN PATTERNS OF DEMAND IN BELGIUM

Peter Scholliers and Chris Vandenbroeke

Among the many possible approaches to social history
one important topic involves a precise description
of the living standard of, and the study of consumer
spending by the population. Central to this topic
are the adjustments which have taken place since the
19th century, when the fabric of society was funda-
mentally changed as a result of industrialization.
It is indeed generally accepted that a marked
improvement in the standard of living of the average
population started during the last quarter of the
19th century, but this trend is least of all to be
considered as a linear process. Until well into the
20th century, numerous, rather abrupt interruptions
will repeatedly occur. Furthermore, a fresh break
can be seen in consumer behaviour since the 1960's,
from which point a growing preference emerges for
tertiary consumption, in general, and leisure, in
particular. Ever more symptoms indicate that interest in material goods has reached a turning point.
In this sense, we can assume with J. Fourastie: "un
peuple dont le niveau de vie s'élève, se préoccupe
de son genre de vie d'une manière croissante; il en
vient même très vite à sacrifier son niveau de vie
à son genre de vie".[1] The restless craving for
wealth and possessions - an attitude which is in-
herent in a capitalist society - is increasingly
contested and exchanged for more deeply-rooted human
values such as sociability, spontaneity, personal
development, diminishing use of labour, and "leisure
preference". One by one, these are values that had
been strongly developed during the Ancien Régime and
the early years of the 19th century, but were
largely lost with industrialization. The recent
interest in, and glorification of the past, which is
to be found almost everywhere, assure us most
emphatically that implicit faith in economic development had led merely to escalating frustrations.

25

Very strong feelings of displeasure are revealed in the evidence of elderly people and employees who were questioned within the scope of Oral History. Notwithstanding all the material acquisitions of recent decades, there is a noticeable nostalgia for the simple happiness of earlier days.[2] In order to place these shifts in consumer spending more accurately, a long-term study of the development of the standard of living is indicated. In this connection, extensive preliminary studies have been undertaken, but we shall merely summarize their essential points.

As a criterion for the Ancien Régime and the first half of the 19th century we have taken the income of the agricultural labourer, which can be traced almost continuously right from the 14th century.[3] More comprehensive information about labour relations and wage structures are available only from the second half of the 19th century on. The integration of these statistical returns allows us to achieve a representative reconstruction of the standard of living and purchasing power spanning six centuries (as shown in graph 1A). Typical for this reconstruction is the stability of purchasing power, when the nominal wage figures are transposed into real terms (litres of rye). Up to the middle of the 19th century, a day's work was equivalent to some ten litres of rye.[4] In a typical family of four or five persons, having a per capita consumption of one litre of rye per day, half of their expenditure went on bread. In these circumstances, there could have been little margin for alternative expenditure.

In the medium term, some important divergences emerge in the purchasing power curve. In no way had the socially acceptable subsistence level been reached by the beginning of the 14th century. The population, hit by chronic undernourishment, fell an easy prey to prevailing epidemics and, more precisely, to the Black Death, which caused serious ravages in the 1340's. A rapidly spreading impoverishment also occurred between 1550-1670 and 1770-1850. On the other hand, a considerable rise in the standard of living was achieved in the 14th and 15th centuries and during the first sixty or seventy years of the 18th century.[5] In each of these periods, the rise in purchasing power at home was a decisive stimulus to a rapid upward trend of the market and to economic expansion. This applies especially to the 18th century, when the foundations of later industrial development were laid. It is by no means accidental that Belgium was the

first nation on the continent to switch to industrialization.[6] Rough estimates of the GNP and of
income per capita before the end of the Ancien
Régime clearly show that Belgium was one of the
wealthiest countries at that time. The picture
painted by Dérival about 1780 is significant: "tous
les habitants des villes des Pays-Bas vivent, si ce
n'est dans l'opulence, du moins dans la plus grande
aisance; mais cette aisance est encore plus grande
dans les campagnes que dans les villes; et dans les
villes comme dans les campagnes, tout caractérise
le bonheur dont jouissent leurs habitants...".[7]

This high standard of living in the 18th century is clearly reflected in the spread of all
kinds of new products such as coffee, tea, tobacco
and cotton. It is obvious that, owing to all this,
a greater accumulation of capital was achieved in
commercial and industrial circles. Besides, the
favourable development of purchasing power at home
coincided with a rapid growth in population and a
greater division of labour. The fact alone, that
the relative portion of the agricultural population
decreased sharply during this period, had a
decisive influence on the development of traditional autarkic structures. Towards the end of the
Ancien Régime, the independent farmers in most
parts of Flanders and Wallonia hardly represented
20 to 30% of the working population. Not only did
the population's dependence on the market increase
rapidly, but the division of labour also led to a
more dynamic pattern of consumption, since saving
for investment in the rural sector now became less
urgent.[8]

The effects of the higher standard of living
are also to be found in an expansion of building
activity and the frequency of rebuilding of every
kind. The Government also stimulated this economic
growth. Much attention was devoted to road
building and the navigability of the waterways, so
that on the infrastructure level, opportunities for
sustained economic development were pretty good
too.

This favourable starting-point in the 18th century led, indeed, in Wallonia, to a rapid expansion
of heavy industry. On the other hand, in Flanders,
where employment was concentrated in the linen
industry, depth investments were very rare. Instead of an economic take-off, a process of dein-
dustrialization started and continued throughout the
first half of the 19th century.[9] Owing to the
density of the population and the fact that most of
the workers made their living both in agriculture

27

and domestic industry, an attempt was made to compete with machinery by reducing wages. Very soon, this would lead to a hopeless social crisis, the culminating point of which occurred about 1850[10], just when the population of Flanders had been reduced to one of the poorest in the world. Up to well into the 20th century there will be a marked discrepancy between Flanders and Wallonia.

Closely connected with this outline of the standard of living, is the problem of the frequency of employment. It is true that we are only sketchily informed about this subject; nevertheless some tendencies are discernible. It is a fact that, up to well into the 19th century, time spent working tended to be in inverse ratio to the family income. With an increase in real wages it was usual to work less. This theme central to the thinking of the Ancien Régime and 19th century has been stressed by several authors, e.g. P. Mathias points out: "there is no potential desire to expand the range of consumption which extra purchasing power would allow to be realized. If real wages rose, enabling that traditional 'basket of goods' to be earned in fewer hours, the gain would be taken out in time rather than in the extra consumption of purchased commodities and services, or by extra leisure ...".[11] Conversely, the tempo of work was increased and people resorted to female and child labour when there was a decrease in purchasing power. Favourable social and economic prospects were interpreted by entrepreneurs and employers in a completely different way, a dilemma that is described in economic literature as a "backward bending supply curve of labour". Just when the entrepreneur reckoned on a maximization of his turnover, the employee signified that this was not on, by working less and setting a high value on his "leisure preference".[12] The reactions to this state of affairs can easily be deduced from the many protests against what are described by the Government and the bourgeoisie as archaic customs such as excessive lay-offs, the celebration of St. Monday, the frequenting of taverns, the high consumption of alcohol and the propensity to feasting.[13] Remarkably enough, all this gave a rise to vigorous protests both in the 16th and 18th centuries. In both cases, a period of economic prosperity is involved, with a real prospect of increased output. In both periods, the Government decided on a review of social policy, characterized by a prohibition of begging and by so-called work-shy people no longer being able to reckon on the support of charitable

institutions.[14] The grounds for these reactions
were self-evident: the mobilization of more labourers and getting them to work longer to increase
sales figures, with wages remaining constant or
perhaps even declining. This implied that the
financial risks of investment in fixed capital were
to be reduced to an absolute minimum. Apart from
the fact that with a reduction of wages the employees automatically became more disciplinable, they
had to cultivate a new way of life. At all times
they had to keep up their performance, apart from
their income. Since the capitalist system strives
for a maximization of profits, it is obvious that
maximum effort and output are expected from the
workers. Hence the pressure brought to bear on the
working classes during the 19th century so that
they finally accepted the proposition that the work
ethic and labour discipline are indeed to be considered as the highest values on earth.[15] Both
education and literature systematically aimed at
such indoctrination. A great wave of moralizing
argumentation always came back to these values. By
the end of the Ancien Régime, this whole design
will take on an additional dimension when, with the
gradual rise in the standard of living, some prospects of acquiring private property were opened
out. At that moment, indoctrination has become
reality.

In contradiction to the attitude prevailing
the Ancien Régime, the rise in the standard of
living becomes, from now on, the starting point of
more exertion and gradually increasing consumer
spending.[16] At first, this change in the behaviour
pattern is transposed into a qualitatively better
extension of primary needs such as food, drink,
sleeping and housing. In a second phase, roughly
speaking between the two World Wars and going on
into the 1950's and 1960's, there is a restless
craving for more secondary goods. This process was
further strengthened by an accelerated urbanization
which had been going on since the 19th century.
But very soon these secondary goods reach satura-
tion point too, all the more because, as the result
of the tremendous increase in productivity, these
products fell very rapidly in price and came within
everyone's reach. This brings us to the 1970's.
characterized by an individualization of the
pattern of needs and an insatiable craving for
tertiary consumption. This is also the period in
which many senseless excrescences of the capitalist
system will be exposed. The exaggerated appraisal
of the work ethic, systematically acquired since

the 19th century, will, from now, be increasingly contested, mainly by the younger generation. The fact that, in some extreme cases, overtime is done to take holidays, from which one returns full of frustrations, is completely in contradiction with the standard of values obtaining in former times. Even in his leisure time, the consumer is manipulated nowadays. The absurdity of that situation is also illustrated by the fact that some executives do not have enough time to profit from their higher incomes. No less revealing are the changes in the clinical picture, now taking place. After the morbid development of psychosomatic affections resulting from an exaggerated craving for achievement, neurotic affections are now increasing alarmingly as a consequence of anxiety about unemployment and redundancy. In the circumstances, it is no longer surprising that there arise all kinds of hostile reactions to the capitalist system in general and the artificially stimulated behaviour code of contemporary consumer society in particular. The work ethic, unlimited economic development and irresponsible purchasing behaviour lead, least of all, to satisfaction.[17]

With this digression into the pattern of needs and the frequency of employment we have, at the same time, defined the most important changes in consumer spending. For centuries, work concentrated on the satisfaction of the most essential needs of life: eating and drinking. The chances of a possible surplus of income were sacrificed for more leisure time and greater sociability. Whenever the standard of living declined, the tempo of work was increased and women and children were enlisted into the production process. It is true that all kinds of protest waves occurred whenever purchasing power was affected; but usually social demands remained limited. What people actually desired was a return to the former situation, when less effort was needed to provide their most vital needs. More radical demands, calling in question the social system and aimed at a so-called improvement of one's lot were mentioned only much later.

The reconstruction of real wages, outlined above, made sufficiently clear that, within living memory, expenditure on food held a dominant position in the pattern of consumption. How all this actually occurred, and what quantitative and qualitative changes were involved, can be studied from several angles. To that effect, we can start from a micro-study of the accounts of some institutions which go back to the late Middle Ages or early

Modern Times.[18] For most of the municipal centres, the dietary pattern can be very appropriately deduced from local excise and "octroi" duties from the 16th and 17th centuries.

From the end of the Ancien Régime on, the opportunities for this approach increase in importance. An integration of the national census returns and customs statistics makes a macro-economic approach possible. In-depth research can then be carried out with the help of existing budget analyses. The shopping basket, as it was at the end of the Ancien Régime or in the early years of the 19th century, is summarized in Table 2.1 A distinction has been made between the average in town and country.

Table 2.1: Composition of the food-basket in Flanders.[19]

	National Average ca.1800	Ghent,first half 19th century	Antwerp ca.1825	Antwerp ca.1855
Cereals (kg)	182	157	124	120
Potatoes (kg)	292	182,5	219	255
Meat (kg)	10	40,6	43,4	38
Butter (kg)	10	12	17	12
Fish (kg)	2,25	6	6,6	4,4
Cheese(kg)	0,35	1,7	?	
Eggs	50	?	288	127
Milk (litre)	30	?	?	?
Buttermilk (litre)	150	?	?	?
Vegetables (litre)	11	?	?	?
Pulses (litre)	–	2,4	?	?
Sugar (kg)	1,65	?	?	?
Syrup (kg)	0,90	?	?	?
Rice (kg)	0,35	?	?	?
Beer (litre)	180	220	250	130
Gin (litre)	6	13	7	5,5
Wine (litre)	4,5	4	7	5,5
Calories per day	2.578	2.435	2.592	2.267

With an average intake of 2300 to 2500 calories per head, per day, the food value of this typical menu is rather low, especially when we take into account heavy physical effort on the one hand, and the over-representation of young people and young workers on the other. Carbohydrates were by far the most important part of this menu (about 75%). Fats (10 to 12%) were very much under-represented, even more so, (animal) protein (about 14%). All this can be summarized as follows: a heavy monotonous diet, mainly based on rye-bread, pulses and potatoes, while dairy produce and meat were rather a rare luxury. In the country, the shopping basket was even less balanced than in the towns, although only a very thin upper stratum of townspeople were responsible for the larger number of variants found in cities and towns.

A long-term study of the dietary pattern reveals a striking preponderance of cereals. Up to the beginning of the 18th century, the daily intake of cereals per person was about one litre (2/3 rye, 1/3 wheat, or maslin), which was equal to more than 2000 calories. Fluctuations in the price of corn were the very linchpin in the spending pattern of the population. In times of crop failure and during the years of dearth, the whole budget might be used to purchase corn or bread. "Bargain" years occurred when their purchase swallowed up less than 30 to 40% of the family budget of day labourers or workers.[20]

The propagation of potatoes was an important innovation in the 18th century, which, at the same time, produced one of the most far-reaching changes which ever occurred in dietary habits. The per capita consumption of corn was thus halved in less than no time. The loss in calories resulting from this was compensated for by the consumption of about a kilo of potatoes.[21] The introduction of this crop into the daily diet had the advantage of maintaining the necessary intake of vitamin C. In this way, specific deficiencies such as scurvy decreased in importance. Originally, the cultivation of potatoes was to be considered as a "culture de misère". Owing to the increasing pressure of population, on the one hand, and the technical inability to raise the productivity of cereal crops and the limited possibilities of a further expansion of the available arable land, on the other, the introduction, into the rotation system, of new crops with a considerably higher yield per surface unit was the obvious method of providing vital necessities. The cultivation of potatoes was the solution to this problem. As this crop made it possible to feed twice as many people as from the same area of corn, it was also possible to make a living on a small farm of barely one hectare. It is, however, true that, in this situation, some additional income had to be earned in rural industry or as a day labourer. But owing to the increased sources of supply, the increase in the price of corn could be kept temporarily under control.[22]

From the end of the Ancien Régime on, supplies, however, were again tight. Instead of promoting free trade, the Government had to switch to a strictly regulated agricultural policy shortly after the turn of the century. The export of cereals was, from now on, almost completely prohibited, while specific tariff laws regulated the import of foreign cereals. In the course of the 19th century, there is a gradual increase in dependence on foreign corn supplies. The Government saw such wholesale importation as an efficient instrument of social policy: low corn and bread prices were an ideal way of achieving wage stability and social peace. During the crisis of 1845-47, average wheat imports rose to about 35 million kg a year, which was about 10% of home production. A few years later, annual imports had doubled. Owing to the improvement in transport towards the end of the 19th century, the import of corn from the New World took on really massive proportions. After an average import of 270 million kg in 1861-70, the home market was flooded with upwards of 866 million kg a year during the following decade[23]. For the first time in history, the population was released from the compelling worry about daily bread (see graph 3). The fall in prices resulting from this massive importation of American cereals was translated into an increase in real wages and an improvement in the dietary pattern. The all too typical, monotonous and bulky character of the daily diet, hitherto characterized by an excessive consumption of farinaceous food, to which, since the 18th century, potatoes had been added, was eventually refined with increasing attention being paid to consumption of (animal) proteins. This finds a clear expression in some approximate figures to do with the consumption of meat. As C. Juglar observed, meat is one of the best social indicators: "la consommation de la viande, qui indique le plus ou le moins de bien-être ... permet de juger le degré des périodes heureuses ou malheureuses".[24] We are able to follow this up particularly for the City of

Ghent, where we have various sources of information about consumption for the period 1650-1900 (see graph 4). The improvements in the pattern of consumption from the middle of the 19th century on are clearly illustrated here. Turnover in the centres of population is, however, to a certain extent, misleading, because the consumption of high-value foods such as meat and dairy produce was always much higher in towns than in the country. Hence we prefer to base our evaluations on national averages.

It can be assumed that, in Belgium just as abroad, a considerable fall in the per capita consumption figures for meat had occurred since the 15th and 16th centuries. In this connection, the disappearance of butchers and slaughterers in most of the rural villages is significant.[25] By the middle of the 19th century, per capita consumption of meat in Belgium was barely 10 to 15 kg. The physician A.J. Meynne observed: "le peuple belge est l'un de ceux à qui le gros bétail fournit le moins de ressources alimentaires".[26] In Flanders, where impoverishment was most pronounced, the per capita consumption of meat was even less than 5 to 6 kg in the first half of the 19th century.

The qualitative shortages of food were so considerable that numerous physical deficiencies were rife, such as we know nowadays in the developing countries, e.g. rachitis (rickets), kwashiorkor and xerophtalmy.[27] With the rise in the standard of living towards the end of the 19th century, there is an immediate increase in the consumption of so-called "protective foods", particularly of meat. From an average of about 15 kg in 1880, per capita consumption had risen to 33 kg by the outbreak of the first World War.[28] Between the wars, adjustments remained somewhat restricted (40 kg in 1930). Especially after the second World War, consumption figures rose further: to 54.3 kg in 1955, 60.8 kg in 1965 and 78.7 kg in 1975.[29] There was also a change in quality, in the sense that trade figures for beef especially were gaining in importance.

On the other hand, we should mention that the dislocation of consumption during the first half of the 19th century is very striking. During this period, there is a qualitative and quantitative decline in the pattern of consumption, both in the country and the towns. The decline is undeniable as far as highly valued products, such as wheatbread, meat and cheese, and drinks such as beer, brandy and gin are concerned. Impoverishment is very clearly reflected in the composition of the shopping basket.[30] The situation became desperate for the country

people of southern central Flanders, where a crisis
in the linen industry led to a process of deindus-
trialization. A quarter or half of the population
was reduced to beggary during the second third of
the 19th century.[31] A reconstruction of meat consumption in the province of East Flanders confirms
the regional inequality of incomes. Reasonable
sales figures were still being noted around 1820-30
in the richer agricultural areas in the north of the
province. In the centre or in the south, however,
where the strongest concentration of weavers and
spinners was to be found, the population was no
longer able to procure proteinrich food. The effects of impoverishment and latent undernourishment
can be clearly traced in the long-term changes in
the physical development of army recruits.

The slowing down in growth between 1780/90 and
1840/50 is conclusive evidence of impoverishment and
undernourishment. Twenty-year-old boys, with an
average height of 1.63 to 1.64 m., at the end of the
Ancien Régime, hardly measured 1.60 during the second quarter of the 19th century. A brief interruption in growth occurred again at the end of the century - as a consequence of difficulties in agriculture and the decrease in purchasing-power of the
agricultural population.[32] With an average height
of 1.63 m. around 1800, the Flemish soldier had a
normal stature, perfectly in line with most neighbouring countries. Differences in stature, however,
will increase in the following decades. During the
second quarter of the 19th century recruits in South
Flanders measured only 1.58 m. By this time, increasing numbers of young men had to be rejected for
the Army because of their stature (less than 1.56
m.). On the other hand, the repercussions of the
social crisis are much better reflected in a breakdown of the figures by occupation. About the middle
of the 19th century, day labourers and textile
workers were 5 or 6 cm. shorter when conscripted
than at the end of the century. The repercussions
of the crisis on the physical condition and stature
of young men was all the more evident as, simultaneously with the deleterious effect on purchasing
power, preferential treatment of some members of the
family became evident. The more the family budget
coincides with the socially acceptable minimum wage
level, or falls short of it, the more usual it is
to favour the main breadwinners: "il importait de
nourrir d'abord les travailleurs pour sauvegarder le
production ... le père est le producteur qui nourrit
la famille et qu'il convient de sauvegarder sa ca-

pacité de production".[33] Under these circumstances, all possible economies were made on the food and clothing of the wife and children. However, there is a great need for protective foods in childhood, which continues to grow in importance in youth, when heavy physical exertion has to be made.

The repercussions of such a dislocation of the pattern of consumption is not confined to a slowing down in physical development. As we noted above, the consequences are manifest in the field of public health and physical welfare. This applies especially to the high sickness figures and death risks, which resulted in a third of children dying before the age of twenty. Owing to this total lack of resistance, the death rate for most infantile diseases was very high. The pre-eminent social diseases, however, were all kinds of tuberculous affections, to which more than a fifth of deaths were attributed in southern and central Flanders.[34]

These diseases were aggravated still further, because impoverishment and wretched housing caused the most elementary hygienic precautions to be overlooked. In spite of urgent appeals by the government, the lower class took conspicuously little interest in physical hygiene and public health.

When, by the end of the 19th century, an improvement in the standard of living became manifest, people concerned themselves first and foremost with adjustments to the shopping baskets and secondly better housing. Only at a later date did they look at standards of hygiene and care of the body. This concern also manifests itself in government policy. From the third quarter of the 19th century on, a little spending on public health was inserted into national and provincial budgets. Up to and including the inter-war years, this item continued to be less important, as it hardly represented 1% of public expenditure. It is not till the 1950's and 1960's that a drastic change will occur. As already noted, this is just when consumer spending moves in a fresh direction. From now on, spending on tertiary consumption will become predominant, with a growth tempo bordering on the unbelievable. Changes in medical consumption speak for themselves. Parallel with the number of medical officers, we see an exponential rate of increase in medical consumption.[35] Recent changes in consumer spending are perhaps even more starkly revealed in the tourist sector. About 1900, Belgian touristsaccounted for approximately 6,000 over-night stays at the seaside. Between 1960 and 1970 this number had increased tenfold. When the number of day trippers and tours

abroad are also taken into consideration, an estimated increase of 2,000-3,000 % is reasonable.

In the meantime, we have once more anticipated
the chronological course of our analyses. As we
have already indicated, the intermediate period
1870/80 - 1950/60 is a very crucial one, because improvement in the standard of living led, for the
first time, to a more varied pattern of consumption.
How these changes actually occurred, will now be
examined in more detail. The many family budgets
for this period form an ideal approach to the problem. Belgium was, indeed, one of the pioneers of
budgetary analysis. Famous economists and statisticians, such as A. Quetelet, E. Ducpétiaux, Ernst
Engel and X. Heuschling contributed to this work.[36]
The evolution of and changes in the budgets can be
tackled in the long term by simultaneously taking a
closer look at certain institutional accounts of the
Ancien Régime and the more modern budgets of working
people. Once more, from this survey we learn that
for centuries, and certainly up to the third quarter
of the 19th century, the price of corn and bread was
the regulating element in determining purchasing
power and standard of living. The wholesale import
of corn from the New World from the 1870's on en-
sured that the unstable equilibrium between demographic growth and supply was consigned to the past.
The lowering of bread prices did not, however, cause
an immediate change in the pattern of consumption
throughout all strata of society. Between 1874 and
1896, the industrially developed countries in Europe
struggled against a downward trend of the market
with low points in 1875, 1885 and 1890. Liberal
agricultural policy was, to some extent, responsible
for these interruptions in economic growth. The
collapse of the price of corn even led to a very
disturbed labour market. Many farmers and day
labourers saw themselves obliged to look out for
other jobs, as a result of which they badly affected
the wage structure in the industrial sectors in
their area.[37] For most of these farmers, emigra-
tion to America and Canada was the only way out.[38]
Owing to a revival in the economic situation by the
end of the 19th century, changes in the labour market continued to increase in importance. Between
1890 (depression) and 1910 (boom), employment in the
secondary sector increased by 45%, while the number
of those engaged in agriculture dropped by 12%. The
number of employees grew by 25% in the same short
period.[39] The tearing down of autarkic structures
and the further increase in the population dependent
on the market was, in itself, already an important

element influencing adjustment in consumer spending. Increasing urbanization, to which we have already referred, was also contributory to this trend. What is more, it is common knowledge that, in the secondary and tertiary sectors, higher wages were being paid, producing an inflationary result.

But a shift towards better remunerated sectors, where a sharp increase in wages occurred after 1896, does not *ipso facto* imply globally increased living standards. The mechanization that had been carried through permitted the use of semi-skilled and unskilled - and therefore cheaper - manpower. These workers may not have perceived from their paypacket whether, or not, they were employed in a so-called "strong" sector. Also, increasing competition from cheap labour in the rural areas (through commuting and decentralization of industry) threatened the frequency of employment and wage levels in many small - scale urban industries.[40] The economic upturn after 1896 may have brought about a polarization of purchasing power (and therefore of consumption potential) among workers employed in a few spearhead industries, and the great masses in more artisanal sectors. It is likely that this polarization was, to some extent, mitigated in the course of the twenties, but contrasts remained acute (see graph 9).

Be this as it may, the economic revival of 1896 enriched a number of social groups. The increase (through labour of capital) of their purchasing power expressed itself not only in a diversified diet, but also in less vitally indispensable purchases. For the highest social categories this meant, for example, buying a car; for the less wealthy, purchasing various home comforts. Industry responded only too eagerly to such a demand. The supply side went in for finished products for domestic and foreign mass consumption. To put it squarely: car assembly established itself alongside the railroad industry. Of course, this development did not begin until the turn of the century, but, in any case, a start had been made.

Obviously, World War I drastically interfered with the process initiated by the factors just mentioned. The stream of vital goods was suddenly cut off by the German invasion of 1914.[41] In the long run, however, war was actually a catalist for these very same factors:

    1.   the import of basic and luxury goods intensified after 1918 (Suffice it to point out that, in 1925, the import of ham and

bacon had increased sevenfold relative to 1910-13);

2. the purchasing power of manual workers in certain sectors increased significantly between 1928 and 1936 (initially because of sharp wage increases and subsequently as the result of a fall in prices). Trade unions, which enjoyed a sixfold increase in membership compared to 1914, exerted a strong influence on wage levels;

3. in the structure of employment, emphasis on the secondary and tertiary sectors was accentuated and, within the former, many more workers were now employed in strong sectors such as metallurgy, the chemical industry and transport;

4. the diversification of the commodity supply spectrum continued. Industry responded to the increased purchasing power of particular population strata. During the 1930-35 crisis, it looked out for new sales potential: e.g. household electrical equipment was "popularized". Expensive publicity campaigns were mounted for this purpose.

All these factors interplayed with the cycle of trade which was, generally speaking, favourable between 1923 and 1930 and unfavourable in 1921-22 and 1930-36. A recovery of economic activity characterized the 1919-20 and 1936-39 periods. Purchasing power (cf. graph 10) fluctuated along with the ups and downs of the trade cycle.

Two new factors now came into play, characterizing not only the period following World War I but also that following 1945. Government (with, for the first time, a socialist-reformist participation) attempted to curb inflation brought about by war (prices were four times higher in 1920 than in April 1914!). In the first place, it applied strict price control to various essential food items and, at the same time, kept down the all too sharp rent increases. The other new factor also relates to inflation and economic policy. Economic and financial troubles twice prompted a government decision to devalue the currency (in 1926 and 1935). As a result of this, price increases were reflected in consumer behaviour.

This series of "consumption determinants" which we consider to have been at work during this important transition period could be supplemented by numerous other factors. While we trust we have indicated the most important factors, the influence of

39

attitudes of mind, fashion, expectations, tradition, prejudices, snobery, credit facilities, age structure, etc. cannot be neglected. In our opinion, of primary importance is the dialectic interplay of product supply, on the one hand, and the purchasing power of the masses, on the other. All other factors merely stimulate or interfere with one of these two basic determinants.

The changes occurring around 1900 no longer allow one to measure the evolution of living standards and consumer behaviour simply and solely by considering food consumption. Still, meat consumption, for example, reveals a great deal about living habits.[42] A wealth of other aspects are, however, bound to be overlooked in this way. Therefore we wish to consider here all possible facets of consumption patterns in order to provide a comprehensive view of their dynamics.

The Belgian statistical service is doubtless one of the very first ever to have employed the method of extensive household budget surveys. It is an unfortunate circumstance that this wealth of data has never contributed to a better understanding of Belgian patterns of demand in the scientific community abroad.[43] As early as 1853, in fact, a budget inquiry (of admittedly limited reliability) was conducted, to be followed by others of increasing refinement. Some were produced on the initiative of the government, others on that of social scientists, workers' or employers' organizations. It seemed a good idea to use these budget surveys as basic data, supplementing them with more in-depth information such as medical consumption figures, tourism statistics and savings ratios. It goes without saying that some surveys are superior to others in terms of representativity, aims and type of details provided (deficits, income and expenditure). A thorough examination of budget survey representativity reveals that the majority refer to better-off working class families. The picture obtained is, therefore, somewhat over-optimistic.

Let us now consider the results of available surveys, annotated according to their credibility:[44]

Table 2.2: Expenditure of working-class families (in %) on:

	1853	1891	1908	1919	1921	1928	1930	1932	1932	1936	1938
Food	56.8	61.6	68.1	77.0	64.8	85.3	54.4	49.5	53.9	41.9	44.7
Clothing	13.3	14.3	2.0	2.9	14.6	15.3	12.2	6.3	7.4	11.7	10.3
Housing	9.9	9.8	13.1	6.4	6.6	9.1	17.5	18.4	14.3	19.7	17.3
Lighting/Heating	5.4	5.2	8.6	3.4	5.5	5.0	8.4	12.1	6.2	5.4	6.3
Health	3.3	1.2	2.8	] 10.1	1.0	1.3	0.8	3.4	3.2	] 21.2	1.3
Miscellaneous	2.3	7.9	5.2		7.5	10.9	6.7	9.9	14.7		20.1
	**	***	**	*	****	****	*	***	***	**	**

Table 2.3: Expenditure of white-collar families (in %) on:

	1914	1922	1922	1928	1931	1938
Food	42.6	44.7	50.3	48.9	45.5	41.8
Clothing	21.4	24.3	16.4	14.0	12.9	13.3
Housing	19.7	12.7	19.8	16.0	22.2	17.8
Lighting/Heating	7.1	7.0	11.9	5.3	6.0	5.2
Health	2.3	2.3	] 1.6	3.7	1.9	1.8
Miscellaneous	6.9	8.4		12.1	11.3	19.9
	*	*	*	****	*	**

*little credibility ; **some credibility ; ***high credibility ; ****very high credibility

Because of their reliability, we shall have to
concentrate on the 1891, 1922, 1928 and 1932 workers'
budgets. The first three resulted from government
surveys, those of the twenties being the more representative. The 1932 budgets were produced on the
initiative of the Solvay Institute in Brussels: one
concerns unemployed, the other, employed workers in
the Charleroi region. The British sociologist
Seebohm-Rowntree drew up the 1908 budget, while that
of 1919 was jointly compiled by miners and the Min-
istry of Labour. A housewife from Nivelles wrote
down her daily expenses during an entire year, thus
providing the 1930 budget. Lastly, the 1936 and
1938 budgets resulted from surveys conducted by the
Christian Trade Union (A.C.V.). The results were
checked by a commission of experts (i.e., housewives) and slightly amended (the budgets served as
evidence in wage negotiations). Four out of six
white collar budgets are quoted here merely as curi-
osities. Only the 1928 budget can be taken seriously. Even a superficial comparison between workers'
and white-collar budgets lead to the conclusion
that, in relative terms, expenditure on food was
substantially lower in the latter group and this
benefitted all other items of expenditure, especially clothing and housing. The marked differences between workers' and white-collar patterns of consumption seem to lessen in the early thirties. In view
of the scantiness of the information available, however, we shall have to refrain from further consideration of the white-collar budgets.

The average budget of a working class family in
1891 differed from that in 1853 by the lower relative share of expenditure on food (-4%). The lower
level of prices (of food mainly) of the recession
years 1874-1896 was responsible for this. Any economies on food were transferred in entirely to the
heading "miscellaneous", which included recreation,
education, transport, insurance, moral and other
needs. Other expenses changed little, if at all.
Increased or decreased expenditure on food determined consumption patterns well into the 20th century. A quick glance at the evolution of relative
expenditure on food throughout the years shows just
this. Only in the late thirties did food cease to
account for more than half of total spending. The
68.1% in 1908 is explained by the higher level of
prices in those years. The 77% (!) in 1919 results
from inflationary prices not offset by wage adjustments (index-linking of prices was introduced by
mid-1920 only). The 1921 results are again comparable with those of 1891. Expenses on food were

higher by 3.2% in 1921, although the global standard of living had improved in the interim. In the light of Engel's law, one would have expected the relative share of expenditure on food to decrease. It seems to us, though, that the increased allocation of income to food in 1921 demonstrates how precarious living conditions were during last century. The greater proportional share of spending on food was concomitant with a substantial quantitative improvement of diet, as is explained below. The great majority of the population was, at last, receiving adequate nutrition. A relative increase of the amount spent on food was essential to this end. In 1928 this was no longer the case, and expenditure on food dropped below 60%. Indeed, in spite of this relative reduction (-6.5%) people ate more and, in doing so, drew on wider spectrum of products. In the course of the thirties, spending on food decreased as a result of substantially reduced food prices (1930-1935). Higher prices during the recovery (1936-37) and pre-war (1938-39) periods again raised the share of expenditure on food to about 45%. In the time-span underconsideration, therefore, the intricate interplay of consumption determinants caused a reduction in the "food" heading from about 65% to 45%. Yet the combination of the five, or seven, factors considered here did not suffice to free the pattern of consumption entirely from the grip of (sometimes violent) fluctuations in food costs.[45]

Expansions or contractions in spending on food were not due solely to the evolution of wages and food prices: rent costs also exerted a considerable influence. Before World War I, rents accounted for about 10% of total expenses. Immediately after the war, they dropped to about 6.5% (rent legislation). Any economy thus made found its way to "food" (compare the 1891 and 1921 budgets). The effect of rent legislation was no longer noticeable in the late twenties: houserents rose sky-high, whereas most other prices *and* wages dropped. Some families in the Brussels area spent as much as 30-40% of their budget on rent. Such high costs characterized the thirties. The benefit gained from lower food costs was, perforce, in part absorbed by increased housing costs. This, then, severely restricts the significance of the drop in expenditure on food from 65% to 45% between 1850-90 and 1930-40. Admittedly, the item "housing" is not limited to rent: it includes maintenance, decorating and domestic equipment, with rent, nevertheless, accounting for the lion's share. Consideration of the remaining budget entries shows clothing costs remaining essentially constant, although subject to abrupt short-term fluctuations. It could almost be considered a general rule that clothing is the first item to be cut down on in times of need. Proportional expenses on lighting and heating changed little, if at all; spending on health rose slightly. Lastly, the heterogeneous heading, "miscellaneous" consisted mainly of expenses which households incurred ar their own discretion. It would, however, be a mistake to equate a rise under this heading with a manifestation of increased purchasing power: in fact, this heading includes the cost of transport, insurance, trade-union contribution, education etc.; i.e. spending which is not entirely avoidable. The benefits of increased purchasing power may be reflected in the "miscellaneous" heading through the increase of effectively discretionary expenses such as, for example, recreation. In 1853, the average household devoted 3.9% of its budget to recreation - in 1891, 5.7% and in 1928, 5.4%. The A.C.V. survey decided it was 3.8% in 1938. It is obvious that these percentages cover different things. On the other hand, it is certainly significant that the average household spent the same proportion of its budget on recreation in 1891 and in 1928, but a smaller proportion in 1938. This shows, once more, that the mass of the population in the thirties and forties did not enjoy the benefits of increased living standards to the extent of breaking free from the traditional consumption pattern where purely physical needs were of prime importance. The small man used his increased purchasing power primarily to meet his essential requirements. For a large part of the population, this still meant having enough to eat in 1930.[46]

The evolution of dietary habits makes this abundantly clear. Belgium possesses a wealth of subsidiary data providing a detailed picture of this evolution. In 1910 and 1923, surveys were conducted, which dealt entirely with the diet of the average working-class individual.[47] Concurrently, macroeconomic data are available on total food consumption from 1897 on, as well as figures on the food stock turnover of several co-operatives from 1914 on.[48] Figures of retail sales, published by the Central Bank, supplement these series from 1927.[49] The information from diet surveys can be compared with the data from budget surveys. As people conducting the surveys used different criteria, the results will be summarized in two tables:

Table 2.4

FOOD CONSUMPTION

	Daily consumption of an adult male based on a selection of 12 foodstuffs						Daily consumption per person of all foodstuffs[50]			
	1891	1910	1921	1923	1928	1932	1891	1917	1929	1939[51]
Calories (approximate)	3140	3570	3785	3480	3370	2890	1910	1815	2185	2865
% calories of animal origin	23	32	34	?	36	?	?	?	?	?
proteins (in grams)	?	84,4	?	101	?	?	?	?	66,8	87,1
distribution according to number of calories (in %)										
1200-3000 cal.		25		35						
3000-4000 cal.		52		35						
4000 + cal.		23		30						

The first table lists the daily calorie intake of an adult male on the basis of a constant set of 12 essential foods. This procedure does not take into account the contribution of other foodstuffs. Up to 1923, this causes no serious problems, as few, if any, other food products were included in the diet besides these 12. The caloric content of the basic selection rose by 14% between 1891 and 1910, a considerable increase, which occurred in spite of the globally higher price level after 1896. Higher nominal wages may therefore be held responsible for the improvement. Unfortunately, we do not know how much the average household had to pay for this quantitatively improved diet in 1910. In view of the rise in food prices, it may well have been more than the 61.1% spent in 1891 (cf. the 1908 budget). Notwithstanding the quantitative improvement in 1910, the results indicate that some 25% of the workers sampled experienced a nutritional deficiency in terms of calories (3000 calories being considered a subsistence minimum and 2000 calories an absolutely necessary minimum). In spite of the rise in caloric intake between 1891 and 1910, therefore, this comparatively high percentage clearly illustrates the precarious living conditions prevailing at the end of last century. A second important conclusion from the 1910 survey is that quantitative and qualitative progress went hand in hand, in spite of caloric deficiencies in 25% of the sample. 32% rather than 23% of total caloric supply was now obtained from animal sources (meat, milk, butter). Minimum protein requirements were exceeded by more than 20%. Another important feature is the improvements which were achieved with "trusted" foods; in absolute terms, the consumption of bread and potatoes remained constant between 1891 and 1910, while more and more "choice" foods were being eaten.

The early years following the first World War saw a continuation of the evolution witnessed in 1910: *per capita* caloric intake of bread and potatoes remained constant, consumption of animal products increased and familiar foods were being eaten more than ever. This trend came to an end around 1923. The 1923 food survey testifies to a deterioration: global caloric consumption dropped by 8% compared to 1921. At the same time, a polarization occurred in the dietary patterns of the different social strata. The distribution of individuals according to caloric intake shows that the middle category (3000-4000 calories), had shrunk considerably and the extremes had gained ground. In 1923, more than one third of the workers examined were inadequately fed. In spite of this, the higher protein figure is indicative of a more varied diet than in 1910.

Whereas this may be far from obvious from the table, the years following 1928 saw a lasting improvement, both in quantity and quality, of the dietary pattern. The 1928 low in calories merely means that people no longer restricted themselves to the basic selection of foodstuffs. A stream of "new" food products appeared on the menu, which had been rarely eaten, if at all, in earlier periods. From the detailed list of food items in the 1928 survey, I list as "newcomers": fresh fish, delicatessen, vegetables, fruit, cheese, canned foods, soft drinks, soda water, herbs, pastries; also chocolate, sweets, jam, syrup and other delicacies. These "new" products accounted for quite an important share of the average worker's budget (no less than 17.8% of total expenditure on food). This trend continued thanks to the low food prices of the early thirties. The so-called basic shopping basket lost ground increasingly to other products in the average worker's budget.

The second table, listing daily consumption per individual (instead of per adult male), reveals the situation in the late thirties: calorie and protein intake increased steadily. The thirties are thus characterized by a nutritional pattern having little in common with that of the years preceding World War I. The preponderance of potatoes and bread as a source of calories belonged to the past, now that meat, cheese, butter and milk had become everyday fare. A varied diet provided enough proteins, carbohydrates, vitamins and other necessary elements. The reader is reminded of the importance of this state of affairs in the light of the global pattern of consumption: the adequate and varied 1938 diet required a proportionally *smaller* expenditure than the monotonous one of 1890-1900. It is here (and, for the greater part of the population, only here) that the improved living conditions effectively made themselves felt. Long-term progress with - sometimes violent - yearly fluctuations is reflected in graph 4, which combines some macro-economic data concerning food consumption. It is possible to see from it how the improvement of nutritional habits, although steady, was hardly linear but proceeded by fits and starts. E.g., the severe inflation, resulting from the 1926 devaluation, is clearly marked in the graphs. Observe also the enormous impact of the depression of the thirties on the consumption of groceries (see graph 12).[52]

It need hardly be repeated that the global improvement in the food situation affected health,
physical development and life expectancy. This
point has often been made in connection with shifts
in the growth of adolescents. Also symptomatic of
improved living standards and a more balanced diet
is the shift in the age of puberty. Many indications point to 15-18 years as the age at which men-
struation began in the 19th century; today it occurs
at 12-13 years. No less significant is the reduced
death rate for children, adolescents and young
adults. These age groups are particularly sensitive
to the pernicious influence of malnutrition. The
reduction in the death rate for these groups dates
back to the third quarter of the 19th century, i.e.
to a time when medical consumption was essentially
non-existent. It was a more adequate diet and,
specifically, a more wide-spread consumption of
protein-rich foods which eliminated social evils
such as tuberculosis.

In the preceding discussion of budget and food
surveys, little attention has been paid to the
diversity in the consumption patterns of different
social strata. Even in our general survey, however,
we had to allude to such differences as obviously
existed.[53] The 1891 and 1928 budget surveys offer
an excellent opportunity to compare the consumption
patterns of high and low income families in both
years, as expenses were reported in Belgian francs
per consumption unit (= Quet). (See Table 2.5 on
next page.)

What strikes one first of all is that the proportional difference in wages is smaller in 1928
than forty years earlier. A comparison between 1891
and 1928 shows that spending on essentials tended to
converge. Differences in expenditure on food between the extreme incomes brackets amounted to 75%
in 1891 and only 35% in 1928. The gap between the
"poorest" and "wealthiest" was therefore less pronounced. This narrowing difference obviously does
not reveal just what the diet of the different
social groups was. For those workers' families of
comfortable means it was of course more varied and
nutritious; choice meat (even veal, chicken and
rabbit), fish, butter, cheese, eggs, fresh vegetables and fruit, beer, wine, etc. were commonplace
items on their menu, e.g., an adult man consumed
half a kilogram of butter a week. The food spectrum
of the less well-off group, on the other hand, remained close to that of 1891 in many respects.
Differences were mainly of quantitative kind, and
consumption of "new" products was moderate indeed,

Table 2.5: Spending (per Quet) of high and low
income households in 1891 and 1928. Relative
differences between the higher and lower income
group.

	1891 cat 1	cat 4	%Δ	1928 cat 1	cat 5	%Δ
Annual Income						
(per Quet)	93,12 Fr.	174,2 F	87	1,366 Fr.	2,111 F	54
Expenditure on						
food	58.5	102.4	75	221	1.106	35
clothing	12.4	28.2	128	200	339	69
housing	10.4	16.2	55	146	154	5.4
heating/						
lighting	5.1	7.8	52	61	63	3
health	0.7	2.4	229	17	23	31
education	1.5	4.2	122	49	22	20
recreation	4.1	11.5	181	52	270	421
miscellaneous	0.4	1.4	276	12	59	233

Difference expenditure on clothes also diminished.
Although clothing is one of the most obvious means
of underlining social distinctions, differences in
dress were doubtless less apparent in 1928 than in
1891.   The development of ready-made clothing may
have played an important part in the process.
"Housing", "heating" and "lighting" display the
most striking convergence. The wide discrepancies
of 1891 dwindled to almost negligible differences
in 1928. Presumably most people enjoyed adequate
heating and lighting. For the wealthier group,
housing costs were mitigated by rent legislation, a
fact which considerably reduced relative differences
compared to 1891. Equally important was the progress achieved by the poorer group in the realm of
individual health care. This shows, among other
things, that even the poorest working-class categories were beginning to call on medical care.
     Levelling was less pronounced in spending on
moral and intellectual needs. The poorest group
lagged far behind as far as "recreation" and "miscellaneous" items were concerned. "Miscellaneous"
expenses, such as vocational expenses, insurance,
debts, taxes, etc. showed about the same relative
differences in 1891 and 1928; the very characteristic item "recreation", on the other hand, displayed
a much greater variance in 1928. The general picture then is one of convergence of expenditure on
primary wants, polarization of expenditure on "non-
bodily" needs. This, again, indicates that the
global increase of living standards between 1890 and
1930 was canalized into spending on food. Only a
happy few better-off workers' families could aspire
to the actual "amenities of life". This privileged
group may already have enjoyed the "charmes dis-
crets" of the expanding consumer society: eating
out, a radioset, visits to the cinema and sporting
events, day-trips to the seaside ... It is therefore
to the latter social group (and to other even
better-off groups) that the curves in graph 13
typically refer.
     Nevertheless, one should bear in mind that the
1891 and 1928 budget surveys provide s "snapshot"
record of a given state of affairs. In times of
economic difficulty (such as the crisis of the
thirties), polarization of purchasing power again
led to an increased divergence between "poorer" and
"richer" groups. This was undoubtedly true of
housing expenses in particular, which had achieved
a close convergence by 1928. The abolition of rent
legislation was largely responsible for this.
Neither should one forget, in considering the above

comparisons, that budget surveys take no account whatsoever of those workers' families living on the verge of poverty. The importance of this group should not be underestimated; their expenditure doubtless lagged even further behind that of the richer groups.

The economic and social changes which started in Belgium at the turn of the century, exerted a far-reaching influence on the average pattern of spending. For the greater part of the population, these meant primarily a sufficient and more varied diet. One group had moved beyond this stage and could, to some extent, afford certain "luxuries". Two other groups presumably did not experience any significant change in their situation: one remained near the poverty line (the unemployed, pensioners and the sick), the other could afford to avail itself immediately of each new product of the consumer society as it came on the market. On the whole, of course, the balance was positive. But, considered from a different angle, it seemd that the powerful industrial apparatus, which achieved an increase in production of 211% between 1880 and 1940, eventually proved capable of providing no more than adequate nutrition for the greater part of the population[54].

After World War II, the dividing line between wants shifted more rapidly, while an increasing number of social groups enjoyed some of society's new benefits. In the fifties and certainly in the sixties, the average Belgian citizen was freed from heavy expenditure on purely physical wants. National tax statistics reveal, however, that, even today, 20% of Belgians live at subsistence level. Their consumption pattern is characterized by spending on food fluctuating around 35% of total expenditure.[55] Sadly, few groups in this "category of the poor" manage to escape from it, whereas new ones continue to join it. Nevertheless, the concept of "subsistence level" has a different meaning today than from what it had 50 or 100 years ago.

NOTES

1. J. Fourastié, "Pourquoi nous travaillons", Paris, 1976, p. 90.
2. Analogous expressions of discomfort already occurred by the turn of the century. In 1896, d' Avenel observed: "never has this (French) people of ours been so happy as it is to-day and never has it believed itself more to be pitied" (W. Minchinton. "Patterns of Demand, 1750-1914", in "The Fontana

Economic History of Europe. The Industrial Revolution", p. 177.

3. The purchasing-power of the agricultural
labourer was taken from C. Verlinden - E. Scholliers
and others, "Documents pour l'histoire des prix et
des salaires en Flandre et en Brabant", Bruges,
1959-1973. For the 14th century, see also C.Pierard,
"Prix et salaires à Mons", in "Annales Cercle Ar-
chéologique de Mons", 1978, pp. 9-80.

4. The wage figures, paid during a period of
about 250 working days, were converted to an annual
base.

5. E. Scholliers - C. Vandenbroeke, "Structu-
ren en Conjuncturen in de Zuidelijke Nederlanden,
1480-1800", in "Nieuwe Algemene Geschiedenis der
Nederlanden", Vol. 5, 1980, pp. 252-310.

6. In connection with the economic development
W.O. Henderson noted: "Belgium was the first Continental country to experience an industrial revolution comparable with that of Britain" ("Britain
and Industrial Europe, 1750-1870), Liverpool, 1954,
p. 102.

7. "Le Voyageur dans les Pays-Bas Autrichiens"
Vol. 1, Amsterdan, 1872, pp. 9-10.

8. R. Braun, "Industrialisierung und Volks-
leben: die Veränderungen der Lebensformen in einem
ländlichen Industriegebiet vor 1800", Stuttgart,
1960.

9. F. Mendels, "Agriculture and Peasant In-
dustry in eighteenth century Flanders", in E. Jones-
Parker (eds.), "European peasants and their markets"
Princeton, 1975.

10. G. Jacquemyns, "Histoire de la crise économique des Flandres, 1845-1850", Brussels, 1929.

11. P. Mathias, "The transformation of England.
Essays in the economic and social history of England
in the eighteenth century", London, 1979, p. 155.

12. D. Landes, "The Unbound Prometheus. Technological change and industrial development in Western Europe from 1750 to present", Cambridge, 1969,
pp. 58-59.

13. The usual behaviour pattern of the labourers was very clearly typified by E.J. Hobsbawm: "The
pre-industrial labourer responded to material incen-
tives, in so far as he wanted to earn enough to
enjoy what was thought of as comfort at the social
level to which it has pleased God to call him, but
even his ideas of comfort were determined by the
past, and limited by what was "fitting" for one of
his station, or perhaps to one immediately above his
his" (Industry and Empire),Harmondsworth, 1978, p.
87.

52

14. C. Lis - H. Soly, "Poverty and Capitalism in pre-industrial Europe", Hassocks, 1979.

15. A reaction of the Chamber of Commerce of Tournai, in 1843, is very striking: "ce n'est pas l'augmentation des salaires qui pourrait améliorer la condition des ouvriers, car l'expérience prouve que ceux qui gagnent assez en deux ou trois jours pour fournir l'entretien de leur famille, restent oisifs les autres jours et se livrent le plus souvent à la débauche" (quoted by J. Puissant, "Le bon ouvrier, mythe ou réalité du XIXe siècle", in "Revue Belge de Philologie et d'Histoire", 1978, p. 881).

16. Especially during the period 1850-1930, a maximization of working-hours is noticeable. Estimates here are beyond all doubt. Working-hours were then perhaps 60-70% higher than during the Ancien Régime. We refer for this to P. Bairoch. "The economic development of the Third World since 1900", London, 1977, p. 166; J. Fourastié, op.cit., p. 91.

17. The hostility manifests itself as much in the formulation of alternative management options; see for instance R. Garaudy, "Il est encore temps de vivre", Paris, 1980.

18. E. Scholliers, "De materiële verschijningsvormen van de armoede voor de industriële revolutie. Omvang, evolutie en oorzaken", in "Tijdschrift voor Geschiedenis", 1975, pp. 451-467.

19. C. Vandenbroeke, "Agriculture et Alimentation dans les Pays-Bas Autrichiens", Ghent, 1975; id., "L'Alimentation à Gand pendant la première moitié du XIXe siècle", in "Annales. Economies-Sociétés-Civilisations", 1975, pp. 584-591; C. Lis-H. Soly, "Food consumption in Antwerp between 1807 and 1859: a contribution to the standard of living debate", in the "Economic History Review", 1977, pp. 460-486.

20. Especially, from the late 19th century on and simultanously with the price fall of bread and corn, a "bakcward-sloping curve" emerged.

21. C. Vandenbroeke, "Cultivation and consumption of the potato in the 17th and 18th century", in "Acta Historiae Neerlandica", V, 1971, pp. 15-39.

22. Already in the course of the 1780's, a comparative price-analysis was inserted in the above mentioned work of Derival: "on trouve à Bruxelles des comestibles excellents et de toutes espèces; s'ils sont chers, ils sont d'un prix très-modéré dans les autres villes. On vit cependant à Bruxelles à un tiers meilleur marché qu'à Paris et pour la moitié moins qu'à Londres et à Amsterdam ...".

23. H. Denis, "La crise agricole. Histoire

des Prix en Belgique", Brussels, 1880; G.
Bublot, "La production agricole belge. Etude économique séculaire, 1846-1955", Louvain, 1957.
24. C. Juglar, "Des crises alimentaires et de
leur retour périodique en France, en Angleterre et
aux Etats-Unies", Paris, 1889, pp. 534-535.
25. The changes in the food-pattern during the
Ancien Régime were very well summarized by W.
Abel: "vom Fleischstandard des Spätmittelalters über den
Getreidestandard der frühen Neuzeit zum Kartoffel-
standard im Zeitalter des Pauperismus" ("Massenarmut
und Hungerkrisen im vorindustriellen Deutschland",
Göttingen, 1977, p. 65).
26. A.J. Meynne, "Topographie médicale de la
Belgique", Brussels, 1865, p. 443.
27. C. Vandenbroeke, "Agriculture et Alimentation ...", op.cit., pp. 597-600.
28. In England, the consumption of meat between 1870 and 1896 was increased by 30-35% (E.J.
Hobsbawm, op.cit., p. 162). In France, we notice an
average increase of 25-35 kg. (J.P. Houssel et.al.,
"Histoire des paysans français du XVIIIe siècle à
nos jours", Roanne, 1976, p. 326). In Germany the
meat consumption per capita was about 45 kg by 1900;
see H.J. Teuteberg - G. Wiegelmann, "Der Wandel der
Nahrungsgewohnheiten unter dem Einfluss der Industrialisierung", Göttingen, 1972, pp. 120-121.
29. Concerning meat consumption in Belgium we
refer to G. Jacquemyns, op.cit., p. 261; A.J. Meynne,
op.cit., pp. 442-443; W. Minchinton, op.cit., p.132;
H. Denis, "Droits d'entrée sur les céreales et les
bestiaux", Brussels, 1885, p. 3; id., "Les phases de
l'histoire des prix depuis 1850 et la corrélation
des phénomènes économiques", Brussels, 1913, pp. 53-
67.
30. There is no question at all, in the Southern Netherlands, of a standard of living debate, as
in England. All symptoms point to a manifest impoverishment of the population during the period
1780-1850.
31. P.C. van der Meersh, "De l'état de la men-
dicité et de la bienfaisance dans la province de
Flandre Orientale depuis le règne de Marie-Thérèse
jusqu'à nos jours", in "Bulletin de la Commission
Centrale de la Statistique", V, Brussels, 1952.
32. C. Vandenbroeke, "De keurlingenlijsten als
sociaal-demografische meter", in "De Leiegouw", 1981.
33. J. Fourastié, op.cit., p. 83; see also D.
Oddy - J. Miller (eds.), "The making of the modern
British diet", London, 1976, p.219.
34. A.J. Meynne, op.cit.
35. C. Vandenbroeke, "De medische Consumptie

        sinds de 16e eeuw", in "Handelingen Maat-
schappij Geschiedenis en Oudheidkunde Gent", 1980.
A very convincing discussion of the increase of
medical consumption since the middle of the 20th
century is to be found in P. Surrault, "L'inégalité
devant la mort", Paris, 1979, pp. 89-90.
        36. E. Ducpétiaux, "Budgets économiques des
classes ouvrières en Belgique", Brussels, 1885; E.
Engel, "Die Lebenskosten belgischer Arbeiterfamilien
früher und jetzt", Dresden, 1895.
        37. This problem was discussed in an interna-
tional context by P. Bairoch, "Commerce extérieur et
développement économique de l'Europe au XIXe siècle",
Paris, 1976, p. 232.
        38. J. Stengers, "Emigration et immigration en
Belgique au XIXe et au XXe siècles", Brussels, 1978.
        39. Changes in employment in Belgium can be
summarized as follows:

	Primary	Secondary	Tertiary
1846	50.9	36.2	12.8
1856	46.8	37.4	15.8
1866	44.4	37.8	17.8
1880	39.6	36.2	24.2
1890	32.1	38.6	29.3
1910	23.2	45.5	31.3
1920	21.7	48.1	30.1
1930	17.3	47.6	35.1
1947	12.5	48.7	38.8
1961	7.4	47.1	45.4

        40. P. Van den Eeckhout, "Onderzoek naar kwan-
titatieve en kwalitatieve wijzigingen in de consumptie, 1840-1890", in J. Hannes, (ed.), "Consumptiepatronen en prijsindices", Brussels, 1981. See also
E. Mahaim, "Changes in wages and real wages in Belgium", in "Journal of the Royal Statistical Society",
1904, pp. 430-438.
        41. P. Scholliers, "Koopkracht en indexkoppe-
ling. De Brusselse levensstandaard tijdens en na de
Eerste Wereldoorlog, 1914-1925", in "Revue Belge d'
Histoire Contemporaine", 1978, pp. 333-382.
        42. See among others: C. Lis - H. Soly, "Pov-
erty and capitalism", op.cit.; P. Scholliers, "Ver-
schuivingen in het arbeidersconsumptiepatroon, 1890-
1930" (to be published in the "Revue Belge d'Histoire Contemporaine",1982).
        43. E.g. A.S. Deaton, "The structure of demand,
1920-1970", in The Fontana Economic History of
Europe, Vol. V, pp. 89-131. The author was not able
to include Belgium in his research.
        44. E. Ducpétiaux, "Budgets économiques ...",
op.cit.; "Salaires et budgets ouvriers en Belgique

au mois d'avril 1891", Brussels, 1892; B.
Seebohm-Rowntree, "Land and Labour. Lessons from
Belgium", London, 1910 (see also: "Cost of living in
Belgian towns. Report of an enquirey by the board
of trade into working class rents, housing and retail prices, together with rates of wages in certain
occupations in the principal industrial towns of
Belgium", in "Bulletin du Ravitaillement", november
1919, p. 39; A. Julin, "Résultats principaux d'une
enquête sur les budgets ouvriers et d'employés en
Belgique (1928-1929)", in "Bulletin de l'Institut
International de Statistiques", 1934, pp. 516-559,
which quotes the results of the 1921-enquiries; "Le
carnet de dépenses hebdomadaires d'une famille
ouvrière de 4 personnes en juillet 1930" in "Le
Peuple", February 24, 1931, p. 4; G. Jacquemyns,
"Enquête sur les conditions de vie de chômeurs as-
surés. Liège, 1932-1934", 5 Vol.; J. Arendt, "Les
conditions d'existence des travailleurs et des en-
treprises en Belgique en 1935 et en 1936", Brussels,
1936. (This enquiry was continued till 1939); "Budget d'employé", in "Revue du Travail", March 1922,
p. 403.
    45. See also P. Scholliers, "Arbeiderconsump-
tie in transitie, 1890-1930", in J. Hannes (ed.),
"Consumptiepatronen en prijsindices", op.cit.
    46. M. Gottschalk, ("Budgets ouvriers en 1891
et en 1929", in "Revue de l'Institut de Sociologie",
1931, pp. 749-773) made a superficial study of the
improvement in nutrition and came to extremely optimistic conclusions.
    47. A. Slosse, E. Waxweiler, "Enquête sur le
régime alimentaire de 1.065 ouvriers belges", Brussels, 1910; M. van Temsche, "Enquête sur le régime
alimentaire d'un groupe d'ouvriers malinois (mars
1923)", in Bulletin Scientifique d'hygiène alimentaire, 1924, pp. 601-648.
    48. L.H. Dupriez, "Indices de la consommation
en Belgique de 1897 à 1933", in "Bulletin Institut
des Sciences Economiques", 1933-1934, pp. 3-29.
Sales figures of co-operative stores between 1919
and 1939 are collected in the archives of the firms
but have not been published.
    49. "Statistiques économiques belges, 1929-
1940", Brussels, s.d. (Chapter "Consommation", pp.
323-329).
    50. Figures for 1891, 1917, 1928 and 1939
refer to the consumption of food by the working
class. The figures used above (see table "Consumption of the food-basket in Flanders") concern the
total population, including the higher social
classes.

51. Calculated from series by G. Bigwood, "Le régime alimentaire actuel de la population belge", Brussels, 1939.

52. The changes in the structure of demand during the thirties have been studied by A. Grauwels, "De impakt van de crisis op het consumptiepatroon tussen beide wereldoorlogen, 1929-1939", in J. Hannes (ed.), "Consumptiepatronen en prijsindeces, op.cit.

53. See, for instance, graph 12: the difference between the consumption of groceries in the co-operative stores of Ghent and Brussels is striking. Wages in Ghent tended to be low, while the working class was better off in Brussels.

54. Figures of industrial production: "L'évolution économique de la Belgique avant la guerre", in Bulletin Institut des Sciences Economiques, 1929, pp. 53-72; C. Carbonelle, "Recherches sur l'évolution de la production en Belgique de 1900 à 1957", in "Cahiers économiques de Bruxelles", 1959, pp. 353-377.

55. "Annuaire Statistique de la Belgique", Vol. 97, 1977 (Chapter "Consommation"), pp. 612-629.

Graph 2.1A: Purchasing Power (Litres of Rye) of a Flemish Labourer

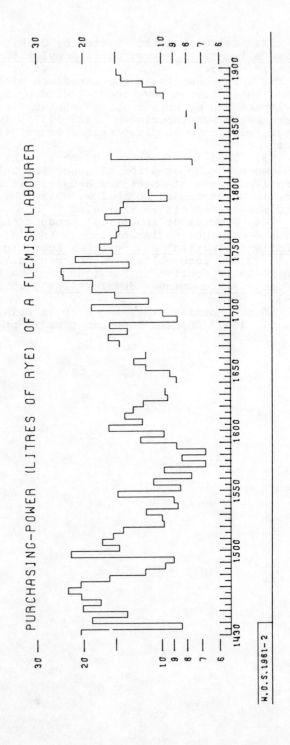

PURCHASING-POWER (LITRES OF RYE) OF A FLEMISH LABOURER

W.O.S.1981-2

Graph 2.1B: Evolution of the Purchasing Power in
Belgium (index 1913/14 = 100)

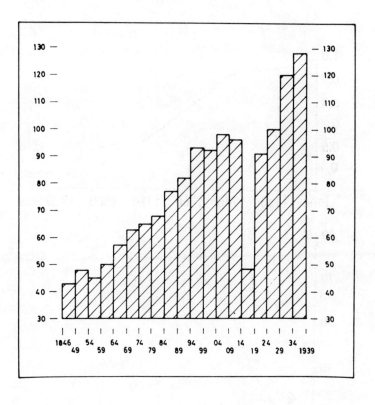

Graph 2.2: Consumption of cereals (1) and
mentions of potatoes in probate inventories (2)

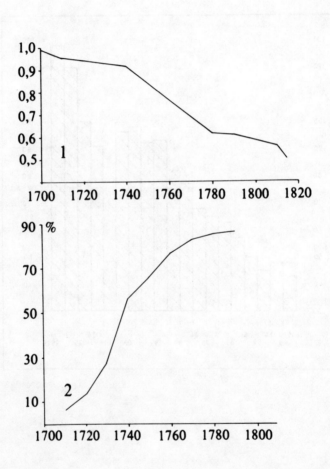

Graph 2.3: Import of corn (---) and price of
bread (———)

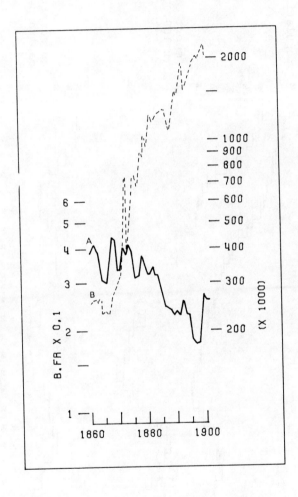

61

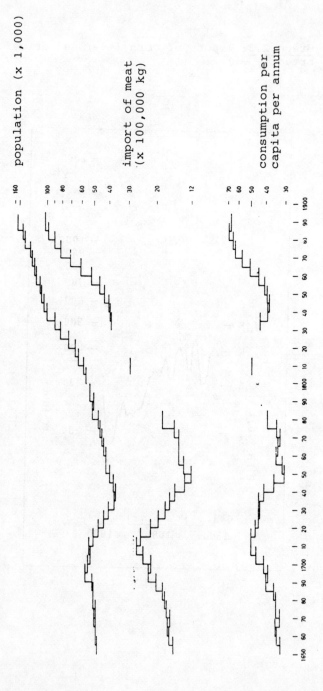

Graph 2.4: Consumption of meat at Ghent

population (x 1,000)

import of meat
(x 100,000 kg)

consumption per
capita per annum

62

Graph 2.5: Consumption of meat in Eastern-Flanders (1820)

Graph 2.6: Medical consumption in Flanders

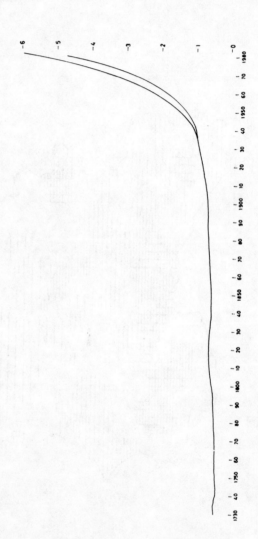

Graph 2.7: Ratio of physicians in Belgium

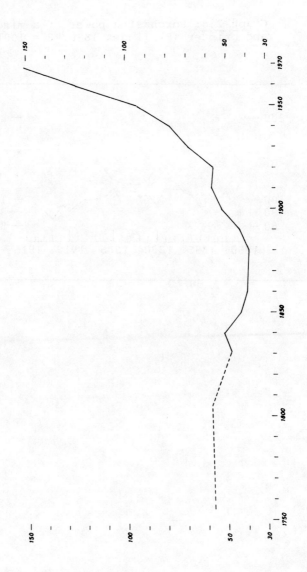

Graph 2.8: Purchasing power of a miner (A) and printer (B) (index 1890/92 = 100)

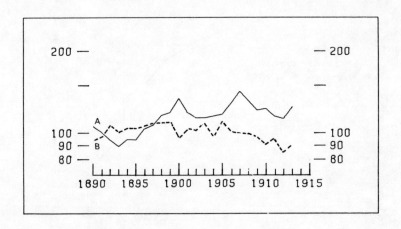

Graph 2.9: Prices (1), Wages (3) and Purchasing Power (2) in all Industries
(index 1913/14 = 100)

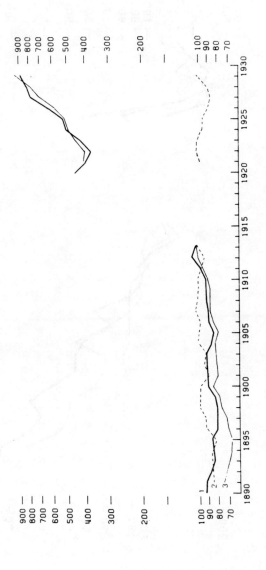

67

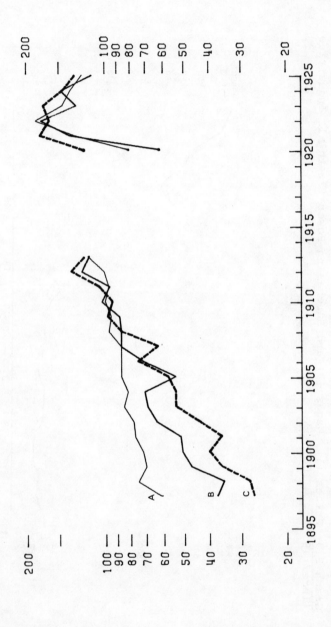

Graph 2.10: Consumption of Cheese (A), Fruit (B) and Cocoa (C) (index 1907/09= 100).

68

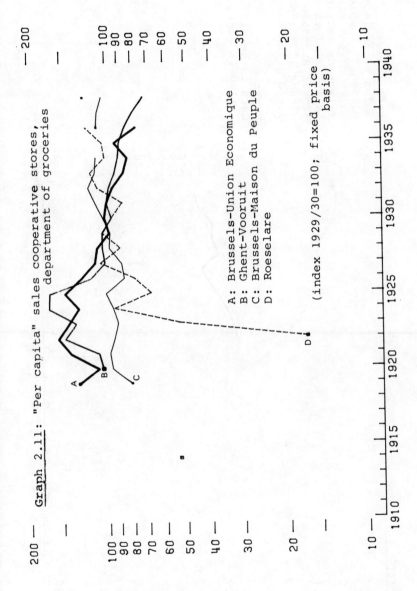

Graph 2.11: "Per capita" sales cooperative stores, department of groceries

A: Brussels-Union Economique
B: Ghent-Vooruit
C: Brussels-Maison du Peuple
D: Roeselare

(index 1929/30=100; fixed price basis)

70

Graph 2.12

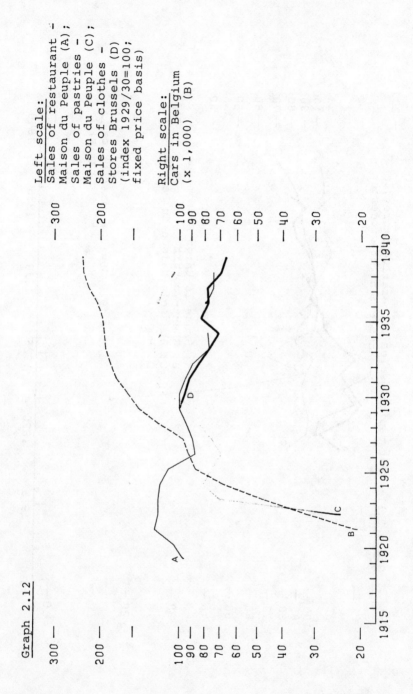

Left scale:
Sales of restaurant
Maison du Peuple (A);
Sales of pastries -
Maison du Peuple (C);
Sales of clothes -
Stores Brussels (D)
(index 1929/30=100;
fixed price basis)

Right scale:
Cars in Belgium
(x 1,000) (B)

Graph 2.13: Risk of mortality in Southern-Flanders

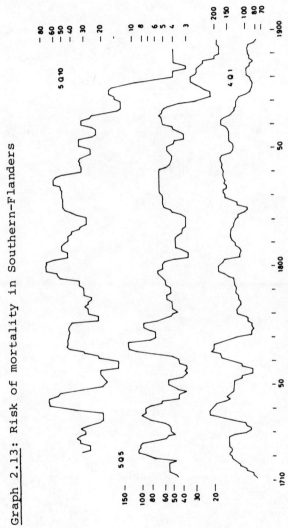

Chapter 3
FOOD CONSUMPTION AND WELFARE 1852-1911

Henri Baudet and Henk van der Meulen

Chapter 3

FOOD CONSUMPTION AND WELFARE 1852-1911

Henri Baudet and Henk van der Meulen

INTRODUCTION

"The consumption of the principal foodstuffs and
stimulants (except alcohol), insofar as this can be
established with sufficient certainty, is without
doubt one of the most important data from which
conclusions can be drawn about tendencies in nal-
tional prosperity over a specified period of time.
A nation is more prosperous the more amply it is
able to provide for its needs".[1] In his behaviour
towards food, the consumer is guided by a large
number of different impulses. Disposable income
and food prices, which we shall, in the main, con-
fine our attention to in this paper, are very important in this connexion, certainly in the period
selected by us. This is, of course, not to say
that there are not other strong impulses: "fact,
fallacy, religion and folklore" also play their
part, sure enough.[2] In a number of observations
which we have already made elsewhere, this 'behavioural' side of consumption came under discussion.[3]
     This paper attempts to establish, as accurate-
ly as possible, given the available figures, the
relationship during the period 1852-1911 which
existed between the development in the quantities
consumed of a number of foodstuffs and stimulants
(always taken to exclude alcohol for the purposes
of this paper), the trend of food prices and the
progress of the estimated (national) income. We
shall be using average quantities (with respect to
amounts) per head of population. So, here, average
means that no attempt will be made to establish a
specific model for specific groups. The working
data do not permit such a disaggregation. In other
publications, attention is given to the results of
budgetary research covering our period, or the

question of the evolution of prosperity in the Netherlands is asked of completely different material: consumption in the non-food sector, taxation data, voters' lists etc.[5] We shall merely have to refer briefly to the results of several of these investigations. Statistical material of a different kind may perhaps permit disaggregation; we shall return to this subject later.

If, with rising income, a diminishing part of this income is spent on prime necessaries (such as food), we see that Engel's Law is confirmed. This is a law which expressly claims that such a phenomenon is characteristic of an industrialized society, an economy with mass production and mass consumption, with rapid economic growth. The results of our research give rise to doubt about the validity in two directions of Engel's Law as interpreted above.

In the time series studied, the depression of the '80's stands out clearly, especially in the evolution of prices. The sharp rise in Theyl's *real* national income in the same period points to the same thing: the depression was primarily one of prices, and, consequently of the incomes of those whose earnings had to come from (agricultural) prices: (small) farmers and farm-labourers. If one takes the view that 'typical' prosperity phenomena are increasing quantities of food consumed and a declining proportion of expenditure on food in the disposable income, and with this occurring at the time of the Great Depression, thought must be given to the position of these disadvantaged groups; they will be left out of the average picture.

DATA

The quotation at the beginning of the Introduction was taken from the "Investigation into the consumption of some foodstuffs and stimulants" by the Dutch Central Commission for Statistics (CCS), later renamed Central Office of Statistics (CBS). This investigation, initiated in 1895, was continued in 1913 and 1920.[6] The researcher into food consumption in the Netherlands in the 19th century will almost certainly have to make do with these figures, if he is looking for material more or less representative for the whole country. Brugmans, Burema, De Jonge, Van Thijn made use, inter alia, of this statistical material, which can be described as unique for the time when it was collected.[7]

In the field of prices, much more work has

been done in addition to the Investigation mentioned here. However, we shall restrict ourselves in this paper to the CCS/CBS figures, because, on the one hand, they are directly matched to the volumes of the "Investigation", and, on the other hand, the other time series used by us are based on the same source: the Meerenberg Institution, a few hospitals, prisons and also a number of shopkeepers' associations.[8] What we lose by this limitation in national representativeness, we gain in consistency within the time series and between them.

For the development of economic activity in the Netherlands, we make use of the best which is to be found about this in the literature: the work of Brugmans, De Jonge, Theyl, Van Stuijvenberg, De Vries and Bos.[9] Consideration of this literature promptly leads to a discussion of the dating of industrialization in our country. Proceeding from the assumption that consumer behaviour does indeed change greatly under the influence of such radical developments, our conclusions lead to a definition of position in this debate. However, dating is not our primary purpose in this paper (see also Section 8).

Finally, a number of observations will have to be based on a collection of (workers') budgets of the selected period. Budgets with rarity value: the 46 (!) known budgets of the period 1852-1897 are repeatedly used - in social history and other literature just as the "Investigation" is. The editions of the budgets which we have used were analysed by H. Klompmaker and H. Vink.[10]

From the material described above, time series were reconstructed, taking into account quantities, prices, nominal expenditure and (national) income. Index figures (1877-1881 = 100) were employed in the presentation of these time series for the sake of positive comparison. Special treatment was required by the two series of estimates of the national income established by Theyl.[11] These figures translated into quinquennial averages were handled in the research by means of interpolation. Theyl's method of estimation produces time series with constant purchasing power (1910 prices).

We calculate what relationship the growth of real spending on ten foodstuffs and stimulants for which complete sets of figures were found, bears to the development of real (national) income, proceeding (again) naturally from the original, non-standardized time series.

An attempt to use *nominal* income development as an explanation for consumer behaviour (to in-

77

troduce some kind of money-illusion) failed, because there is no satisfying index of consumer-prices with which to adjust Theyl's figures. A trial with the unweighted mean of the Meerenberg prices produced highly inconsistant results. On the other hand, money-illusion is not very likely, given the heavy deflation during the 80's and 90's. Thus all income elasticities were constructed on the basis of volume-data.

Expressed as a formula : $Ey = \dfrac{\Delta C}{\Delta Y}$

where Ey = the income elasticity of consumption

ΔC = growth of consumer spending

$$\Delta C = \frac{C_t - C_{t-1}}{C_{t-1}}$$

ΔY = growth of nominal income

$$\Delta Y = \frac{Y_t - Y_{t-1}}{Y_{t-1}}$$

Now when $Ey>1$, the share of consumption increases, when $Ey<1$, the share decreases: Engel's Law. A typical prosperity phenomenon arises when $Ey<0$ (with income rising). However, we can hardly say anything with any force of argument about inferiority and Giffen goods, unless we have more detailed statistical material.[12] The same is true of a special study of the development in the period of income elasticities with regard to certain articles of consumption, the so-called Engel curves.[13] We look upon the series of income elasticities met with merely as a rough indication of consumer behaviour relative to food.

Finally, the separate values for income elasticities are averaged, *nominal* spending serving as weights. Three combinations have been made: All ten foodstuffs and stimulants, foodstuffs excluding meat, and stimulants and meat. The last two combinations are an attempt to distinguish between 'absolute necessities' and 'luxuries'. The time series for these three combinations eventually give us, in our opinion, a reasonably justified picture of the reaction of food consumption on economic development in the Netherlands prior to the First World War, a picture, again, on the highest conceivable level of aggregation.

RESULTS

In the tables (see Annexe) we find, in the first
place, an overall picture of the index figures, of
quantities, prices and expenditure per head of
population. Consumption was calculated by the com-
pilers of the "Investigation" from production, cor-
rected for the balance between imports and exports
and for losses in processing, non-consumer use etc.
In a number of cases, accurate correction appeared
to be impossible. In the case of rye, peas and
beans especially, human consumption could not be
separated from their use as cattle feed. For the
beans category, an approximation for human consumption eventually appeared to be possible; in our
subsequent calculations we left rye and peas out of
consideration. The time series for sugar which
have been included, were compiled by us from various sources. For tea, currants, raisins and figs,
we have no reliable prices, so that they too do not
appear in further calculations.
   There is quite a different story to tell about
meat consumption. We appreciate that precisely
this important source of high-value protein should
be recorded, if one wants to be able to draw intel-
ligent inferences about the quality of the diet.
This fact was also appreciated by the statisticians
of the time. However, on the basis of the available data, it was impossible to construct good time
series for pork, mutton and lamb, and horseflesh,
not to mention, of course, game and poultry. Tendencies are indeed indicated: for pork and mutton
perhaps slightly increasing consumption, with the
quantities of mutton and lamb being pretty well
negligible in the Netherlands, for horseflesh
probably increasing consumption too. Only the
figures for beef and veal were considered to be
usable and have been included by us in the calculations.
   Finally, in this sereis of tables, some non-
food data have been included, that is to say,
spending on (new) gold and silver work, and also
the indirect tax levied on this, all three per head
of population. The tax time series could have a
special use as a kind of individual indicator of
prosperity, against which food consumption as well
as income development can be measured. The CSS/CBS
had indeed to do this in the absence of income figures. We shall further give, without commentary
here, Theyl's two sets of income figures: the first
estimated by use of the production function method
and the second by means of the tax quota method.

The development of population serves as the last time series. This was used all the time for calculating values per head.[14]

Some preliminary conclusions which can be drawn from these time series are the following:

1. The volumes consumed increase considerably in nearly all cases. Exception: buckwheat which is losing its importance as a foodstuff.

2. Cereals gain relatively on potatoes. This phenomenon is incidentally reported by many authors as seen as an indication of increasing prosperity and a 'modern' dietetic pattern - no longer potatoes with *every* meal.

3. Unfortunately, a shift from rye to wheaten bread cannot be established with certainty. In view of the development of prices and the increasing popularity of rye as cattle feed, such a shift is very likely to be mentioned. This too is generally seen as as indication of prosperity.

4. The high-value protein sector (beans, peas, beef) has increased relatively fast, also as far as spending is concerned. We must, however, be cautious with regard to peas, as reported, and, with regard to meat, we must give thought to the increase in consumption of pork and horseflesh. To sum up, we may conclude that the diet has made rapid improvements in quality. (See, however, Section 4).

5. Stimulants and 'luxury' foods share in the growth, tobacco especially. Figs lose ground completely.

6. Thus altogether, our period shows growth in the volumes, often (more than) a doubling in 60 years. If we look at spending, this obviously lags far behind in the case of cereals and potatoes and not at all, or hardly at all, in pulses, sugar, meat and stimulants. Naturally an explanation for this state of affairs is to be found in price development: prices in the first named category fell heavily in the 1880's and 90's, those in the second category rose througout the depression.

7. The above-mentioned phenomenon is illustrated again in Graphs 1 and 2.

In Section 4 we return to the general picture provided by the figures: with the CSS/CBS we cannot fail to conclude that consumer behaviour points to

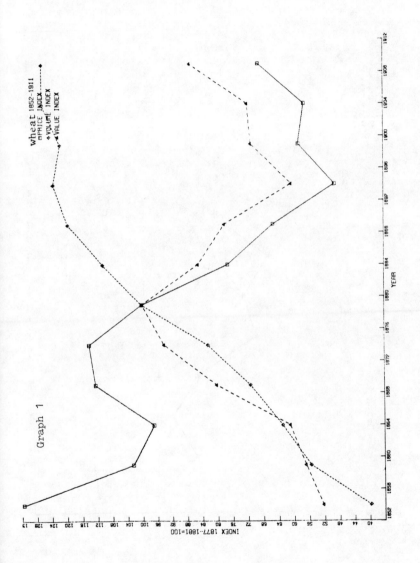

Graph 1

wheat 1852-1911
□PRICE INDEX
◆VOLUME INDEX
▲VALUE INDEX

INDEX 1877-1881=100

YEAR

81

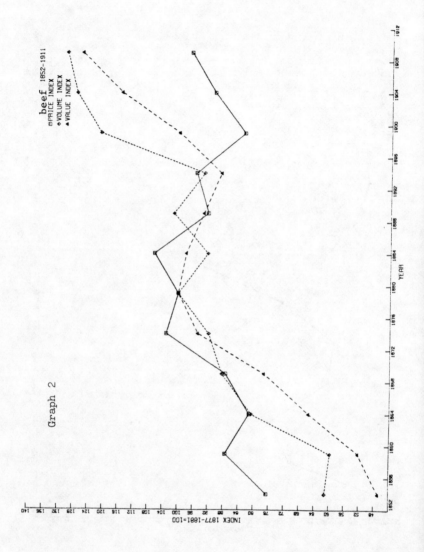

Graph 2

beef 1852-1911

□ PRICE INDEX
◇ VOLUME INDEX
▲ VALUE INDEX

INDEX 1877-1881=100

YEAR

82

increasing prosperity througout the period. The
question then arises whether this improvement in
living conditions put an end to the rather serious
shortage situation which the Netherlands met with
halfway through the 19th century.

Drinking is not included in these time series
(one could even speak of excessive drinking). This
omission is not caused by a lack of data; the use
of alcohol kept contemporary researchers into social matters terribly busy.[15] The relationship of
the consumption of alcohol to economic conditions
is, however, completely different from that of food
consumption. In a certain sense, an inverse relation can be assumed. (In fact, this occurs explicitly in the literature.) Moreover, in our opinion,
social and psychological influences are at work
here to a great(er) extent. See, in this connexion,
inter alia, the copious literature about the temperance movement in England and in the Netherlands.[16] However it may be, the use of alcohol in
the Netherlands declined considerably during our
period (after reaching a peak in 1835). Finally,
in the distribution of the consumption of alcohol
over the 11 provinces of the Netherlands, it is a
notable fact that the province where you now are,
namely Groningen, always achieved the highest
score and, in this province, the City of Groningen
was at the top of the league.[17]

A second set of figures consists of the prices
paid by the Meerenberg Institute for seven foodstuffs. These prices had also been used in part
by the CCS for the "Investigation". The unweighted
average of these time series is used in this paper
as a price index figure for food consumption and is
shown to be useless for our purposes (see page 78).
Graphs 3 and 4 give a clear picture of price development: white bread and butter plotted against the
general index, illustrating to what extent the
depression around 1881 influenced food prices.
White bread reacted strongly (cereal prices!),
butter prices (Dutch production, important export)
did not.

The third group of figures shows the results
of income elasticity calculations. Here too we are
making use of an assumption which is arguable.
Theyl's time series are based on an estimate (in
two ways) of real national income against factor
costs. We have used these figures intentionally,
as if it were here a matter of available family
income.
This is tenable only if:

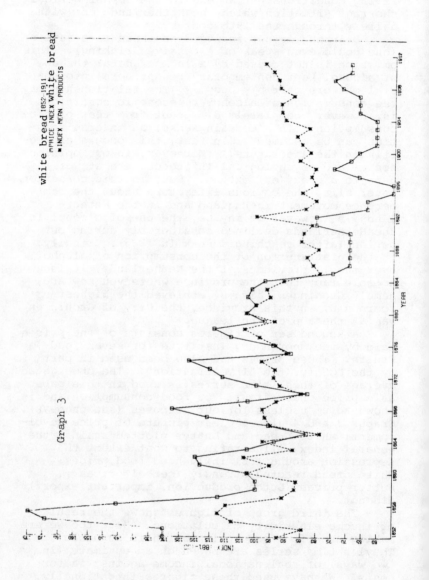

white bread 1852-1911

□ PRICE INDEX ✳ white bread

✳ INDEX MEAN 7 PRODUCTS

Graph 3

INDEX 1881=100

YEAR

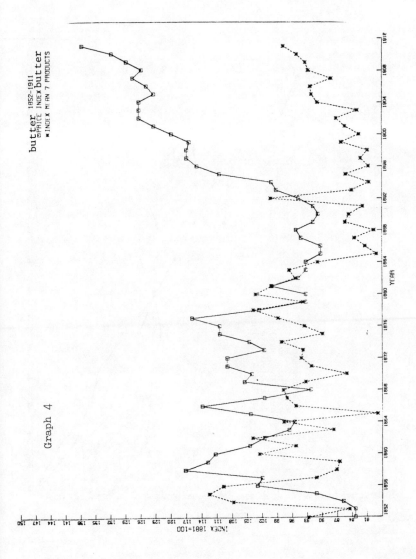

Graph 4

butter 1852-1911
□PRICE INDEX butter
✳INDEX MEAN 7 PRODUCTS

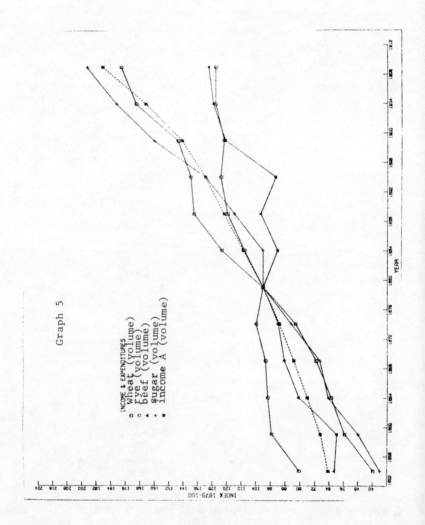

Graph 5

INCOME & EXPENDITURES
wheat (volume)
rye (volume)
beef (volume)
sugar (volume)
income A (volume)

INDEX 1879=100

YEAR

1. use alone is made of the (quinquennial) *growth* figures - which we do use - and
2. the assumption that available family income grew just as rapidly as national income can be made plausible - and this is what we assume.

Grounds for this assumption are provided especially by the observations of De Jonge and, to a lesser extent, Brugmans writing about wage and price development after 1850. The budgets too are indicative of continuous real improvement, although the depression did bite into agricultural incomes, as we have already stated.

The results of the various products can consequently be looked at with Ey greater or smaller than 1? as criterion. And the picture does not really vary greatly from what was expected. Cereals and potatoes score - certainly after 1877/81 - lower than pulses, sugar, meat and stimulants; the first category declines relatively in volume within the budget, the second category does not decrease or does so to a much smaller extent. That a product such as sugar behaves pretty much like meat (e.g. beef) in the development of its consumption is an indication of the, relatively, luxury character of both, that is to say, luxury in the eyes of the consumer in the second half of the 19th century. In the 18th century, sugar (molasses) was of all things a cheap substitute for meat among the poorest.[18]

The last three time series are weighted averages of the 10 elasticities: for the whole selection, for cereals and potatoes and for pulses, sugar, meat, coffee and tobacco. As was to be expected, the first and second sets of averages comply with Engel's Law (decreasing share of the budget). The third group does not. Nevertheless, this conclusion appears to be more agreeable than it really is.

DISAGGREGATION

An investigation, as previously described, derives its force of argument as well as its weak association with a multiform reality from a high level of aggregation. On the one hand, it can boast of a certain accuracy by reason of the institutional origin of the statistical material: CCS (CBS), the Meerenberg Institution, hospitals, prisons, traders' associations etc., and furthermore because of the spread of sources both geographically and chronologically (1852-1911). On the other hand, information solely about aggregated consumption does give an insight into the totality of society, but not into social reality, i.e. if not into individual consumer behaviour, at least into socially grouped consumer behaviour.

Information gained from budgetary research (mainly workers' budgets) as previously undertaken (and now being undertaken by ourselves), does provide a similar insight, but up to a very relative level. Representativeness and spreading are the problems here. Nevertheless, an analysis of family budgets cannot, for this reason, be set aside. Every indication of a possible detailed picture is, in our opinion, important. We have said this already. The literature of social history obviously subscribes to our opinion, and besides, it can be postulated, with regard to Engel's Law, that the use of budgetary material in cross-section form appears to be theoretically more plausible than the use of time series, which was what we did in the first instance. In the introduction to the proceedings of this conference which will be published in due time, this theoretical bakcground will be discussed in greater detail.

Thus, there is sufficient reason for undertaking an analysis of available family budgetary material. This involves:

1. The large collection of housekeeping books of 1891: 26 families who each filled in a prescribed book designed, distributed and edited by J.A. Tours and C.A. Verrijn-Stuart;[19]
2. A collection of housekeeping books covering the period 1910-11, designed etc. by the Social Democratic Study Circle (SDSC) and relating to the households of 70 working-class families;[20]
3. The author's own collection of private housekeeping books.

In our concluding remarks, we bring together, only in an indirect way, the data from 20 known budgets, dating back to the period 1854-1891.

We have focused, or tried to focus the analysis on the three sectors, which can be regarded as central to present-day historical research into consumption. They are: (1) consumption and standard of living; (2) consumption and innovative behaviour; (3) consumption and market tendencies.

Within the limitation selected for this contribution, the first of these sectors is the main

subject of discussion here. Nevertheless, some observations will be made about the other two sectors
as a result of the experience gained from the research.[21]

1891 : 26 BUDGETS

As expected, working with this type of material
seems to involve some specific difficulties, which
were partly diagnosed at that time too. Not the
most important fact is that the budgets are relatively small in number and their representativeness
is restricted. More critical is the doubtful reliability notably of a part of the 1891 information.
The working-class families referred to were not
much good at filling in and, what is more, keeping
housekeeping books. They harboured understandable
suspicions of the interest shown by the well-off
who were "looking at their ha'pennies". All kinds
of expenditure and income particularly were sup-
pressed, and could, when checked, be only partially
detected. Carefulness which needed to be maintained for a whole year (1st July 1889 - 1st July
1890) was frequently too taxing and therefore far
to seek. Over and over again, considerable differences between outgoings and income did not appear to be justified anywhere in the budget nor
were these differences susceptible of satisfactory
explanation. Moreover, not in all cases, was the
size of the family known, so that statistical
treatment according to consumption units was not
possible. That in the end 18 of the 26 budgets
were, for all that, considered to be reasonably
usable, meant that they had to be judged manifestly
deficient in no more than *one* of the senses mentioned.
     In spite of the narrow compass of such a
limited set of data, obtained, at that, not by non-
selective, random sampling, and also with so many
reservations, there was no reason to suppose that
the budget of the average Dutch working-class family
in 1890 differed greatly from the average of the
figures obtained by Tours (see Table 3.1).
     The 52% of income spent on food showed in this
set of data a remarkably small variation. That
could indicate that the incomes considered were the
lowest with respect to minimum physical needs.
Around 1900 the share of expenditure on food, according to later estimates, amounted to about 50%
in comparable income groups.[22] That could support
the acceptability of the 1891 estimate.
     But the evaluation of such a percentage is

Table 3.1.

	Average of 26 budgets	Average of 18 more or less reliable budgets
Weekly income in guilders	11.1	12.2
Weekly expenditure in guilders	11.2	11.9
Percentage of expenditure on food	54	54
Percentage of expenditure on housing	21	21
Percentage of expenditure on clothing	14	14
Percentage of expenditure on education and pleasure	5	5

always a difficulty. Ernst Engel obtained a result for Belgium in 1853 that showed, on an average, a working-class family consisting of a man, his wife and three children (just about the average), spent 65.83% of his outgoings on food. This corresponds, according to his table, to an average annual income of approximately 800 francs.[23]

Table 3.2.

Annual family income in francs				Percentage of expenditure on food
200	.	.	.	72.96
300	.	.	.	71.48
400	.	.	.	70.11
500	.	.	.	68.85
600	.	.	.	67.70
700	.	.	.	66.65
800	.	.	.	65.69
900	.	.	.	64.81
1000	.	.	.	64.00
1100	.	.	.	63.25
1200	.	.	.	62.55
1300	.	.	.	61.90
1400	.	.	.	61.30
1500	.	.	.	60.75
1600	.	.	.	60.25
1700	.	.	.	59.79
1800	.	.	.	59.37
1900	.	.	.	58.99
2000	.	.	.	58.65

Annual family income in francs			Percentage of expenditure on food
2100	.	. .	58.35
2200	.	. .	58.08
2300	.	. .	57.84
2400	.	. .	57.63
2500	.	. .	57.45
2600	.	. .	57.30
2700	.	. .	57.17
2800	.	. .	57.06
2900	.	. .	56.97
3000	.	. .	56.90

In 1891, prices of foodstuffs were near enough equal to those in 1853, but wages and the standard of living had risen considerably as a result partly of somewhat violent movements in prices and volumes between these two years. Recent research, such as that of Peter Scholliers also gives a clear impression of this.[24] But is is scarcely to be supposed that the average percentage of expenditure on food could therefore have declined to 50, even if the rise in wages between 1853 and 1891 could have amounted to more than 50%, which we can, at least, assume to be broad view.

Engel produced in 1853 a reasonably positive judgment of labour relations in Belgium and the development of the standard of living of working-class families.[25] His opinion of the situation in the Netherlands was probably no less favourable. Such an aggregated validity does not mean that numerous working-class families were not living below the level.

1912 : 70 BUDGETS

The same can be said mutatis mutandis in respect of the results of the research undertaken by the Social Democratic Study Circle (SDSC) and published in 1912. In this research 70 working-class families co-operated: they were a selection from the 131 who had spontaneously reacted to an appeal in the trade press. They formed a varied and, in every respect, well spread company who had to keep housekeeping books for the period June 1910 until June 1911. Incidentally, the method followed was, in the main, similar to, or, at least, highly comparable with that used in 1891.

One certainly has the impression that the families of the 1912 group achieve, as a whole, a higher score socially than those of the 1891 group.

The SDSC made no secret of the fact that the appeal
had reached mainly organized workers and that the
budgets showed markedly that they originated from
well-regulated households running fairly smoothly,
and even, for the most part, exemplary households.
There were no unemployed in the group. A further
indication that these families were hand-picked was
to be found in their average income (F. 876.77),
their average composition of a man, wife and three
children, the age of the head of the family and the
type of occupation.[26]
   That the average percentage of the outgoings
spent on food was now a few points lower (50.2%)
than twenty years previously, with the cost of living
remaining pretty well the same, ought perhaps to be
ascribed primarily to this fact.[27] An indication of
a distinct improvement in the standard of life of
Dutch working-class families in general is not, in
any case, to be gathered from this without further
study.
   We in the Netherlands are not over-indulged
with data on wages and wage development during this
period. The latter particularly is something which
we fail to track down from the incidental information contained in this type of budgetary research.
Besides, structural change in the spending pattern
has reason unexpectedly to point to some places in
the housekeeping books, and probably it is a factor
of significance, if not primarily from the point of
view of spending, then surely from the standpoint of
change in behaviour and mentality. However, for
this point, shopkeepers' accounts should be regarded
as the primary source (following the classical opinion of Stanley Jevons) in preference to the family
housekeeping books of the organized surveys discussed here and of other surveys.[28]

THE PRIVATE COLLECTION

The collection of private housekeeping books which
has been at our disposal for some time, more recently supplemented by the collection deposited in the
Dutch Economic History Archives, appears to contain,
nonetheless, an interesting stock of data. We shall
discuss this in greater detail in due course.
   The main difference between the information
derived from these collections and that emanating
from the budgetary research previously discussed,
lies in the diachronic character of these private
collections, which, in general, cover long to very
long periods, even decades. The question how these
can be turned to good account, is less easy to

answer than may perhaps appear at first sight.

Besides, it happens that, as a 'fortuitous' difference between the two groups of housekeeping books, the private collections, in the vast majority of cases, come from 'better' social circles with higher incomes: the family of a teacher, a judge, and similar people. A comparison of the spending of incomes in this category with that of working-class families can indeed be interesting from all sorts of points of view, but it is not easy to see how they can contribute to a study of the standard of living within the meaning decided upon above. It is precisely these divergent private housekeeping accounts which can furnish important contributions to the study of changing patterns in consumer behaviour especially when discretionary purchasing power is available. However, in the context of this paper, that subject does not come under consideration.

It is tempting to speculate whether this promising material is possibly applicable to the third aspect distinguished by us, i.e. consumption and market tendencies. Our line of thought could then lead to the following questions among others:

1. How has the dependable (macro-economic) picture of market prospects stood out, in point of fact, against the private sector?
2. How has the private sector reacted in fact to movements in the market, i.e. how has it been expressed in spending and saving?
3. Is there here a case - particularly when seen over a relatively short time span, as the 1880's and our 1930's - for showing a striking similarity between consumers having discretionary purchasing power at their disposal, or, alternatively, a striking difference between these as a category and working-class families at the level of, let us say, the 1912 survey?

In practice, however, budget research does not easily solve this kind of problem. Time series are not, for obvious reasons, the best data for interpersonal budget comparisons, being intended for intertemporal analysis. Budget surveys like those of 1891 and 1910 were based on cross-sections with a great amount of comparable data obtained by means of meticulously constructed questionnaires. The time series in the private collections had a different purpose. Housekeeping books were intended to record what was happening daily, weekly and monthly in a given family, but, in the end, they recorded, without

meaning to, the long-term course of household expenditure and, in some cases, of family income too.

These private accounts have, for that reason,
both advantages and disadvantages. They give us a
succession of pictures (not just a snapshot) of consumer behaviour - and, deriving from that, also pictures of fundamental aspects of human behaviour in a
wider sense - of (mainly) middle-class families.
Although our research so far indicates a considerable
similarity in the behaviour of the diverse families -
they react, for example, on the whole, in a surprisingly similar way to the vicissitudes of the
economy - our results still fail to be representative
when compared with the findings of surveys of
workers' families.

Monographs on the spending of one family over a
long period, particularly in unsettled years, should
be seen, first and foremost, as a positive opportunity for studying the data of this kind available in
private sources. Habits, behaviour and reactions to
circumstances, contained in their pages, can be
properly elicited and displayed by sophisticated
analysis.

No doubt, such monographs provide a start in
answering the questions formulated above. However,
these answers are, for the time being, far from con-
stituting pronouncements or any kind of generalisa-
tion. It would appear that priority has to be given
to a different kind of research, which should smooth
the way to providing the vital, missing link between
the different levels of aggregation in macro-economic
data and individual family records.

We have already put forward the view that
changes in the pattern of consumption - innovative
consumer behaviour - are some of the obvious, important subjects within our field of research. This
subject also plays a really important part in the
relationship between consumption and the economic
climate.

SOME CONCLUDING REMARKS

As budgetary research of the 1891 or 1912 type (or
much research of more recent date) stands, in many
respects, squarely on the follow-up of one or more
individual families in time, using their housekeeping books, so, in this paper, macro-time-series
also stand in respect to meso- and micro-budgets.
Time series and cross-sections appear to be mutually
exclusive where a number of hypotheses about food
consumption behaviour are concerned. Thus, time
series should lend themselves to research into causal

relations between individual behaviour and economic variables such as prices and incomes. A cross-section, like a snapshot, enables as insight to be gained into the (social) stratification of food consumption. Income can also be used, in this connexion, as a (stratification) criterion.

At the same time, a combination of the two kinds of research can also be useful. Basically, both examine the same problems of relations between people and the material environment. After evaluating the macro-time-series and the various pieces of budgetary research, we reach a number of final conclusions:

1. The economy of the Netherlands, measured by food consumption behaviour, is certainly not a "full grown" society at the end of the period under review, i.e. the eve of the First World War, which affected the larger part of Europe directly and the Netherlands indirectly (through the economy among other things). It is true the national product is growing fast but there is as yet no question of mass production and mass consumption. Rather there is (and still is) a question of a pre-industrial deficiency (both in quantity and quality) in necessary foodstuffs for a large part of the Dutch population.

2. If, in the time series, there are indications of a continuous increase in food consumption (stemming from "prosperity", as the CCS/CBS terms it), investigation of working-class budgets collected between 1854 and 1912 in terms of caloric value and high-value protein content shows that there was indeed improvement during the period but the final result: an average number of kilocalories *below* 2,800 and an average quantity of high-value protein *below* 75 g. (both for an "average" person per day) points to malnutrition: both quantitatively (energy value in k cal.) and qualitatively (protein value). These deficiencies have been calculated from budgets of families where the breadwinner was in work and receiving a wage probably somewhat higher than the minimum.[29]

3. The increasing purchasing power of the Dutch wage-earner during our period was due partly to the growing productivity of labour, but partly also to food prices which were on average sharply falling in

95

the post 1880 period. These food prices
were also falling relative to other prices
during the "Great Depression".
These two factors : real progress and relatively falling food prices explain to a
considerable extent the growth of food consumption and the improvement in the quality
of the diet. This also explains the fact
that the share of nutrition in the total
budget declines slightly *at the same time*:
increased prosperity does not in itself
supply the explanation (this is an interpretation which is indeed given to Engel's
Law), but, at least, partly the changed
price relationship of foodstuffs to other
consumer goods does. The agricultural deflation mentioned here emphasizes the fact
that the 80's and 90's were relatively less
favourable to a number of disadvantaged
groups such as farm labourers, small farmers, peat-cutters and others than to industrial workers and, more generally, inhabitants of the urban (western) areas of
the Netherlands. This picture is confirmed
by the budgets of farm labourers with which
we are acquainted for this period.

4.   These final observations bring us to a
final consideration of time series and
cross-sections. Engel's Law had, and still
has, no pretention to causal relationship.
Such a causality between income and consumption is also difficult to deduce from
cross-section research. On the other hand,
time-series analysis makes research into
(possibly causal) relationships between
consumption and other economic variables
possible. Houthakker estimates, with the
help of regression calculation, the connexion between the consumption of various
foodstuffs and explanatory variables such
as prices, incomes and the quantities consumed themselves, the latter naturally
lagging behind. He does this with post
1929 data obtained from the USA. Through
extrapolation on the basis of connexions
already found, he then makes predictions up
to 1970.[30] In the meantime, we began with
comparable statistical research based on
statistical material (1852-1911). Some
provisional results give an indication of
one and the same conclusion which Houthakker
arrived at. The movement in the prices of

foodstuffs explains far more of the development in quantities consumed than the other explanatory variables (income, lagging quantities, lagging prices and others). In other words, the consumer reacts, as an individual, primarily to price changes and not so much to income development during the period under review. As a result of this, a phenomenon as described in Engel's Law can be found in cross-sections. This is a matter of the consumption *pattern* of a society at a specified time. Really, a better illustration of the ideas of Ernst Engel could not be wished for.

NOTES

1. "Onderzoek naar het verbruik van sommige voedings- en genotmiddelen", Bijdragen tot de Statistiek van Nederland (Centrale Commissie voor de Statistiek), II, The Hague, 1895.

2. See for instance, Magnus Pyke, Food and Society, Fact, fallacy, religion and folklore - the background to scientific nutrition, London, 1968.

3. H. Baudet, "Mensen en Dingen", Tijdschrift voor Geschiedenis, 1969; H. Baudet (et.al.), "Consumenten en Innovaties II" (ZWO-reports), Groningen, 1977; H. Baudet and H. van der Meulen, "Productinnovatie - een algemene beschouwing en een ongerijmd voorbeeld", Paper Maatschappijconferentie 1979, Groningen, 1979.

4. Sources for family budget analysis are for example: Bijdragen van het Statistisch Instituut, 1886 and 1891; I.J. Brugmans, De Arbeidende Klasse in Nederland in de 19e eeuw, Utrecht, 1971[8]; L. Burema, De voeding in Nederland van de Middeleeuwen tot de twintigste eeuw, Assen, 1953; Th. van Tijn, "Het sociale leven in Nederland (1873-1914)", in Algemene Geschiedenis der Nederlanden, XIII, Haarlem, 1978. Other sources: For some standard (text-) books on Dutch 19th and 20th century economic and social history see note 9. To give here two examples of specific sources and how these can be used, we mention: Joh. de Vries, "Het censuskiesrecht en de welvaart in Nederland 1850-1917", ESHJ, XXXIV, 1971; L. Blok and J.M.M. de Meere, "Welstand, ongelijkheid in welstand en censuskiesrecht in Nederland omstreeks het middel van de 19e eeuw", ESHJ, XLI, 1978.

5. J. Teyl, "Nationaal inkomen van Nederland in de periode 1850-1900", ESHJ, XXXIV, 1971.

6. These are very consistent explorations. In the 1913 report, some of the 1895 time series have been recalculated on the basis of new insights.

7. I.J. Brugmans, "De arbeidende klasse", op. cit. ; I.J. Brugmans, Paardenkracht en Mensenmacht, The Hague, 1960; L. Burema, "De voeding in Nederland" op.cit. ; J.A. de Jonge, De Industrialisatie in Nederland tussen 1850 en 1914, Amsterdam, 1968; Th. van Tijn, "Het sociale leven", op.cit.

8. See: Maandschrift (voor de) Statisitiek, 1911, 1912, 1913. The "instellingen" (institutions) are, among others: The "Gesticht Meerenberg", hospitals in Amsterdam and prisons in 's-Hertogenbosch, Leeuwarden, Leiden and Hoorn. The retail-prices come from shops which are members of retailer co-operations such as: "Eigen Hulp" (Self Help) in Amsterdam, Haarlem, Arnhem, Utrecht and Leeuwarden and shops of another co-operation, former members of "Eigen Hulp". The food prices paid by Meerenberg are the only series covering the entire period 1852-1911. These series have therefore been used in the "Onderzoek", op.cit.

9. I.J. Brugmans, "Paardenkracht en Mensen-macht", op.cit.; J.A. de Jonge, "De Industrialisatie" op.cit.; J. Teyl, "Nationaal Inkomen", op.cit.; J.H. van Stuijvenberg, "Economische groei in Nederland in de 19e eeuw: een terreinverkenning", in Bedrijf en Samenleving, Alphen a/d Rijn, 1967; Joh. de Vries, De Nederlandse Economie tijdens de 20e eeuw, Utrecht, 1973; R.W.J.M. Bos, "Van periferie naar centrum: enige kanttekeningen bij de Nederlandse industriële ontwikkeling in de 19e eeuw", Maandschrift Economie, XI, 1975/76; R.W.J.M. Bos, Brits-Nederlandse Handel en Scheepvaart 1870-1914, Tilburg, 1978.

10. (See also note 4) H. Klompmaker, H. Vink, "De voeding der arbeidende klasse 1850-1900", 1977; J. Winkler, "Het kritieke minimum", 1980; both essays, written for the economic history department, State University of Groningen.

11. J. Teyl, "Nationaal Inkomen", op.cit.

12. "Inferiority" is meant here strictly in its economic definition. For the micro-economic theory of consumer behaviour, see, for instance: W.J. Baumol, Economic theory and operation analysis, London, 1972.

13. Econometricians have done much research on Engel's Law and on the Engel-curves: H.S. Houthakker and L.D. Taylor, Consumer demand in the United States 1929-1970, Analysis and projection, Cambridge, USA, 1966; S.J. Praix and H.S. Houthakker, The analysis of family budgets, Cambridge, USA, 1971.

14. J. Teyl, "Nationaal Inkomen", op.cit.

15. See e.g. Maandschrift (voor de) Statistiek, 1920 (supplement to the 1st issue pp. 1-41), in which one finds avery detailed (partially historical) survey of Dutch alcohol-consumption.

16. A.E. Dingle, "Drink and working-class living standards in Britain, 1870-1914"; D.J. Richardson, "J. Lyons and Co Ltd.: caterers and food manufacturers 1894-1934", both in: D.J. Oddy, D.S. Miller (eds.), The making of the modern British Diet, London, 1976.

17. Maandschrift Statistiek, 1920

year	Netherlands	Prov.of Groningen	litres of 50% alcohol-solutions per capita Groningen/town
1899	8.04	10.21	-
1913	5.24	7.68	9.31

18. D.J. Oddy, "A nutritional analysis of historical evidence: the working-class diet, 1880-1914" in D.J. Oddy, D.S. Miller (eds.), The making of the modern British Diet, London, 1976.

19. Bijdragen van het Statistisch Instituut, 1891. The budgets were collected by J.H. Tours and analysed by the "Statistische Instituut" in The Hague, 1891.

20. Jaarbudgets van 70 arbeidersgezinnen in Nederland. Report of an inquiry made by the "Sociaal-democratische Studieclub", Report nr. 69, Amsterdam, 1912.

21. At this point we would like to stress the co-operation of some of our students with respect to the budget-part of our research: A. Beetsma, J. Dölle, E. Jansen, H. Klompmaker, H. Vink (all history students).

22. A. van Braam, "Welvaartstoeneming en inkomensbesteding bij arbeidersgezinnen", in Socialisme en Democratie, 1960, pp. 510-521, Spec. 515.

23. Ernst Engel, Die Lebenskosten Belgischer Arbeiters-Familien früher und jetzt, p. 123; Ernst Engel, Die Produktions- und Konsumptions-verhältnisse des Königreichs Sachsen, pp. 29-31, both in: Bulletin de l'Institut International de Statistique, Tome IX, Première Livraison, 1895. Compare: H.S. Houthakker, An international comparison of household expenditure patterns, commemorating the centenary of Engel's Law, in Econometrica, 25, 1975, pp. 532-551, Spec. pp. 547-9. Compare: W.H. van der Goot, De besteding van het inkomen, The Hague, 1930, pp. 82-6.

24. Peter Scholliers, Lonen in de Brusselse drukkerij Hayez, 1865-1934, Centrum voor Hedendaagse Sociale Geschiedenis, Brussels, Free University of

Brussels, 1980, p. 16 passim

25. Ernst Engel, "Lebenskosten", op.cit, p.123.
26. Arbeidersbudgets, in Maandschrift van het Centraal Bureau voor de Statistiek, 8e jrg., nr. 5, 1913, pp. 280-1.
27. Compare: J.A. de Jonge, De industrialisatie in Nederland tussen 1850 en 1914, Amsterdam, 1968, p. 435. Compare: Maandschrift C.B.S., 1913, t.a.p. 280-81. Compare: A. van Braam, op.cit., p. 517.
28. This problem was seen very early by Frédérique Le Play. He introduced in 1856 the concept of the family monograph in which single families are followed through longer periods. Their behaviour then should be typical for certain groups; F. Le Play, Les ouvriers européens, 1855.
29. See H. Klompmaker, H. Vink, "Voeding arbeidende klasse", op.cit., and Nederlandse Voedingsmiddelentabel, The Hague, 1975[29].
30. H.S. Houthakker, L.D. Taylor, "Consumer Demand", op.cit.

APPENDIX

Tables

Table 3.1: Products for which price, volume and value are given (per head index 1877-1881=100)

Year	1. WHEAT			2. RYE		
	Price	Volume	Value	Price	Volume	Value
52-56	132	40	52	112	81	91
57-61	102	56	57	88	96	89
62-66	97	63	61	84	97	82
67-71	112	71	80	105	99	104
72-76	114	82	94	101	104	105
77-81	100	100	100	100	100	100
82-86	77	110	85	73	123	90
87-91	65	119	78	65	138	99
92-96	49	123	60	47	140	65
97-01	58	121	71	59	147	86
02-06	57	126	72	59	170	99
07-11	69	126	87	67	178	119

Year	3. BARLEY			4. BUCKWHEAT		
	Price	Volume	Value	Price	Volume	Value
52-56	94	100	94	108	105	113
57-61	89	97	86	98	98	96
62-66	87	97	84	97	98	94
67-71	104	116	120	115	100	115
72-76	108	106	115	113	95	107
77-81	100	100	100	100	100	100
82-86	78	106	83	82	71	58
87-91	70	106	74	79	61	48
92-96	54	158	85	65	44	28
97-01	67	97	65	78	37	28
02-06	66	190	125	75	29	22
07-11	76	200	152	89	22	20

	5. RICE			6. POTATOES		
Year	Price	Volume	Value	Price	Volume	Value
52-56	127	80	101	80	76	61
57-61	101	51	51	77	90	70
62-66	99	39	39	57	119	67
67-71	105	75	79	82	104	85
72-76	97	104	101	77	122	93
77-81	100	100	100	100	100	100
82-86	81	103	83	71	132	94
87-91	91	145	132	73	102	74
92-96	83	155	129	49	136	67
97-01	75	124	93	57	133	76
02-06	71	130	92	71	115	82
07-11	79	142	112	74	103	76

	7. BEANS			8. PEAS		
Year	Price	Volume	Value	Price	Volume	Value
52-56	91	63	72	96	46	45
57-61	86	71	73	100	42	43
62-66	91	78	82	90	57	51
67-71	100	80	89	97	89	86
72-76	93	82	81	100	80	80
77-81	100	100	100	100	100	100
82-86	92	107	92	79	147	116
87-91	85	125	94	81	133	108
92-96	80	152	100	72	134	96
97-01	72	251	141	72	142	103
02-06	88	205	189	73	217	159
07-11	119	304	246	105	193	202

	9. BEEF			10. COFFEE		
Year	Price	Volume	Value	Price	Volume	Value
52-56	77	61	47	65	66	45
57-61	88	60	52	80	62	50
62-66	81	81	66	96	56	54
67-71	88	88	77	81	68	55
72-76	103	92	95	118	115	136
77-81	100	100	100	100	100	100
82-86	106	92	98	66	125	82
87-91	92	101	93	112	87	98
92-96	95	93	89	116	100	116
97-01	83	121	100	82	116	95
02-06	91	127	115	65	105	68
07-11	97	130	126	83	100	83

	11. TABACCO			12. SUGAR		
Year	Price	Volume	Value	Price	Volume	Value
52-56	88	55	49	144	36	52
57-61	101	89	90	102	48	49
62-66	105	74	77	95	65	61
67-71	84	76	64	101	69	70
72-76	130	105	137	102	85	86
77-81	100	100	100	100	100	100
82-86	85	111	95	85	100	85
87-91	76	102	78	69	116	79
92-96	86	99	85	61	131	80
97-01	78	97	76	65	160	104
02-06	100	93	93	61	181	109
07-11	126	93	118	68	197	133

Table 3.2: Products for which volume or value is given (per head, index 1877-1881=100)

	13. TEA	14. CURRANTS	15. RAISINS	16. FIGS	17. GOLD	18. SILVER
Year	Volume	Volume	Volume	Volume	Value	Value
52-56	62	17	65	107	88	101
57-61	70	49	67	100	85	103
62-66	80	68	63	121	88	103
67-71	88	84	70	118	88	95
72-76	100	93	76	143	117	109
77-81	100	100	100	100	100	100
82-86	104	108	93	107	71	91
87-91	110	128	100	125	51	92
92-96	120	150	157	114	44	95
97-01	130	148	96	118	56	119
02-06	144	177	146	100	63	140
07-11	162	166	154	82	71	150

Table 3.3: Other items (per head, index 1877-1881=100)

	19. INCOME A*	20. INCOME B*	21. TAXATION*	22. POPULATION
Year	Volume	Volume	Gold/Silv.	Index
52-56	65	62	86	80
57-61	69	65	89	83
62-66	76	70	91	86
67-71	83	76	90	90
72-76	91	88	115	94
77-81	100	100	100	100
82-86	111	107	77	106
87-91	121	114	59	113
92-96	132	121	54	121
97-01	145	132	69	128
02-06	164	152	80	138
07-11	188	176	89	147

*INCOME A : National Income, volume per head, estimated on productionfunction basis.
*INCOME B : National Income, volume per head, estimated on tax quota basis.
*TAXATION : Indirect taxation of Gold and Silver objects (value-index).

Table 3.4: Prices as paid by 'Meerenberg' (index 1877-1881=100)

YEAR	23. WHITE BREAD	24. RYE BREAD	25. BUTTER	26. BEEF	27. RICE
52-56	144	122	89	72	127
57-61	102	74	109	87	101
62-66	95	80	101	80	99
67-71	101	84	101	87	105
72-76	102	85	106	101	97
77-81	100	100	100	100	100
82-86	85	95	91	105	81
87-91	69	78	92	91	91
92-96	61	80	103	94	83
97-01	65	83	117	82	75
02-06	61	86	124	89	71
07-11	68	86	129	96	79

YEAR	28. POTATOES	29. PEAS/GREEN	30. MEAN
52-56	92	82	102
57-61	98	79	93
62-66	94	72	93
67-71	91	81	93
72-76	79	89	94
77-81	100	100	100
82-86	81	85	89
87-91	91	83	83
92-96	86	96	86
97-01	83	79	84
02-06	110	80	89
07-11	89	109	93

Table 3.5: Income-elasticities on the basis of Income A

YEAR	31. INCOME A1	32. WHEAT	33. BARLEY	34. BUCKWHEAT	35. RICE	36. POTATOES
57-61	.03	13.4	-1.1	-2.4	-12.4	6.3
62-66	.06	2.2	0.0	0.0	-3.8	5.3
67-71	.05	2.5	3.7	0.5	17.3	-2.4
72-76	.05	3.3	-1.7	-1.0	8.1	3.7
77-81	.03	8.0	-2.3	1.9	-1.5	-6.7
82-86	.04	2.5	1.6	-7.0	0.8	7.6
87-91	.03	2.5	0.0	-4.1	11.9	-6.6
92-96	.01	2.5	39.8	-23.0	5.8	27.0
97-01	.04	-0.4	-11.0	-4.7	-5.7	-0.6
02-06	.06	0.6	16.4	-3.4	0.9	-2.3
07-11	.07	0.0	0.7	-3.6	1.3	-1.5

YEAR	37. BEANS	38. BEEF	39. COFFEE	40. TABACCO	41. SUGAR
57-61	4.5	-0.8	-2.1	21.2	11.3
62-66	1.6	5.8	-1.6	-2.9	5.8
67-71	0.6	1.8	4.1	0.6	1.3
72-76	0.5	0.8	14.5	7.9	4.6
77-81	8.2	3.3	-5.0	-1.8	6.8
82-86	1.7	-1.9	6.0	2.7	0.0
87-91	5.0	2.9	-8.9	-2.6	4.6
92-96	17.4	-6.5	12.3	-2.3	11.1
97-01	18.6	8.4	4.4	-0.4	6.2
02-06	3.0	0.9	-1.6	-0.6	2.2
07-11	0.4	0.3	-0.7	-0.0	1.3

INCOME A1 = (Income A(t)-Income A(t-1))/ Income A(t-1)

PRODUCT 1 = (Product(t)-Product(t-1))/Product(t-1)

All elasticities : Product = $\dfrac{\text{Product 1}}{\text{Income A1}}$

Table 3.6: Income elasticities on the basis of
Income B

YEAR	42. INCOME B1	43. WHEAT	44. BARLEY	45. BUCKWHEAT	46. RICE	47. POTATOES
57-61	.01	60.4	-4.9	-10.7	-55.8	28.4
62-66	.04	3.2	0.0	0.0	-5.6	7.7
67-71	.04	3.3	5.0	0.6	23.5	-3.2
72-76	.11	1.4	-0.7	-0.4	3.4	1.6
77-81	.07	3.2	-0.9	0.8	-0.6	-2.7
82-86	.01	18.9	12.0	-55.4	6.0	58.7
87-91	.01	11.4	0.0	-18.7	54.8	-30.1
92-96	-.01*	-2.4	-37.8	21.6	-5.4	-25.4
97-01	.03	-0.5	-12.1	-5.2	-6.3	-0.6
02-06	.07	0.6	14.0	-2.9	0.7	-2.0
07-11	.08	0.0	0.6	-3.0	1.1	-1.3

* So: <u>decreasing</u> income.

YEAR	48. BEANS	49. BEEF	50. COFFEE	51. TABACCO	52. SUGAR
57-61	20.1	-3.5	-9.6	95.2	50.9
62-66	2.3	8.4	-2.4	-4.3	8.4
67-71	0.8	2.4	5.5	0.8	1.8
72-76	0.2	0.3	6.1	3.4	2.0
77-81	3.3	1.3	-2.0	-0.7	2.8
82-86	13.0	-14.6	46.3	20.7	0.0
87-91	23.0	13.3	-40.8	-11.7	21.3
92-96	-16.4	6.1	-11.6	2.1	-10.4
97-01	20.5	9.2	4.9	-0.5	6.8
02-06	2.6	0.8	-1.4	-0.6	1.9
07-11	0.4	0.2	-0.6	-0.0	1.1

All elasticities are derived in the same way as
with income A1:
$$\text{Product} = \frac{\text{Product 1}}{\text{Income B1}}$$

Table 3.7: Weighted averages of income-elasticities.(Weights are the product-values per head)

YEAR	53 AA	54 BA	55 CA	56 AB	57 BB	58 CB
57-61	4.9	6.1	2.5	22.0	27.2	11.1
62-66	2.7	2.8	2.6	4.0	4.0	3.8
67-71	1.4	1.0	2.3	2.0	1.4	3.1
72-76	4.8	2.8	7.7	2.0	1.2	3.2
77-81	0.3	0.3	0.3	0.1	0.1	0.1
82-86	2.9	3.9	1.2	22.1	30.5	9.3
87-91	-1.3	-0.9	-1.8	-5.9	-4.2	-8.1
92-96	9.5	15.3	3.3	-9.0*	-14.4*	-3.1*
97-01	2.1	-1.7	6.4	2.3	-1.8	7.1
02-06	0.7	1.0	0.4	0.6	0.9	0.3
07-11	-0.2	-0.5	0.1	-0.2	-0.4	0.1

* Income B1 < 0. This means that an elasticity <1
reflects an increasing share for food; E 1>reflects
a decreasing share for food.

On the basis of Income A

AA : all elasticities
BA : elasticities of Wheat, Barley, Buckwheat,
     Rice and Potatoes
CA : elasticities of Beans, Beef, Coffee,
     Tabacco and Sugar

On the basis of Income B

AB, BB, CB (see above).

Chapter 4

DIETARY CHANGES IN EUROPE FROM 16th TO 20th CEN-
TURY, WITH PARTICULAR REFERENCE TO FRANCE AND ITALY
Maurice Aymard

Chapter **4**

DIETARY CHANGES IN EUROPE FROM 16th TO 20th CENTURY,
WITH PARTICULAR REFERENCE TO FRANCE AND ITALY
Maurice Aymard

One might well expect that the history of diet would
be one of long, steady evolution. In fact, it is
now clearer than ever that it is marked by a distinct break in the 19th century. Between 1800 and
1860 the main European countries began to keep statistics which were more accurate, more reliable, and
which related to the availability of food (and sometimes to its actual consumption) for the whole of
the population. Furthermore, this development coincided with important quantitative and structural
changes in diet. Both the sources and the nature of
the questions to be examined changed; around the end
of the 18th and the beginning of the 19th century
the perspective of the historian changes. Both before and after this date an agreement emerges on a
certain number of conclusions, and these constitute
the general framework of our research.

BEFORE 1800

Before 1800 there are very few statistical sources,
and those that exist are incomplete, fragmentary and
often indirect. They concern specific categories,
such as the army, the navy, convents and colleges
rather than the whole populace; privileged groups
(the accounts and registers of the nobility) rather
than the lower class; the towns (records of levies
and taxes on consumption and decisions concerning
the supply of grain) rather than the rural population (in the latter case effective research is rendered almost impossible by the large amount of home-
produced food that they consumed). They concern
certain key products (those which were likely to be
in short supply and which were also more heavily
commercialised), a fact which increases the strong
impression of dietary monotony, by ignoring the very
considerable categories of fresh fruit and vegeta-

bles, dairy and poultry products, which, moreover, constitute the most important sources of vitamins and mineral salts. A final reservation about these statistics is that they usually set dietary norms which, given the difficulties of supply, were rarely matched by reality. They do however indicate:

1. The constant low level of per capita averages before 1800 (1800-2000 calories). These appear to have risen only in periods of severe reduction in the population, such as in the 15th century. Furthermore the regular occurrence of bad harvests and famines means that even this vital minimum must be seen as a fragile ideal which was frequently not attained.

2. The small amount of progress achieved before the 19th century. Any sustained increase in the population involved a reduction, or at least the absence of any increase, in food supplies. While population growth was related to the price of wheat, agricultural production could not keep up with this increase. However, a study of price movements and the demographic effects of poor harvests suggests that an improvement may have come about in the 18th century in the form of a greater regularity of supplies. The periodic crises in which deaths outnumbered births became less severe, and the corresponding bulges on the graphs derived from parish records virtually disappear.

3. The primacy of cereals up to the 19th century, if not into the 20th, *as the main source of both calories and proteins*. The preference for bread as the staple foodstuff leads to all winter and spring cereals capable of being used in the making of bread, either alone or in combination (including maize for example), being referred to as "corn". During periods of shortage a great variety of other foodstuffs were mixed with these cereals for the making of bread, including potatoes, mixed in Parmentier's proportions.

4. With certain exceptions the insufficiency of animal products (meat and dairy products) and of fresh fruit and vegetables. Alongside the regular quantitative inadequacy of bread consumption, there was an insufficiency, in terms both of quality and variety, of other foods (*companage*). The availability

of proteins (whether from animal sources or
from leguminous plants rich in lysin), of
vitamins, and of minerals salts appears to
have been low and unreliable. In any case
these complementary foodstuffs could not
compensate for a shortfall in the supply of
cereals; in fact there were often simulta-
neous shortages of both. At best, certain
periods, (such as the end of the Middle Ages)
or certain countries, (such as Hungary in
the 16th and 17th centuries when stock farming predominated) or certain provinces within a country, (such as Bray, which had rich
pastureland in comparison with the neighbouring area of Beauvaisis, which produced
only cereals), seemed to have enjoyed a
greater margin of safety, due mainly to a
geater availability of meat (though at a
level considerably below that which we enjoy
today).

5. The marked vulnerability of the urban or
   agricultural labourer who had to buy most or
   all his food. In the long term any sustained population increase in the 16th as in
   the 18th century resulted in a corresponding
   reduction in real income (expressed as the
   quantity of cereal purchasable). This reduction itself reflects a reduction in agricultural productivity. To this must be
   added that in the short term these labourers
   were the first victims of the instability of
   prices. This in turn reflects the inadequa-
   cies of the market, which collapses when
   harvests are poor, under pressure both from
   peasant farmers, who tend to consume their
   own products and decrease both the quantities they offer for sale and their contrac-
   tual deliveries, and from better-off pur-
   chasers. This factor both inhibited urban
   development and retarded the specialisation
   in cash crops by those regions less suited
   to the cultivation of cereals.

FROM THE 19th TO THE 20th CENTURY, A BREAK IN THE
PATTERN

In contrast, sources which become available in the
19th century - though the dates vary from country to
country - show a certain number of quite clear
transformations:

1. The availability of foodstuffs increased as a result of improvements in agriculture. It is reported to have increased in France from 1800-2000 calories in about 1800 to 3200 by the end of the century (J.C. Toutain, 1971). The size of the increase, even if it is not evenly spread among all western European countries (for example Italy), is such that after 1850-1860 all, or almost all, of the population is above starvation level.

2. These improvements were all the more notable in that they occurred in all categories of foodstuffs. They occurred in cereals - now supplemented by the potato, the cultivation of which spread too late for it to replace cereals and so bring about a qualitative regression in diet (except for certain regions such as Ireland perhaps) - but they were also seen in the provision of meat and dairy products, fresh fruit and vegetables, and in new or exotic foodstuffs such as sugar, coffee and chocolate. The consumption of all these products now began to increase with the development of urbanisation.

3. As both cause and consequence of these increases there was an improvement in the market for food products. Larger and more frequent surpluses were produced by a more productive and more specialised agriculture. A national market was created through the development of new methods of transport. Importations from new countries were now easier, making up for insufficiencies, whether permanent or temporary, in home production. From the end of the 19th century there were improvements in techniques for preserving and conditioning food. The retail trade developed and became better organised and was supplied with better quality products, particularly fresh products. A more demanding urban clientele developed whose standard of living, even among the working class, showed a marked improvement for the first time since 1500. From around 1880-1890 wage earners were able to spend a smaller proportion of their income on food and still to eat better. The improved quality of the statistics available owes much to the more strongly developed network of monetary exchanges against the background of which food production took place.

4. One comfortable caloric levels had been

reached (3000-3200), this same period, 1880-
1900, saw the beginning of a transformation
in the dietary structure in France. (For
other countries the dates vary.) With
regard to carbohydrates, the increase in the
consumption of sugar only partially compen-
sates for the dramatic decrease (by more
than 50%) of cereals and, a little later, of
potatoes. Bread thus ceased to be the main
source of calories and proteins. The increased consumption of eggs and dairy products resulted in two changes. Firstly, the
majority of proteins now came from animal
products, whereas for centuries meat and
vegetables had rarely risen above the minimum 20-25% level in the provision of proteins. Secondly, animal fats, along with
vegetable oils, now account for an increased
consumption of lipase, which came to repre-
sent 40-50% of the total intake of calories.
It is as a result of this that justified
anxiety is now being expressed over the consequences of a change which only 10 or 20
years ago was taken as a symbol and condition of all economic progress. The particular focus of this anxiety is the development of diseases related to an excessive
level of fat (cardiovascular diseases) or of
sugar (diabetes).

A comparison of two graphs will more clearly
reveal the real extent of this structural change
which took France, like the United States and the
other western European countries, into a new dietary
system characterised by the absence of one basic
foodstuff providing the bulk of calorie input, and
by the predominance of proteins from animal products: (see next page)

Graph 1: An analysis of food consumption in
France, 1850-1966 (based on J.C.
Toutain, 1971)

Graph 2: A classification drawn up in 1969 by
the FAO of the composition of diets
throughout the world, in relation to
levels of income.

What stands out from these graphs is the
abruptness of the change which has taken place over
a period of less than a century. In 1880-90, just
as in 1800, and despite a per capita availability of

Graph 1

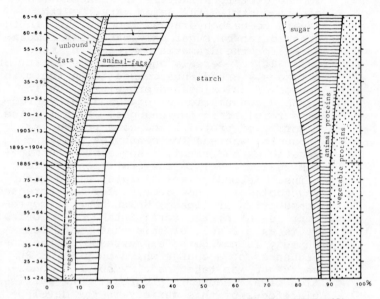

Source : J.-C. TOUTAIN, *La consommation alimentaire...*, Genève, Droz, 1971.

Graph 2

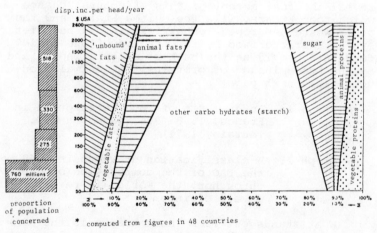

Source : La consommation, les perspectives nutritionnelles..., Rome, 1969.

3000-3200 calories, France still provided an example of a diet comparable in its structure and in the origin of the different categories of calories, with countries at the bottom of the scale of average income per head in 1962 (in which availability was nearer to the 1800-2000 calories of 1800 than it was to the 3200 of 1880-1890). The diachronic diagram in Graph 1 seems to provide the key to the interpretation of the synchronic presentation of Graph 2: having experienced an increase of 70-80% in the availability of foodstuffs in the course of the 19th century, France, like the other developed countries, changes its diet in the 20th century, abandoning its base of wheat and other comparable cereals (barley, rye, etc.) which it had used since at least the Middle Ages, in favour of a diet based on animal products.

This transformation in dietary structure, while most advanced in the United States, is well established in all the main industrialised European countries and those with a population of European origin. It raises a number of questions:

1. Its dynamic force - is it complete? Or is meat going to continue to advance until it becomes the primary source not only of proteins but also of calories, and so really becoming a new staple? Three developments seem possible: a progression - perhaps indicated by the gap between the United States and a country such as France, currently in the order of 35-40% (500-700 calories); a levelling off, brought about by the fight against cardiovascular diseases; or a regression, based either on the substitution of cheaper calorie sources (including vegetable proteins) to take the place of increasingly expensive animal-based products, or, on the other hand, on the adoption by the richer countries of new, more diversified dietary structures.

2. Its relative chronology. Outside France this remains largely unknown for want of comparable statistical data on the availability of foodstuffs at national level. It can be seen as simply the result of industrialisation, urbanisation and the in-increase in per capita revenue. But these are three independent factors and their relationship with earlier dietary traditions is rarely examined. Uniformity of consumption through the market does not

necessarily imply uniformity in culinary practices.

3. Its role as a model. This is clear when one considers that the whole of Europe from the east down through to the Mediterranean is undergoing the same transformation, albeit at different stages in different countries. The more recently the process began, the more rapidly has it advanced: in Italy (see table) it only got underway after 1960 as far as meat is concerned, though for sugar it began as early as 1900. It was held back by the unreliability of the supply of cereals, which during the Great Depression (1880-1900) and the Second World War fell from 1900-2000 calories to 1500 (St. Somogyi, 1973, pp. 882-84). But a new stage has now been reached. The model is no longer confined to Europe, it has become worldwide. Its impact is particularly noticeable in newly industrialised countries and in the leading developing countries. A qualitative change in sources of supply precedes or coincides with a quantitative advance, or at least a consolidation, of the availability of supply. Traditional patterns of diet and cooking methods are abandoned in favour of "modern" rules in which meat and other animal-based foodstuffs are given preference. The very conditions under which the "transition" takes place are altered. For the new model costs infinitely more than the old, and its rapid adoption results in a widening of the gap between the privileged few and the poorer masses. The break with tradition is all the more severe when it occurs - or is imposed - in regions previously dominated not by wheat or rye, but by rice, maize or millet, and where meat never occupied the same place in the minds and the practices of the well-to-do classes, for the change to a meat-based diet is often accompanied by the adoption of wheat and bread.

On a number of points the analysis of these dietary transformations is worth expanding.

An analysis of the "transition", that is the change from a cereal-based diet to a meat-based diet. In every case the phenomenon is recent (it has been in progress for less than a century), rapid (spread over a maximum of two or three generations), and it is still in progress. Nowhere can it be said with certainty to be complete, stabilised, or irreversible. An awareness of the recently discovered dietetic "optima" underlies a concept of linear progress and a binary opposition between the past and the present, such as is found elsewhere in history, with the same resultant distortions. We, for the moment at least, shall not accept that there is anything inevitable or automatic about the phenomenon under discussion. We see instead the victory of a *European* model which can be explained and dated historically, and which is manifested in a large number of different varieties. It is tempting to contrast the long internal gestation which is characteristic of countries such as France (or the United States), where the old cereal-based "régime" had reached the full flower of its development, with cases where the transformation was more abrupt, where, under pressure of external influences, the stage during which earlier gains were consolidated and social divisions were reduced, was bypassed. This would seem to be the case with non-European industrialised countries such as Japan, and certain developing countries.

The psycho-sociology of diet. People do not eat nutriments - protids and lipids, carbohydrates and mineral salts - but food. And the different foods are subject to a relatively rigid system of values, rules, and symbols which evolves only very slowly. Within a given diet there will be some very stable elements and others which are extremely volatile. There are thus certain possibilities for substitution, but only within a fixed framework. Observations concerning 20th century migrants, who remain attached to their methods of preparation, to their ingredients and their spices, are relevant here, as are observations made by historians of both the Middle Ages and of the early modern period, who are quite familiar with the changes in the composition of bread. In times of shortage almost any sort of foodstuff may be used - cereals, vegetables, herbs and tubers. It was not that the content was unimportant, or that anyone was deceived by the "appearance". It was rather that the latter gained in symbolic importance precisely because the content *was* in question.

The history of the old cereal-based régimes. The height of their development was seen in 19th cen-

tury western Europe, when regularly recurring famine
was finally vanquished. But it would be wrong to
think that there were no changes before 1800.
Changes did occur prior to that date, and though,
from the standpoint of the second half of the 20th
century, they may seem minor, they were nonetheless
real. But if they are not to be lost sight of in a
long period in which relatively little changed, they
must be measured by reference to their own times
rather than to ours. We will look at a few examples from the period of the 12th to the 18th century.

The change from gruel to bread. Many historians see
the main stage of this transition as being during
the 14th and 15th centuries, coinciding with the decline of barley in favour of winter cereals, (particularly wheat) which is firmly attested in the
Mediterranean area. Not that gruel has disappeared
everywhere by then. The ready acceptance of maize
from Aquitaine to the Balkans between the second
half of the 16th century and the first half of the
18th century is a good indication that *polenta* was
still popular at that time. Another change seems
to have occurred in southern Italy and in Sicily,
where semolina (attested in the 14th and 15th centuries) gave way, first to couscous (consumed in
Palermo in the 16th century, but then abandoned to
the "Berbers") and then to edible pasta, which was
a luxury in the 15th and 16th centuries, "bourgeois"
in the 17th, "lower class" in the towns in the 18th,
spreading to the country areas only in the 19th and
20th centuries.
    In all cases changes in dietary habits strongly
affected the relationship between the availability
and the actual consumption of food. Certainly bread
is easier to carry, to keep and to eat at the work-
place. Though eaten cold it is the result of a
cooking process, something the poor would not have
been able to afford. It is also true that as a
result of the introduction of bread there was an
increase in productivity of food preparation. To
the extent that we can compare moisture content with
modern bread (which is reckoned to contain 240-250
calories per 100 grams, compared with 330-340 for
cereals and flour), it seems to have involved a
considerable - and poorly understood - waste of resources. One would expect 120-125 kg of black bread
from one quintal of wheat. But all estimates found
in urban authority records from the 16th and 17th
centuries, based on the most careful observation of
costs and the results of the different stages in the

120

"production chain" for bread, normally give 100 kg
only, rising exceptionally to 105-110. Thus a
ration of 600 grams corresponds to 1980 calories in
wheat, but to 1440 in bread - a discrepancy of 20-
25%, which undermines all our calculations.

The victory of winter cereals over spring cereals,
and the elimination of millets and sorghums etc.,
in favour of a combination of wheat and rye, and
particularly of maize. This had a dual result.
Firstly, an increase in the cereal productivity of
most rural areas in the west, and secondly, the
"regression" of some of them from millet to maize,
which has fewer and inferior quality proteins.
This regression was more marked in areas such as
Northern Italy when, between the 17th and 18th centuries, maize became the exclusive staple of the
working classes, giving rise to deficiency diseases
such as pellagra. With some exceptions, notably
Ireland, the potato, as we have noted, became established too late to provoke another, more cata-
strophic, regression - from cereals to tubers,
which are virtually devoid of proteins. It appeared in the 19th century, as a *supplement* to
bread rather than as a replacement for it.

The late mediaeval maximum of meat. This has
always particularly fascinated historians in that
it plays a crucial role in the Malthusian explana-
tions which underlie the analysis of the growth of
rural society between the 13th and 18th centuries.
It also confirms the constraints imposed by that
"long-term prison sentence" which, according to F.
Braudel, represents the choice any civilisation
makes of one cereal rather than another. Figures
relating to the sparse population of Hungary in the
16th and 17th centuries also make the point. Any
progress made by a sedentary agricultural population limits the contribution that can be made by
extensive stock farming and hunting - at least
until the development of fodder crops, which make
intensive stock farming possible. This occurred in
the Milan region as early as the 16th century, and
in England in the 18th century.
    Nonetheless, this ideal remains relative - we
must not exaggerate its importance. For available
figures relate to the privileged classes: the
nobility and those at the top of the ecclesiastical
hierarchy, their officers, soldiers and immediate
entourage. By contrast, average figures everywhere
stand at much more modest levels: around 20 kilos
per head per year in Carpentras and in Palermo in

the 15th century - (this was the average for the whole of France in 1840); less than 40 kilos in the indulgent Rome of the Counter-Reformation in 1600, to which should be added about 10 kilos of fish (fresh, smoked or salted). It should be noted that all the examples are of towns. Their superiority in this respect over rural areas is not to be explained simply in terms of sources, or by the administrative support provided by the system of urban butcher's shops, for it is a constant feature over a long period. As early as 1816 the chief towns of the French *départements*, and towns of more than 10,000 inhabitants, passed the level of 50 kilos per person per year, whereas consumption in the rural areas remained at less than 15 kilos (G. Désert, 1975, p. 523).

Even more important are the maximum levels indicated by L. Stouff (1970: 305-315 grams per meat day at the table of the Archbishop of Arles in 1429-42) and by P. Charbonnier (1975, p. 470: 935 grams per meat day, and 187 kilograms a year at the Court of Vic of the Counts of Auvergne in 1380). These figures confirm that meat occupied a secondary position compared with bread. The latter provided 50% of the calorie intake at Vic, and 62% at Arles, while meat provided 25% and less than 10% respectively. These very high rates of 4500-5000 calories are, almost certainly, far in excess of what was actually consumed. It would seem that this 14th and 15th century "ideal" simply meant that the richer members of society were happy to eat more bread, meat, eggs, and fish, while their diet continued to be firmly based on wheat, which provided the bulk of the intake of calories and proteins. As for the poorer classes, the part played by meat in their diet was more modest but nonetheless real, and helped to prevent them, in a good year, from crossing the upper threshold of 75-80% of calorie intake from wheat which should not be exceed if a qualitative deficiency of proteins (a lack of lysin) is to be avoided. In years of shortage, meat partly made up for the shortfall in cereal intake. This is an important contribution, but one which is frequently observed in the 17th and 18th centuries in mountain regions where stock farming played a more important role.

New dietary hierarchies in the 16th-18th centuries: the first signs of change. There can be no doubt that there was a considerable reduction in the standard of living of the common people in the 16th and 17th centuries in Italy and in France. There

was less bread, and what there was was blacker and
often of dubious quality, and even less meat.
Though there was a little more wine, especially in
the towns. There was an improvement, it is true,
in the 18th century, in that supplies became more
regular, even though they remained at fairly low
levels (1800-2000 calories in France in 1800, according to the estimation of J.C. Toutain, 1971).
This would seem to be confirmed by a certain
lessening - in France at least, not in Italy - of
the devastating impact of the cereal crises. Other
explanatory factors include a softening of the
climate, better care of the crops, and greater ef-
ficiency and openness of the market resulting from
improvements in the transportation of products.
But alongside this basic tendency there emerged
another. For the popular masses the cereal-based
diet was consolidated and strengthened. Only a
lucky few were able to bring some variety to an
otherwise monotonous diet, thanks to the resources
provided by their vegetable garden and what few
animals they could rear. By contrast the privileged classes during this period were forging ahead.
Being better off than ever, they were eating
better and, more importantly, they were beginning
to *change* their diet. Whereas as in the 14th and
15th centuries the ostentation of the nobility took
the form of simply increasing two- or threefold the
quantities of the same basic diet (for a very considerable period thereafter this remained the case
for army and naval officers), there now began to
emerge an alteration in the actual composition of
meals. It was not that bread disappeared from the
tables of the rich. But it was more and more the
case that the bread they ate was white bread, made
from pure wheat flour, bolted to a level of 50 or
60% (which widened further the gap between availability and actual consumption). Consumption remained at the same level. Increases *are* recorded
for other foodstuffs, such as meat and fish, but
also for drinks, fresh fruit and vegetables, and
dairy products, and, when they became available,
for new items from the colonies (sugar, coffee,
cocoa, etc.). These are of course no more than
tendencies, but there is a significant amount of
evidence to support them.
First, there is the map already referred to,
which shows the consumption of meat in France from
1840-1852. This map in fact shows a situation
which already existed in 1816, and most probably
before that (G. Désert, p. 520-22). It reveals two
series of divergencies: between towns and rural

123

areas (the former consumed three times as much butchered meat as the latter), and between regions. On the one hand there is a beef-eating zone stretching "from Alsace to Calvados" and "taking in Lorraine and Champagne, with an extension down into Burgondy ... and the central region of the Paris basin and upper Normandy", and another, mutton-eating zone consisting of the Bas-Languedoc and Provence. In these two zones consumption levels were between 25 and 32 kilos. On the other hand there was "a large depressed area lying diagonally across France from Poitou and Périgord to the Nivernais and the Allier", in which they are 50% lower (12.4 to 15.8 kilos). "The cattle-rearing bocage areas" of France sent their fat cattle to Paris, their cast cows to small local towns, and ate their own dairy products and pork. It is true that the correlations with net income per head are not absolute. But they do show - given the regions concerned, north of a line from St. Malo to Geneva - that the consumption of meat is no longer, as it was in the 14th and 15th centuries, the result of depopulation and an increase in stock rearing on the abandoned land, but that rather it is the result of a certain form of economic development, initiated by the towns, which are themselves the principal beneficiaries.

A second piece of evidence, which is more detailed and more complete, is the table drawn up by Lavoisier showing foodstuffs consumed in Paris for a "typical year, prior to the Revolution" (R. Philippe, 1961, pp. 564-568). Per capita availability is uncertain, for the total population of the town is not known, but it probably varied between 1669 and 2336 calories, levels which were in any case very moderate and even inadequate. Taking account of fruit and vegetables, cereals still provided 58% of calorie intake, but only 53% of proteins, compared with 13% and 43% respectively for meat, fish and eggs taken together. These percentages correspond to the lower limits of the cereal-based régime. Bread remains by far the main source of calories, but tends no longer to be the main source of proteins. The table of expenditure of food confirms this decline in the importance of bread: it represents less than a seventh of total expenditure (less than double that on colonial products), compared with more than one fifth on drinks and more than a quarter on butchered meat alone:

		% of expenditure
- Bread		13.57
- Drinks: wine	21.41)	
brandy	1.58)	
cider	0.08)	24.12
beer	0.79)	
vinegar	0.26)	
- Meat	26.68)	
- Eggs	2.31)	
- Fish, fresh & salted	4.02)	34.59
- Cheese, fresh & salted	1.58)	
- Oil	3.95)	7.45
- Butter, fresh & salted	3.50)	
- Fruit and vegetables		8.22
- Sugar	5.14)	
- Coffee	2.06)	7.53
- Cocoa	0.33)	
- Other items		4.52

These figures may be compared with the estimations
of J.C. Toutain (1961, tables 72 and 74) according
to which cereals constituted 40% of total French
agricultural production around 1840. Even if only
a proportion of this is made into bread, the capital still enjoys an enormous advantage, spending
only 14% on bread. However, Lavoisier's figures
relate to a total population in which rich and poor
are not distinguished. If we were to suppose that
they all ate the same amount of bread, then this
would give a per capita average of 400 to 500 grams,
depending on the figure we assume for the total
population (5-700.000). This represents between 960
and 1320 calories, i.e. 50-70% of a "poor" diet of
1800-2000 calories a day, or 30-40% of a "rich" diet
of 3200 calories. It is clear that we are no longer
looking at the old cereal-dominated régime, though
the question of exactly how many Parisians benefitted from the change remains open.

A good counter-example to the new link which is
established in modern times between levels of urban
consumption and economic development is providid by
figures from papal Rome (J. Revel, 1975, pp..563-
74). For here per capita availability decreases
rather than increases: for cereals from 290 kilograms per head around 1600 to 167 around 1790, and
for meat from 38.3 kilograms to 21.5-24.7 kilograms

between these same dates. Even in the case of wine
the increase observed between the 16th and 17th
centuries (from 210 to 270 litres) is checked in
the 18th century.

Finally, the third source of evidence, useful
despite its more rigid character - the dietary
norms which prevailed in well-organised and well-
fed collectivities, such as colleges and religious
establishments. The populations concerned consist
of homogeneous groups of adolescents and adult
males, similar to the "middle classes" rather than
to the aristocracy, reflecting, in their rejection
of ostentatious sumptuousness and wastage, the
practices and aspirations of the urban bourgeoisie.
In all cases consumption levels are very high:
3500-4400 calories in the Collèges de St. Jacques
de Compostelle, where they show hardly any change
from the mid-16th to the mid-19th century (A. Eiras
Roel and M.J. Enriquez Morales, 1975, pp. 454-64);
more than 3500 calories at the Jesuit Noviciate at
Palermo in the 17th century (M. Aymard and H. Bresc,
1975, pp. 597-98); and from 4000 to almost 5000 in
the French colleges on the eve of the Revolution
(W. Frijhoff and D. Julia, 1975, pp. 491-504).
Bread retains an important place in that it
provides 1800-2200 calories, this being about 50%
of the total calorie intake. But the quantity
consumed shows a significant tendency to decrease:
from 920 grams at St. Jacques in 1555-88, to 860
grams in 1751; about 750 grams at Palermo around
1680, 775-868 grams at Molsheim, and 721 grams at
Beaumont en Auge, compared with more than a 1000
grams at Auch and Toulouse. At Molsheim this
reduction in bread consumption is matched by a
considerable increase in dairy products and in
fruit and vegetables. The table of expenditure at
Molsheim is comparable to Lavoisier's data for
Paris:

Bread	16.0-27.0%	(depending on the price of wheat)
Wine	22.0-30.0%	
Meat	25.0-30.0%	
Fish	6.0- 8.0%	
Butter and eggs	7.0-11.0%	
Oil	1.3- 3.5%	
Spices and sugar	3.0- 5.0%	
Fruit and vegetables	3.0- 9.0%	

Thus a relatively well-off and protected part of the population spent more on meat and drink than on bread, and diversified its diet by the regular consumption of fruit and vegetables. Between the 16th and 18th centuries it evolved new rules, methods of cooking, and composition of meals which placed it at the lower limits of the cereal-dominated pattern and set up a new ideal of an "abundant" and regular diet. Despite attempts by the rich bourgeoisie to maintain its status through an incredible voracity (J.P. Aron, 1973), the increase in availability of foodstuffs in the 19th century brought about a reduction of the gap between the extremes of this hierarchy. Its wide distribution over different regions and different social categories helps explain the process which, through a greater homogeneity of patterns of consumption, prepared the way for the dietary changes of the 20th century.

* In the above article in stead of "calorie" read kcalorie in all places (eds.).

Table 4.1: The Dietary Pattern in Italy - Per Capita Availability in Calories (from Somogyi, 1973, table 24, p. 884).

Years	Cereals	Potatoes	Dry Vegetables	Fruit and Vegetables	Dry Fruit	Sugar	Vegetable Oils	Wine/Beer/Alcohol
				VEGETABLE PRODUCTS				
1861-70	1902	65.5	117.5	65	333	26	195	187
71-80	1926	63.3	128.4	70	284	28	214	187
81-90	1526	54.6	102.1	78	222	29	133	198
91-1900	1373	50.2	98.5	83	214	26	138	184
1901-10	1903	83.4	129.3	84	264	35.4	140	235
11-20	1949	63.4	131.1	109	214	52	116	231
21-30	2068	70.7	108.5	118	160	81.2	163	222
31-40	1942	88.8	109.4	101	105	77	143	170
41-50	1592	80.3	47	110	81	80	96	148
51-60	1807	106	48.8	150	82	169.7	148	204
61-67	1731	105.8	49.7	210	67	253	239	233

Table 4.1 (cont'd)

	ANIMAL PRODUCTS							TOTALS		
Year	Meat	Butter	Milk	Cheese	Eggs	Fats	Fish	Vegetable products	Animal products	All products
1861-70	90	6.2	50.1	12.3	34.6	56.9	12	2891	262	3153
71-80	100	12.4	50.3	20.5	30.2	66	14	2901	293	3194
81-90	116	14.4	59.2	26.3	26.6	77.1	16.6	2342	336	2678
91-1900	108	14.4	59.8	24.6	22.6	69.7	17.7	2166	316	2482
1901-10	98	16.5	64.1	29.6	23.5	60.6	15.2	2884	307	3191
11-20	124.5	22.7	61.5	36.1	29.3	75.2	16.8	2865	366	3231
21-30	131	22.7	63.7	36.1	28.8	67.9	23.5	2991	373	3364
31-40	127	24.7	68.2	42	31.5	66	24.4	2736	383	3119
41-50	82	20.6	65.2	36.1	22.6	42.2	16.2	2234	285	2519
51-60	128	33	98.7	53.4	35.5	55.1	27.8	2715	431	3146
61-67	182	35	199.6	73.1	41.7	29.4	34.7	2888	515	3403

Chapter 5
INTERRELATIONS BETWEEN CONSUMPTION, ECONOMIC GROWTH
AND INCOME DISTRIBUTION IN LATIN AMERICA SINCE
1800: A COMPARATIVE PERSPECTIVE
David Felix

Chapter 5

INTERRELATIONS BETWEEN CONSUMPTION, ECONOMIC GROWTH
AND INCOME DISTRIBUTION IN LATIN AMERICA SINCE 1800:
A COMPARATIVE PERSPECTIVE
David Felix

As the title suggests, the focus of this paper is
more analytic than descriptive. Its intent is less
to describe in detail long term changes in the aggregate size and composition of consumption in Latin
America, than to causally link underlying characteristics of Latin American consumer behavior to persisting *problématiques* about the Latin American
growth process using the experiences of developing
countries elsewhere to buttress the analysis. But
before discussing the *problématiques* a summary description of the long term trends in output and consumption per head is in order.

Let us begin with the 20th century. Except for
Haiti, all Latin American countries show, according
to their national accounts, per capita output growth
in the period since World War II. Average annual
growth rates through 1976 range from Brazil's 3.0
percent to Uruguay's 0.4 percent, the averages con-
cealing, however, sizeable shorter-term oscillations. Aggregate output series are much sparser for
the first half of the 20th century, only three reach
back before World War I. These show Argentina's GDP
per head to have grown about 1.4 percent per annum
between 1900 and 1950, roughly equivalent to its
post-World War II growth rate; Mexico's to have
grown at around 1.6 percent per annum during 1895-
1950; and Chile's at about 1.0 percent between 1908
and 1957.[1] The annual growth rates for Brazil and
Uruguay during the first half of the century must
also have been at least 1.0 percent, with lower,
positive rates of growth likely for most of the remaining countries.

Nineteenth century output growth was much
weaker, as is also the evidence on which the conclusion is based. During the first half of that
century per capita output probably fell somewhat

133

in Argentina, Mexico, Brazil, Colombia, and perhaps in most of the other countries.[2] For the majority of the countries output per head probably rose only slightly if at all during the second half of the century, despite a pickup in the growth of their exports and imports.[3] Some, however, began to grow quite rapidly. Argentine output per head rose at perhaps 1.5 percent per annum between 1850 and 1900; Mexico's may have achieved a similar growth rate from the mid-1880's to 1911, and Chile's growth rate was perhaps 1.0 percent from 1855 to 1908.[4] Output per head must have also been growing in Uruguay in this period, though quantitative guestimates are lacking.

The GDP growth estimates probably overstate the growth of aggregate consumption per head during the 1850-1930 era. This is because at least until World War I, the investment/GDP ratio was rising along with the foreign ownership share of the productive capital stock. GNP thus rose less than GDP, and if Latin American residents like their post-World War II descendents kept their private domestic savings to GNP trend ratio relatively flat, aggregate consumption had to rise less than GDP. If they increased their savings/GNP ratio, the GDP estimates would overstate consumption growth even more.[5] The direction of bias is reversed during the 1930's and 1940's, when the foreign ownership shares declined and GNP rose relative to GDP, compensating in part for the earlier upward bias of GDP as a proxy for consumption.

Diverging secular growth rates have helped to widen 19th century inter-country differences of productive structures, urbanization ratios and various other socioeconomic indicators, most of which point to rising heterogeneity in the region. Absent other comprehensive secular data, the urbanization ratios of Table 1 are offered as a crude proxy of the increasing heterogeneity. However, the differing speeds of urbanization have been the result of other influences than mere income growth differences. The rank correlation between the 1975 rankings of the countries by urbanization ratio and by GNP per capita, though a significant 0.76, leaves ample room for such influences.

M.D. Morris' Physical Quality of Life Index, also gives us a systematic measure of trends in a few dimensions of the "quality of life" during the post-World War II years. The PQLI is a simple average of indices of infant mortality, life expectancy at age one, and adult literacy, normalized to a range of 1 to 100.[6] In 1950 the PQLI ranged from

36 in Guatemala to 77 in Argentina; in the early 1970's from 43 for Bolivia to 90 for Puerto Rico. All seventeen Latin American countries for which such data are available increased their PQLI's between 1950 and the early 1970's, albeit at different speeds. The correlation of the Latin American countries in the mid-1970's between their GNP per capita rank and their PQLI rank is a robust, 0.68, but the correlation between the relative increase of their PQLI and the relative increase of their GNP per capita during the interval, 1950 to the mid-1970's, is a feeble 0.15.[7] As with the urbanization ratios , other factors than economic growth have influenced trends in the physical quality of life.

One obvious candidate for "other factor" is difference in social and economic policy. In fact, the homogeneity of socio-economic policy in the region persisted much longer than its structural homogeneity, substantial policy divergences setting in only with the Great Depression. Indeed, many Latin American historians use economic strategy as te main criterion for dividing the post-1850's era into two sub-periods; the mid-19th century until the 1930's world depression, when the shared growth strategy was *crecemiento hacia afuera*, export-led growth, and the 1930's to-date, when strategy shifted to *crecemiento hacia adentro*, domestically-led economic growth, built chiefly around import substituting industrialization (ISI). Like all such periodizing, this one oversimplifies, especially for the later period. But *grosso modo* the division is useful, and we use it in this paper.

During the first period policy homogeneity was indeed high, the divergences of growth rates reflecting, in the jargon of political science, differences in policy outputs, not inputs. The common set of inputs were: liberal trade policies; an eager *abrazo* for foreign capital and European immigrants; public infra-structure investments oriented primarily to reducing transport costs from the interior to coastal ports; social policies geared mainly to keeping the raw labor supply elastic and labor costs down; and land distribution and wealth taxing policies that promoted large-scale capitalistic agriculture. Mexico and Brazil around the turn of the century did adopt moderately protective tariffs and tax subsidies intentionally to encourage ISI, mainly in textiles, but in most other countries, the political battle between protectionists and free traders was won by the latter. Free trade was not implemented fully, but mainly because tariffs were relied on heavily for fiscal revenue. By World War

Table 5.1: Percentages of National Population of Latin American Countries Residing in Towns and Cities, 1890–1970

Country	1890[a]			1950			1970[b]			1975
	I	II	III	I	II	III	I	II	III	I
Cuba	30.7	15.0	0.0	56.5	4.6	19.6	58.4	10.9	19.6	62.0
Uruguay	30.0	28.7	0.0	56.6	27.8	0.0	84.2	0.0	53.0	81.0
Costa Rica	28.4	0.0	0.0	33.3	17.4	0.0	37.2	24.6	0.0	40.0
Argentina	27.1	16.8	0.0	63.3	15.1	30.5	80.5	22.3	39.0	80.0
Venezuela	22.8	0.0	0.0	45.2	20.3	0.0	76.4	16.2	20.7	82.0
Chile	21.8	14.1	0.0	54.3	5.5	21.0	73.7	9.7	27.3	83.0
Guatemala	16.9	0.0	0.0	24.9	10.5	0.0	36.6	14.9	0.0	35.0
Paraguay	16.5	0.0	0.0	32.9	16.3	0.0	35.8	18.7	0.0	37.0
El Salvador	15.4	0.0	0.0	36.5	8.7	0.0	39.8	13.6	0.0	40.0
Mexico	12.7	3.3	0.0	42.6	6.4	8.7	58.2	9.6	11.7	63.0
Ecuador	12.3	0.0	0.0	28.5	14.6	0.0	37.5	21.3	0.0	42.0
Brazil	10.9	5.8	0.0	36.1	6.9	10.6	53.5	10.4	23.5	60.0
Colombia	9.4	2.9	0.0	37.0	17.4	0.0	55.0	18.3	17.0	62.0
Honduras	8.4	0.0	0.0	17.7	0.0	0.0	25.9	10.4	0.0	28.0
Bolivia	8.0	0.0	0.0	20.6	9.9	0.0	25.3	15.1	0.0	37.0
Peru	7.4	3.9	0.0	35.5	11.4	0.0	46.1	3.5	19.4	57.0
Panama	n.d.	n.d.	n.d.	36.0	15.9	0.0	46.8	30.0	0.0	51.0
Nicaragua	n.d.	n.d.	n.d.	34.9	10.3	0.0	43.7	17.6	0.0	48.0
Dominican Rep.	n.d.	n.d.	n.d.	23.8	8.5	0.0	33.0	17.5	0.0	44.0

a Actual date of estimate varies from 1876 for Peru to 1905 for Colombia, but with most years in the 1890's.

Table 5.1 (cont'd)

b Percentages based on projections by Kingsley Davis and colleagues according to methods described in Chapter IV of cited source.

Category I: Total population in urban areas, with varying lower-bound definitions of "urban". It is all towns and cities over 10,000 in the 1890 estimates, while the 1950-70 estimates include towns under 10,000, with cut-off minima varying between countries.
Category II: Cities between 100,000 and 1 million.
Category III: Cities over 1 million.

Sources: 1890 estimates from Nicolas Sánchez-Albornoz, The Population of Latin America: A History (Berkeley,University of California Press, 1974) Table 5:13. 1950-70 estimates from Kingsley Davis, World Urbanization, 1950-70, Population Monograph Series No. 4 (Berkeley, University of California Press, 1969) Vol. I, Table C. 1975 figures from The World Bank World Development Report, 1978 (New York, Oxford University Press, 1978) Annex, Table 14.

I, the "social question" was forcing modifications in a few of the countries of the social Darwinism that had dominated the region's labor policies. But prior to the 1930's legalization of non-agricultural unions and some incipient social security measures were limited to the more affluent "Southern Cone" countries and post-Revolutionary Mexico. The differences in growth rates during the export-led period derived primarily, therefore, from inter-country differences in the relative richness and variety of their exploitable natural resources and their accessibility, given the technologies of the time. Argentina was the outstanding success story mainly because of the wide range of alternative uses to which its accessible humid pampa could be put. Its relatively high sustained output growth was the shifting composite of briefer but usually overlapping export booms in various animal and cereal products. Mexico's export growth also benefited from varied mineral resources that supplemented the limited flexibility of its agricultural resources, as did Chile's. Most of the tropical countries were, however, less well-endowed by nature for such allocative flexibility; the periods of stagnation between their export booms were longer and their export growth trends lower.

The inward-directed growth period was initially an unplanned effect of the collapse of primary export markets and prolonged balance of payments weakness during the 1930's depression. Import and exchange controls plus fiscal deficits and emergency credits to financially pressed but unfluential business groups such as the large farmers, combined to create pockets of excess demand for manufactured imports. In the larger countries the pockets were large enough to induce import-substituting investments by native and European refugee entrepreneurs. At first, the investments were mainly in textiles, houseware, and building materials, for which capital and technological requirements were moderate and the home market relatively sizeable. But during World War II, when exports recovered while industrial imports where sharply curbed by the conversion of the overseas industrial powers to war production, the range of import substitution spread to other metal products, including some machinery and spare parts. The larger Latin American countries thus managed to revive economic growth despite sharply declining import coefficients; an historic first for Latin America.[8]

Formalizing ISI into a general growth strategy came after the War, with the United Nations, Economic Commission for Latin America, under the dynamic leadership of its first director, Raúl Prebisch, playing the leading intellectual role in modeling the strategy. The goal was to have GNP grow faster than the economy's capacity to import, set by the growth of foreign demand for its primary exports, would allow. This meant progressive lowering of the ratio of imports to GNP, using selective import restrictions and industrial subsidies to direct ISI through a succession of stages. Consumer ISI was the first stage, since home markets for such goods were generally the larger and their technologies the less exiguous. The first stage expansion called the "easy stage", would, in turn, expand demand for intermediate materials and capital goods, so that these could be phased seriatim into the ISI effort. The expansion of aggregate demand, plus the growth of industrial experience and industrial capital accumulation, would then progressively carry the economy successfully through the "hard stage", when consumer imports were dwindling toward zero and ISI had, perforce, to concentrate on intermediate and capital goods imports. In addition to using its import control and tax subsidy instruments, the state was to support industry-led growth by redirecting its transport, communications, energy and educational investments toward connecting internal markets and supplying the expanding energy and skill needs of industry.

In the larger countries formal adoption of ISI as a general strategy was less from intellectual conversion than from responses to the increased political clout of industrialists and urban workers which accompanied industrial growth during the informal ISI years. ECLA's theorizing provided intellectual reassurance, but the programmatics remained quite ad hocish. With these new political forces came also various *conquistas sociales* by the urban working classes: retirement and medical programs, minimum wage legislation, overtime and severance pay, controls on basic food prices and the like. In the smaller countries, enthusiasm for ISI was tempered by their small home markets, although ECLA helped promote the short-lived effort of the Central American countries to augment their ISI potential by forming a common market.

ISI strategy trends notwithstanding, the import coefficients of most of the countries began to turn up again in the 1950's or early 1960's.[9] The differences in post-war GNP growth rates turned out to be more strongly related to different rates of primary export growth than to rates of expansion of the industrial share of national product.[10] The expanding shares, moreover, were not matched by growth in the industrial share of total employment,[11] but were associated with rising shares of foreign ownership of the growing industrial sectors, through multi-national corporation take-overs of established firms and dominance of investment in many new product areas. Neither of these developments had been anticipated in the earlier ISI theorizing.

By the end of the 1960's, rising inflation, disgruntled middle classes, and disillusionment with ISI, were ushering in a partial return to *crecemiento hacia afuera*, particularly in Brazil and the more industrialized "Southern Cone" economies, with industrial exports, usually heavily subsidized, supplementing the promotion of primary sector exports. The export-led strategy called for holding down wage costs and lifting price controls on basic foods, and the domestic and foreign business groups promoting the strategy encouraged military take-overs to roll back the *conquistas sociales* and reduce real wages. A number of Latin American social scientists see this as a prolonged new era, meriting a distinctive sobriquet, Authoritarian Capitalism; i.e. fascism without its populist face.

So much on general growth and policy patterns. What of the persisting *problématiques*? This paper focuses on three that have accompanied economic growth in the Latin American countries since the mid-19th century: (1) the tendency for already high levels of concentration of income and consumption to worsen during both the pre-1930's and the post-World War II growth periods; (2) the tendency for structural dualism to intensify rather than diminish in most of the countries; (3) an unabated vulnerability of all the countries to frequent balance of payments crises despite different rates of economic growth and structural diversification. I shall first expand on the three *problématiques*, then discuss their interactions with Latin American patterns of consumer behavior.

On income distribution it's best to begin with the current period, for which data, albeit of varying reliability, are much more abundant. In Table 6.2 the income shares of the lowest 40 percent and of the top 20 percent of income recipients, usually households, are compared for 57 countries, 14 of them Latin American. The 57 countries are placed in three GNP per capita groups, the lowest two made up of LDC's. Note that the Latin American contingents of each of the two groups shows a quite different dispersion than the other LDC regions. With one ex-

140

ception. (Uruguay), the Latin American countries are in the low half of the range, as regards the income shares of the lowest 40 percent and in the high half of the range as regards the income shares of the top 20 percent. In contrast, the European capitalist and socialist LDC's are distinctly in the egalitarian halves of the respective ranges, while the African and Asian LDC's sprawl across both halves of the two ranges. Of the two Latin American countries in the highest income group, one (Argentina) fits in with affluent capitalist Europe's moderate inequality, while the other (Venezuela) has the high income concentration of its poorer Latino neighbours. In sum, the Latin American propensity for income inequality is unusually strong among the LDC's, and higher GNP levels scarcely seem to weaken it.

Limited quantified estimates of trends in income distribution are also available for five Latin American countries. These all show increasing concentration post-World War II: slight in Argentina, more vigorous in Brazil, Puerto Rico, Colombia and Mexico. For the first three countries the estimates are based on only 2 or 3 observations from the 1950's and 1960's, a fragile basis for long term generalizing, although there's strong reason to suspect from the decline of real wages since the imposition of "Authoritarian Capitalism" in the 1970's, that the trend toward concentration is persisting in Argentina since Videla, and in Chile since Pinochet. For Colombia and Mexico, on the other hand, the rising concentration has been tracked statistically from the late 1930's to the mid-1970's.[12]

Are these trends part of a parabolic Kuznets curve pattern in which sustained growth of per capita income eventually reverses the trend toward greater concentration? One can only say that the economic dynamics are against the likelihood of a sustainable turnaround in the next few decades. The economic case for the universality of Kuznets curves is based mainly on domestic two-sector models, in which inequality increases during early "modern growth", when the growing urban sector is increasing its output per head relative to the rural sector. The turnaround then comes as enough rural labor is drawn to the city to generate labor scarcity, rising capital-labor ratios and rising wages in the countryside, so that the inter-sectoral productivity gap begins narrowing. The turnabout takes longer if inequality is higher in the urban than the rural sector, and can be further delayed, indefinitely at the limit, if inequality is also increasing in both sectors.[13] In the Latin American countries for which

Table 5.2: Income Inequality of Countries Grouped by Region and Income Level, circa 1960's

	A. Whose Income Share of the Poorest 40 Percent Was:				B. Whose Income Share of the Richest 20 Percent Was:			
	Below 10%	10-13%	13-17%	Over 17%	Below 40%	40-50%	50-60%	Over 60%
GNP per capita in 1971 U.S. $								
I. Below $ 300								
1. Latin America	2	1	0	0	0	0	1	2
2. Africa	2	4	4	3	0	4	3	6
3. Asia	2	2	3	4	0	6	4	1
II. From $300 to $750								
1. Latin America	4	4	1	0	0	1	4	4
2. Africa	2	0	0	0	0	0	1	1
3. Asia	0	3	0	0	0	0	2	1
4. Caribbean	1	0	1	1	0	2	0	1
5. Capitalist Europe	0	0	0	2	0	2	0	0
6. Socialist Europe	0	0	0	2	1	1	0	0
III. Over $ 750								
1. Latin America	1	0	1	0	0	0	0	1
2. Asia	0	0	0	1	0	1	0	0
3. Capitalist Europe	1	1	5	1	1	5	2	0
4. Socialist Europe	0	0	0	3	3	0	0	0
5. Australasia	0	0	0	0	0	0	0	0
North America	0	0	2	3	2	2	1	0

Table 5.2 (cont'd)

a Data of observations range from 1956 to 1971, with most observations in the 1960's.

Source: Montek S. Ahluwalia, "Income Distribution: Some Dimensions of the Problem", in Hollis Chenery, et al., Redistribution with Growth (Oxford University Press, 1974) Table 1.1, pp. 8-9.

income distribution statistics exist, the ratios of urban to rural income per head ranges from 1.2 (Argentina) to 2.7 (Peru), and in all except Argentina and Venezuela urban inequality appears to be higher than rural. As for trends within each sector, intertemporal data are too sparse as yet for confident generalizing.[14] The information that exists, therefore, does not support an early turnaround in the overall concentration trends.

Leveling revolutions and/or reformist policies can, in principle, reverse polarizing forces of the market via land tenure reforms, *conquistas sociales*, and egalitarian taxes and public expenditures. However, Mexico, which had such a revolution, has been ruled since by a coalition committed in principle, and intermittently in practice, to such reforms, and which has increased its output per head more than five-fold since 1885, illustrates the resiliency of the forces for concentration. Mexico's 1975 Gini coefficient, 0.579, was one of the highest in Latin America, and probably as high as in 1910, the eve of the Revolution.[15] Since Porfiriato income growth from 1885 to 1910 was substantial and notoriously concentrated, Mexico's Gini coefficient must have been lower in 1885 than in 1975. In retrospect, 1911-1939, with its Revolution, intermittent reform and slow growth, was only an egalitarian interruption between two periods of rapid growth and rising concentration, with the second period's momentum still alive, thanks to the recent oil discoveries. Mexico's growth-inequality pattern is not unique in Latin America, but it stands out when compared to the secular growth experiences of other regions and epochs. E.g. when Britain's Kuznets curve peaked at the end of the Victorian era, its Gini may even have exceeded Mexico's today. But Britain's inequality peaked after about seven decades of a per capita income growth rate that was only two-thirds as high as Mexico's; and the downswing since the 1880's has not been associated with a lower growth rate,[16] nor has been in the other industrialized economies for which long term Kuznets curves have been traced.

The pattern of a secularly rising inequality trend temporarily reversed only during periods of slow economic growth, has also been traced statistically for Colombia for the period, 1935-1974.[17] Partial data for Argentina and Chile suggest that the 1930's and 1940's, a time of slower GNP growth, falling import coefficients, "easy" ISI, and advancing *conquistas sociales*, was also an interlude of reduced inequality in those countries. In the non-industrialized countries of that period, a similar

144

reversal probably occurred, mainly because the income and consumption of the landed and mercantile classes was proportionately more depressed by falling export earnings and a reduced capacity to import than was the predominately in-kind income and consumption of estate workers and tenant farmers who made up the bulk of the labor force in these countries.

During the earlier *crecemiento hacia afuera* era, the pervasiveness of the above pattern is also strongly implied, despite the absence of Lorenz type statistics, by three general features of export-led growth in that period. One is its association, particularly before World War I, with an intensification of land concentration, by arrant land-grabbing as well as through conventional market transactions. Legislation, judicial chicanery and armed seizure carved up public lands with their squatter settlements into latifundia and allowed large estates to grow by encroaching on lands that colonial decrees had formally reserved for the Indian villages.[18] The second general feature, a widespread tendency for rural labor earnings to stagnate or decline during periods of per capita GNP growth, was doubtlessly related to the increased supply of landless labor and land-short peasants created by the land concentration process. A third feature, the decay of artisan manufacturing, cottage and workshop, interacted with the first two. During export-led growth surges consumer imports surged, and, aided also by transport improvements from port to interior, enabled the landed classes to rapidly substitute imports domestically for home-produced consumer goods, while concurrently the demand for popular artisan consumer goods was being depressed by the falling incomes of lower class households. Stagnation and/or decline of demand for artisan products in turn contributed to the decline of rural labor income and to the stagnation and/or decline of real wages in the small towns and cities of the interior. In the larger countries the expansion of factory type production in the ports and capital cities during the export booms was usually an incomplete offset to the decline of artisan employment. Skilled labor, much of it immigrant, benefited from the expansion, but the scattered evidence suggests no sustained improvement in the real income of unskilled urban labor prior to World War I in most of the countries for which such data has been collected.[19]

In contrast to the immiserating export-led growth of the pre-1930 era, income gains trickled down more deeply in the post-1930's era. In Mexico

the income shares of the lowest sixty percent of
households fell during 1950-75, but only the real
income of the lowest quintile also fell absolutely.
Households in the 80th to 95th percentiles increased their share of income the most, but the share of
the next quintile also rose slightly, while that of
the top 5 percent fell slightly. Brazilian income
gains, 1960-70, were more narrowly concentrated:
only the top decile's share increased, while those
of the lowest 8 deciles fell. Colombian data, covering 1935-74, also show a rising share only for
the top decile, with falling shares for the lowest
seven. Evidently the populist rhetoric of Mexico's
ruling party had some real, if limited, basis in
fact.[20]

Nutritional data, however, throw a darker
light on the distribution of material gains. Thus
a recently completed Brazilian survey found that
the 68 percent of Brazilians in 1975 consumed less
than the FAO/WHO minimum daily caloric requirement
for normal physical activity, that 37 percent of
the children suffered from first degree and another
21 percent from second degree malnutrition.[21] Long
term comparisons are even more startling. Surviving records from six haciendas near Bogotá show
that an estate worker in 1791 could command alternatively with his annual earnings, 30 percent more
corn, 230 percent more meat, 80 percent more flour
and 85 percent more potatoes than could a Colombian
agricultural worker in 1962.[22] On a Zacatecas
hacienda of 418 square miles, "medium size according to the standards of the day" the surviving records show that peon families in the 1840's could
command enough corn, beans, meat, etc. to meet the
U.S. National Research Council's Recommended Dietary Allowance, with less than 60 percent of their
cash and in-kind income. In 1968 the lowest 40
percent of rural households in Mexico devoted 66
percent of their cash and in-kind expenditures to a
bundle of food containing about the same quantity
of corn and beans per family member as their 1840's
ancestors, but much less meat.[23] The apparent deterioration in each case was not monotonic; the
1960's diets were better than those of 1900.
Neither, however, has the improvement since 1900
been monotonic. Rural real wages in Colombia did
not rise during 1935-1968, and Mexican studies show
declining output per head in minifundia agriculture
containing almost half of Mexico's farm population,
during 1940-1970.[24]

The second *problématique*, the intensification
of structural dualism or, more accurately, the

widening of labor productivity differences within countries, obviously interweaves with the income concentration trends. But contrary to the emphasis on *inter-sectoral* productivity differences of the two-sector models referred to earlier, in Latin America the strongest dualistic trends since World War II have been *intra-sectoral*. As cited previously, the ratios of average urban to rural incomes of Latin American countries in the 1969's range from 1.3 to 2.7, with most clustering above 2.0 and Argentina the low outrider at 1.3. If we use these ratios as rough proxies for inter-sectoral value added per worker ratios, they turn out to be only moderately higher than Britain's peak ratio of 1.5 in 1841, and considerably lower than Japan's peak of around 5.0 in the late 1930's.[25]

Consider, on the other hand, the enormous intra-sectoral productivity differences for Latin America in the 1960's revealed in Table 3. Let us take Argentina as the most technologically modern, the Central American group as the least modern, and the average for Latin America as approximating the intra-sectoral productivity ranges of the other ISI countries.[26] As one moves up this "modernization" ladder what stands out is the lack of any consistent narrowing of the intra-sectoral productivity ratios. This is so whether one compares Modern with Primitive, Modern with Intermediate or Intermediate with Primitive. What does occur along the ladder is a shift of intra-sectoral employment shares from Primitive mainly to Intermediate and, less strongly, to Modern in each sector, and a shift in intra-sectoral output shares primarily, except in manufacturing, to the Modern sector. The notion of a modernization ladder is, of course, a deceptive metaphor. The Primitive in Argentina has been of minor importance for many decades, while the characteristics of the mining sector in Latin America have been shaped far more by resource availability activated by foreign enterprises than by a process of indigenous technological upgrading.

This extreme intra-sectoral dualism, and its resiliency is what marks off Latin America comparatively. In Britain, with its agriculture organized in large tenant farms, the productivity variance of agriculture in the early 19th century must have been much narrower. The same was no doubt the case then for British industry, whose expansion was still heavily dependent on the growth of artisan output. In early 20th century Japan, agriculture was rather uniformly small tenant farming, with no important agribusiness overtones; the average value added per

Table 5.3: Estimated Composition of Employment, Product, and Relative Value Added per Worker by Sector at the End of the 1960's

	Latin America				Central America			
	Technological Strata							
	Modern	Inter-mediate	Primi-tive	Total	Modern	Inter-mediate	Primi-tive	Total
Employment and Product as percent of each sector's total:value added per person as percent of each sector's average								
All sectors Combined								
Employment	12.4	53.3	34.3	100	8.1	33.6	55.0	100
Product	53.3	41.6	5.1	100	42.6	48.0	9.4	100
Value Added per Worker[a]	328	99	19	100	528	144	17	100
Agriculture								
Employment	6.8	27.7	65.5	100	5.0	15.0	80.0	100
Product	47.5	33.2	19.3	100	43.9	30.6	25.5	100
Value Added per Worker[a]	700	120	29	100	877	204	32	100
Manufacturing								
Employment	17.5	64.9	17.6	100	14.0	57.4	28.6	100
Product	62.5	36.0	1.5	100	63.6	30.4	3.3	100
Value Added per Worker[a]	359	55	8	100	468	55	11	100
Mining								
Employment	38.0	34.2	27.8	100	20.0	60.0	20.0	100
Product	91.5	7.5	1.0	100	57.2	40.0	2.8	100
Value Added per Worker[a]	240	21	1	100	285	67	14	100

Table 5.3 (cont'd)

	Argentina			
	Technological Strata			
	Modern	Inter- mediate	Primi- tive	Total
Employment and Product as percent of each sector's total: value added per person as percent of each sector's average				
All sectors Combined				
Employment	21.3	65.8	5.3	100
Product	58.6	40.5	0.9	100
Value Added per Worker[a]	276	61	1	100
Agriculture				
Employment	25.0	57.0	18.0	100
Product	65.1	32.3	2.6	100
Value Added per Worker[a]	260	57	2	100
Manufacturing				
Employment	25.6	70.6	3.8	100
Product	62.1	37.5	0.4	100
Value Added per Worker[a]	240	53	10	100
Mining				
Employment	50.0	40.0	10.0	100
Product	77.8	21.6	0.6	100
Value Added per Worker[a]	156	54	6	100

[a] Index of value added per worker, with sectoral
average of each group of countries = 100.

Source: CEPAL, La mano de obra y el desarrollo
económico de América Latina en los últimos anõs,
(E/CN.12/L.1), as summarized in Aníbal Pinto, "Notas
sobre estilos de desarrollo en América Latina",
CEPAL Working Paper ECLA/JDE/Draft/103, December,
1973.

worker of Japanese factories ranged from 2.3 times
that of the artisan sub-sector (5 workers) in 1909
to 2.8 in 1937; and in the latter year the artisan
production still supplied 26 percent of Japanese industrial output.[27]
Some economists have contended that the post-
war income concentration trends, the 1960's structural features of Table 3, and the increasing unemployment and underemployment afflicting Latin American countries, largely result from product and labor
market distortions brought on since the 1930's by
excessive ISI policies and *conquistas sociales*. The
comparison of Mexican and Japanese industry trends
during 1895-1930, as summarized in Table 4, suggests
otherwise.

Table 5.4: Output and Employment in Manufacturing,
1895-1930 in Japan and Mexico

	Index of Manufacturing Output		Manufacturing share of Gross Domestic Product		Labor Force	
	Japan	Mexico	Japan	Mexico	Japan	Mexico
1895	100.0	100.0	.097	.125	.152	.116
1900	–	123.0	–	.132	–	.122
1905–7	176.0	–	.130	–	.181	–
1910	–	176.1	–	.127	–	.115
1915–17	367.3	–	.191	–	.181	–
1925–27	503.3	–	.196	–	.258	–
1930	–	270.5	–	.167	–	.099

Sources: Japan: Ohkawa and Shinohara, *op.cit*. p.232,
Table 13.5; pp. 278-79, Table A-12. Mexico:
Reynolds, *op.cit*. p. 60, Table 2.1; p. 386, Table
E.2; Donald Keesing, "Structural Change Early in
Development: Mexico's Changing Industrial and Occu-
pational Structure from 1895 to 1950" *Journal of
Economic History*, XXIX, No. 4 (December, 1969) Table
1.

In both countries the dominant strategy then was
export-led growth, unionization was negligible, and
minimum wage and other "distorting" labor market
legislation was largely absent. There were some de-
viations from purity, offsetting ones, however, as
concerns the comparison. Japanese tariffs were
lower, but Japan discouraged foreign investment
while Mexico welcomed it. Mexican policy became
less hostile to unionization after the Revolution,

but Japan in the 1920's was initiating its life-tenure system in the larger industrial firms. These minor falls from grace can hardly explain the contrasting trends in Table 4, in which Japan's industrial share of employment rose along with its industrial share of GDP, whereas Mexico's industrial share of employment fell as its industrial share of GDP rose. Nor can they explain why in Japan the agricultural shares of both employment and output fell sharply while in Mexico only the output share fell, while the employment share rose.[28] Neither can they account for the contrasting wage trends in this period. The emergence of wage dualism in Japan was the consequence of factory real wages rising faster than the *rise* of agricultural and artisan real wages, while in Mexico during the fast growing 1895-1910 sub-period, all three real wage categories fell.[29]

The relative speeds with modern factory products displaced artisan output is the key to the contrasting structural trends of early Mexican and Japanese industrialization. On Mexico, Keesing observes, "In these early years expanding industrial production must have displaced handicraft industries more than imports. During each period of rapid industrial growth up to 1930 people seem to have been thrown out of work in the traditional rural occupations faster than the modern sector could absorb them."[30] In Japan, on the other hand, craft output rose 230 percent and craft employment 20 percent between 1895 and 1925. Indeed, between 1925 and 1937 craft output rose another 80 percent and employment a further 21 percent.[31] The Japanese craft sector was a technologically progressive sector, with rising productivity and real wages, not a technologically stagnant employer of last resort. Behind these different speeds were major differences in the pattern of demand for consumer manufacturers. In Japan imported consumer manufacturers were a diminishing fraction of the total final goods supply during the periode 1895-1911, despite the 5 percent cap on tariffs which the "Unequal Treaties" with the major Western Powers imposed on Japan. In Mexico, despite higher tariffs, imports supplied a rising fraction of total consumer goods during 1898 to 1911.[32] Speed of displacement, linked more complexly to consumer behaviour, also helps to account for the intensity of structural dualism in Mexico and other Latin American countries in the inward oriented growth era after 1930. But more on that later.

The third *problématique*, the chronic vulnerability of Latin American Economic growth to balance of payments crises needs little elaboration. Briefly, the initial decade of independence, the 1820's, experienced the first of a succession of such crises. Excess demand for consumer imports, sustained for a time by British mercantile credits and some longer term loans extended the trade deficits and intensified the payment crises that struck before the end of the decade. This was the recurring pattern until around the 1880's.[33] The pattern was then modified as the periods of export expansion lengthened, as capital goods to facilitate that expansion became an important component of import demand, and as foreign portfolio and direct investments became a more important means of extending the periods of import surpluses. Nevertheless, both parts of the *crecemiento hacia afuera* era were periods of intermittent currency depreciation in most countries. Another modification came with the ISI era. The demand for consumer imports, which now could be expressed by a broader segment of the population, was deflected by import controls to domestic substitutes. Since World War II the imports of the more industrialized countries have consisted primarily of raw and intermediate materials, fuels and capital goods, destined mainly for industry and its ancillary services. Nevertheless, the frequency of balance of payments crises and the severity of exchange rate depreciation have both increased in this period. Comparatively, the Latin American experience with exchange rate deterioration since the early 19th century is unequalled in its pervasiveness, intensity and persistence by the experience of any other group of countries.

Two general observations of <u>Latin American consumption</u> are commonplaces in the historiography on the region. The first is that from the colonial era to the present the effective demand for consumer manufactures other than foods and, to a more limited degree, textiles, has been dominated by the higher income households. Prior to the 1930's this meant at most the top quintile.[34] By 1970 the prime market for non-food manufactures had broadened in many of the countries to encompass, as is shown in Tables 5 to 7, perhaps 40 percent of the households. Only Table 5 covers an entire country and a time-span of observations. Table 5 and the supplemental fact that average household income increased by one-third in Mexico between 1963 and 1975, suggests that the post-war income elasticity of trickling down has been positive for recreational equipment, weakly positive for household "software" and durables, and negligible for vehicles. The other two tables, as they cover only the most affluent area of the respective countries, the metropolis, understate the concentration of consumer effective demand nationally. São-Paulo's household expenditure concentration in Table 6 appears to be similar to Bogotá's in Table 7, but higher than that of Asunción, Lima and Caracas; although variations in the sampling and the definitions of expenditure categories muddy the comparison of Table 6 with 7. If the concentration differences are valid, they are not readily explainable by either per capita income or income concentration differences between the cities. São Paulo's 1971/72 average income was probably equivalent to Caracas of 1968, and was substantially above that of Asunción and Lima, while Bogotá's was considerably higher than Asunción's. The highest in income concentration among the cities in Table 7 was Asunción's (about equal to that of São Paulo) with Lima the second highest of the group.[35]

We cite these anomalies as introduction to the second general observation about Latin American consumption: the intense and persistent addiction to foreign consumption goods --European until World War I; mixed U.S.-European since-- of the affluent classes of Latin America. The observation runs through Latin American historiography from the colonial era to the present. Thus from an 18th century English historian:

"Quito is the only province of South America that can be denominated a manufacturing country: hats, cotton stuffs and coarse woolen cloths,.. ... furnish a considerable article for exportation to other parts of South America ..... But among the ostentatious inhabitants of the New World, the passion for everything that comes from Europe is so violent that I am told the manufactures of Quito are so much undervalued as to be on the decline."[36]

A half-century later British travelers described the central market areas of Quito, Valparaiso, Santiago and Bogotá as surrounded by shops dealing in "imported textiles and all kinds of hardware and cutlery of the latest fashion for a small upper class for which price was not everything".[37] Around the end of the century a Porfiriato writer remarked that

"The owners of our spinning and weaving mills .. ... dress themselves in European textiles, they

153

Table 5.5: Shares of National Household Outlays on Selected Household Items by Family Income Class: Mexico, 1963, 1968 and 1975

Income Percentiles	Household "Software"[1]	Telephone	Electricity	Household Durables[2]	Recreational Equipment[3]	Vehicles and Accessories[4]	Vacations, Other Recreational and Cultural Services
81-100							
1963	47.5	87.3	53.0	62.2	57.6	90.6	78.9
1968	56.6	91.9	52.0	52.8	59.5	94.8	81.1
1975	52.2	n.a.	n.a.	48.5	50.3	83.5	n.a.
61-80							
1963	26.1	8.7	27.5	25.9	28.1	6.6	15.3
1968	23.6	5.6	22.3	26.2	24.3	3.6	26.6
1975	22.6	n.a.	n.a.	31.4	22.2	10.5	n.a.
41-60							
1963	12.6	2.3	11.6	6.8	9.5	2.0	3.8
1968	11.6	2.0	14.0	12.1	10.9	1.1	13.1
1975	10.9	n.a.	n.a.	11.2	16.5	2.8	n.a.
0-40							
1963	13.8	1.7	7.9	5.1	4.8	0.8	2.0
1968	11.4	0.5	11.7	8.9	5.3	0.5	2.2
1975	17.2	n.a.	n.a.	8.9	10.9	3.0	n.a.

1 Clothing, shoes, hats, linens and drapery, candles, laundry, cleaning, personal grooming materials; 2 Furniture, utensils, kitchen, heating, cooling and cleaning durable equipment; 3 Toys, radios, T-V receivers, tape recorders, phonographs, cameras, musical instruments; 4 Automobiles, motorcycles, bicycles and accessories.

Table 5.5 (cont'd)

Sources: Encuesto Sobre Ingresos, 1963, Cuadro 26-7; La Distribucíon del Ingreso, 1968, Cuadro IV-2; Encuesta de Ingressos, 1975, Cuadro 8-2.

Table 5.6: Percentage of Expenditures in each Category by Household Income Class in the City of Sao Paulo, 1971/72

Income Class	Articles for the Home	Car Purchase	Car Maintenance	Clothing	Property Acquisition
Top 20 percent	67.0	69.3	78.6	60.8	79.5
Next highest 20%	16.3	26.9	19.2	20.2	13.4
Lowest 60%	16.7	3.8	2.2	19.0	7.1

Source: Computed from John R. Wells, "The Diffusion of Durables in Brazil and its Implications for Recent Controversies Concerning Brazilian Development", Cambridge Journal of Economics, Vol. 1, No. 3 (September, 1977) Table 6. Original data from Instituto de Pesquisas Econômicas, Orcamentos Familiares na Cidade de São Paulo, 1971/72.

Table 5.7: Distribution of Private Consumption Expenditures by Quartiles for Four Latin American Capital Cities; Late 1960's Year

Consumption Category	Percentage of Total Expenditure on Each Category per Quartile															
	Lowest Quartile				2nd Quartile				3rd Quartile				Highest Quartile			
	A	B	L	C	A	B	L	C	A	B	L	C	A	B	L	C
Food & Beverages	17.5	12.8	17.3	16.4	20.0	18.1	20.5	20.4	26.4	24.5	19.9	25.8	36.1	44.6	42.3	37.4
Durables	4.2	2.0	9.1	4.7	10.2	4.4	17.2	16.6	22.8	20.1	19.6	24.6	62.8	73.5	54.1	54.1
Household Non-durables	16.2	12.4	14.9	14.1	14.9	14.9	17.6	19.1	25.8	22.6	25.5	23.8	43.1	50.1	42.0	43.0
Cloting & Footwear	10.3	6.3	10.3	10.3	16.6	11.5	13.4	17.9	27.2	22.2	25.9	23.8	45.9	60.0	50.4	48.0
Housing	7.8	8.2	8.5	9.0	13.0	15.7	12.8	14.7	26.2	23.8	22.3	24.4	53.0	52.3	56.4	51.9
Transportation & Communication	4.5	7.7	5.6	8.8	11.9	9.1	12.0	15.5	19.5	16.1	20.6	28.1	64.1	67.1	61.8	47.6
Recreation	6.7	4.0	9.2	10.3	13.1	11.1	14.6	15.9	29.2	19.6	23.3	22.8	51.0	65.3	52.9	51.0

	Relative per Capita Income of City
	100.0
	148.9
	165.7
	195.6

% of Total City Expenditure Covered by Above 8 Categories
89.9
87.6
85.8
83.8

Notes

A = Asunción, Paraguay
B = Bogotá, Colombia
L = Lima, Peru
C = Caracas, Venezuela

Source: Computed from Tables A-2 to A-5 of Arturo Meyer, "Patterns of Consumption in Latin America", in Robert Ferber, ed., Consumption and Income Distribution in Latin America (Washington, Organization of American States, 1980).

use European or American hats, they lay out money for European or American carriages, they decorate their houses with European art objects, and prefer, in short, everything foreign over the national; even the painting, the literature and the music ..... have to carry the foreign seal."[38]

After World War II a technical term, "the international demonstration effect" was given this predilection, conveying for some the misconception that this long standing Latin American behavioral trait was mainly a product of Hollywood and Madison Avenue.

The contrast with observations of other regions is striking. At the hearings in 1813 before the House of Lords on the renewal of the East India Company's charter, a parade of export witnesses appeared whose observations of Indian consumption is capsulized in the following excerpt from the interrogation of Sir Charles Warre Malet, former Governor of Bombay:

"Does it appear to you that the more oppulent Hindus, who have intercourse with Europeans, have much taste for European articles, or use them much? In the course of my journey from Surat to Delhi ..... and visiting the principal zamindars and rajahs in my route, I recollect very little of European articles, or European manufacturens."[39]

The testimony of Sir Charles and the rest of the witnesses was partisan, the East India Company being intent on downplaying the size of the Indian market as part of its case against allowing non-Company merchants to enter the India trade under the renewed Charter. The company lost its case, but enough of the Indian artisan sector did survive colonial free trade and the Suez Canal to become one of the building blocks of industrialization planning in post-World War II India; an option that in Latin America, artisanía for the tourist trade excepted, would be dismissed as romantic necrophilia.

In China, the ability of artisan cotton cloth production to expand until the 1930's, despite increasing inroads of imported and local factory cloth, is also attributed in good part to the tenacity of home preferences for the indigenous.[40] Most striking is the adherence of the Japansese affluent classes to traditional consumption styles well into the 20th century. In Tokyo of the 1930's,

"the crowds of men and women, mostly dressed
in Western costume ... and going to work in the
huge ferro-concrete buildings ... give the appearance of a thoroughly modernized society.
But when they go home in the evening, they live
in small wooden houses, each with a small garden, in a manner not much changed since the beginning of Meiji. They want to wear Japanese
cloths and to eat and drink what their parents
had been accustomed to consume."[41]

This impression was firmly quantified by a 1955
urban household income-expenditure survey which
showed that 48 percent of household possessions, 73
percent if housing is added, consisted of items of
pre-Meiji design, with the propensity for the traditional declining only moderately with household
income level.[42]

How do these two persisting characteristics of
Latin American consumer behaviour interrelate with
the *problématiques*? Except for *aperçus* of the recently emerging but still amorphous Dependency school
of Latin American social scientists, the "hard"
technical analysis by economists of recent trends of
the *problématiques* have incorporated only the concentration of consumer demand into their analysis.
The hypothesis of a causal circle from concentration
of income to concentration of consumption to high
structural dualism back to high income concentration
etc., has motivated a number of econometric studies
to test the effect of breaking the circle with large
simulated redistributive transfers of income, using
input-output tables and consumption functions of
various Latin American countries. Generally, the
effects of income redistribution on employment and
import demand turned out to be quite small.[43] The
import demand finding might be taken as support for
attributing the balance of payments *problématique*
to monetary and foreign exchange mismanagement
rather than to structural factors, though to do so
requires ignoring the contrary implication of the
comparison between Porfiriato Mexico and Meiji Japan
presented earlier. The imperviousness of structure
to income distribution remains a puzzle to the
authors and to the comparative minded historian cog-
nizant that 19th century Britain, despite a concentration of land ownership and income distribution
matching the Latin American norm, had an expanding
artisan sector through most of the 19th century, a
moderate and reversible trend of economic dualism,
and a turnaround by the end of the century of its
Kuznets curve.

Bringing consumption style characteristics into the analysis can solve much of the puzzle, provided one is willing to junk some core concepts of neo-classical theory about production processes and consumer behaviour. This conceptual house-cleaning is needed because neo-classical theory is basically constructed to demonstrate a normative point: how substitution in production and consumption motivated by changing market prices can be the ubiquitous servo-mechanism that keeps a decentralized market economy on a steady expansion path; and this normative objective, rather than concern for fidelity to technological fact has shaped its conceptualization of production processes and consumer behaviour. Thus, efficient scaling-up of a productive process is assumed to require merely scalar multiplying all inputs; all changes in input proportions are assumed to be responses to relative input prices; and the capacity of productive units to respond is assumed to be independent of their varying capacities to innovate technologically. So outfitted, each market economy is shown to be capable of servicing the full gamut of consumer predilections by producing the desired goods, or trading for them. Sociological analysis of preference behaviour becomes superfluous detail, and the theory can, with no loss of essentials, be simplified by postulating that each consumer's preference are unaffected by what others around him say or do.

The simulation studies referred to above were informed by this theoretical framework. Their authors were aware that limitations of the data used, including excessive aggregation, affected the results. They deplored not being able to track the relative price changes which the simulated income transfers would bring about and the transfer feedbacks on the choice of techniques and on the composition of consumer demand. Absent in the litany, however, were complaints about the need to analyze feedbacks on the scale economies, on the relative technical dynamism of different activities, and on consumer preferences. Neo-classical theory is not set up to raise or to handle such questions. As Lindert and Williamson have put it:

> "The long-term demand forces --in particular the degree of imbalance in technological progress between sectors using machines, skills and raw labor with varying intensity-- have been understated as determinants of inequality trends. Indeed such technological imbalance has not been well-appreciated in explanations

of accumulation and growth."[44]

However, the recent theoretical and empirical critiques of neo-classical production theory, which sum to the conclusion that the theory has been clothing the production process with imaginary garments , frees us from its thrall. Thus, it's safe now to recognize that in the real world of technology changing the scale of production efficiently does usually require changing input proportions; and changing either does usually require some capacity for technological innovating. These interdependencies between scale, substitution and innovation provide theoretical underpinning for the following generalizations about modern growth and technical change.[45]

1. Process technologies, due to basic physical and probabilistic laws, have the potential to generate technical economies of scale; the extent of the potential varying, however, among processes and products.
2. Realization of these potentials requires the expansion of specific limitational inputs, rather than scalar multiplication of all inputs.
3. Redesigning, and hence innovating, is an essential element of efficient scaling up; the element's importance also rising periodically, when qualitative improvements of the limitational inputs are also needed for further scaling up.
4. The cognitive sources of skills for identifying and innovating around strategic bottle necks to scaling up have been a changing mix of "learning by doing" and formal principles of applied science and engineering, with the latter increasing in relative importance in the course of modern technological progess.
5. Since the changing composition of consumer demand helps determine the changing sub-set of processes to be expanded and discarded, differences in national consumption styles help to explain the variations in the technological trajectories and productive structures among the early industrializing countries of the 19th century, as well as among the later industrializers of the 20th century.

The first four generalizations imply that the course of modern economic growth has been toward ever larger productive units, and that the later the industrialization effort the higher the barriers against access to the "state of the arts" technologies, set by increasing scale requirements and the rising cognitive requirements for innovating. These familiar points should require no special documentation here. The fifth, which implies that these tendencies have been moderated in varying degree by differences in national consumption styles, may need some clarification of that concept, as well as elaboration of its role.

The concept has for its main theoretical underpinning the 18th century classical economic distinction between "necessities" and superfluities,[46] and the associated classical proposition that the consumer's utility from superfluities derives as much from their role as indicators of social standing as from their contribution to creature comforts. Since the status value of a superfluity depends on its relative inaccessibility to those below, it also becomes a mark of success to the upwardly mobile, so that the consumption style of those at the top is filtered with varying intensity to the lower income layers above the non-mobile masses. The values of the elite that guide their choices of status goods determines, therefore, which of the possible set of superfluities will have high income elasticities of demand. Finally, aristocracies built around enduring titles and family names are more protected against social climbers than *soi-disant* aristocracies of wealth. Capitalist societies with no strong aristocratic heritage have, therefore, been especially prone to frantic pursuit of new status goods to restore social distance.

As for non-Latin American examples of the importance of consumption style, I very briefly note just two. One is the thesis, by now fairly widely accepted, that differences in consumption styles between the 19th century rural and small town elites of the Northern United States and the aristocratic style setters of Britain helped shape the diverging technological trajectories of the two countries; the first toward superiority in mass-producing and marketing consumer goods; the second toward sustaining and modernizing craft technologies. The other is the importance of Japanese elite preferences for traditional status goods in protecting late industrializing Japan against too rapid inundation by mass-produced consumer imports and the Latin Americanizing of its productive structure.[47]

As for Latin America, from the data and arguments already presented, the effect of the elite consumption style during the *crecemiento hacia afuera* era should be evident: it reinforced the immiserating tendencies of growth in most of that region during that era. In effect the Latin American elite administered a double blow to the rest of society. The first, the land-grabbing, forced labor and other manifestations of Marxian primary accumulation, was advertent; the second, the stagnation and decay of the artisan sector from the deflection of elite demand toward status imports, was largely inadvertent. Regardless, the consequence was to depress artisan employment, and to remove a basic stimulus to capital accumulation and technical advance from the artisan sector. By reducing the internal linkage effects during export growth it also augmented the frequency of balance of the payment overloads.

The links between consumption style and the *problématiques* during the later ISI era do merit further probing. They are no less important, but are less visible.

Thus, most critics and supporters alike of ISI as a development strategy took it as self-evident that when imported consumer goods were reduced to a minor proportion of total imports by "easy phase" ISI, the role of "leading sector" during the "hard phase" of ISI would necessarily shift from consumer manufactures to intermediate and capital goods. In fact, after the early 1950's the fastest growing industries of Brazil, Argentina and the other advanced ISI economies of Latin America were the consumer durables including the passenger car industry, and technically sophisticated new consumer nondurables. What was occurring was a substitution-chaining dynamic within two, three and four digit-industries, whose different speeds accounted for much of the differential growth rates between these statistically-fixed industry categories. The main difference between the "easy" and "hard" phases of ISI was that in the latter the consumer industries were no longer replacing competing artisan products and imports, but older import substitutes with new products.

This substitution dynamic is of course a basic characteristic of modern economic growth with its continual outpouring of new products. The problem for the Latin American countries in the post-war period has been that because the new products are overwhelmingly of foreign design, a balance is needed between the speed of the substitution-chaining and the lags in developing domestic sources of specialized inputs for producing the succession

162

of new products. Since new products are initially
more import-intensive than the older products they
are displacing; beyond some critical speed of
chaining, the import intensity of industrial output
rises, despite ISI, putting the balance of payments
at risk. This is, indeed, what has been occurring
since the eraly 1950's. For example, with the aid
of Argentine input-output matrices for 1953 and 1960
I've shown that the 1960 vector of final demand mul-
tiplied by either matrix produced substantially
higher raw and intermediate imports per unit of
final demand than did the 1953 final demand vector.[48]
Similar links are traceable from the extent of
"foreignness" of the new products, to the extent to
which the low labor using technologies must be imported, to the intensification of the other two
problématiques: structural dualism and income concentration. In sum, Latin American countries with
their ISI strategies have been navigating ineffec-
tively against the strong current of their consumer
dynamics.

Would an export-led growth strategy have improved matters significantly? A recent study of
post-war Puerto Rico's experience with export-led
industrial growth suggests not. With tariff-free
access to U.S. markets and exemption from U.S. taxes
of the earnings of the U.S. owned firms domiciled in
Puerto Rico allowed under the island's commonwealth
status, Puerto Rico is unusually well-situated for
exploiting export-led industrial growth. Indeed,
the strategy worked well during the first two post-
war decades before success bred failure. In its
autopsy of the Puerto Rican "Miracle", the study
found a rising import content of domestic consumption, in particular, a persisting rise of imports in
the same industrial product classes that had led the
export expansion. The exports were less expensive
labor-intensive goods, as called for by the strategy,
but income growth, increased income concentration,
and preference shifting turned Puerto Rican consumption increasingly toward more expensive imports in
the same product classes. The study summarizes its
findings as system overload due to the speed "of the
reshaping of the island's consumption into the
'American way of life'".[49]

The speed of consumer product substitution in
the ISI economies has been propelled in good part
by rising household incomes and its concentration.
It's a commonplace that the large consumer manufacturing firms in post-war Latin America find it most
profitable to pursue a "skimming the cream" marketing strategy, aiming their new products at the top-

third of the urban income strata.[50] But the following pieces of evidence indicate that the contribution of consumption style and its diffusion by mass communication channels must not be overlooked.

The experience of Chile and Argentina with ISI during the 1930's and 1940's is one piece of evidence. This interlude, during which the Great Depression and World War II cut back both industrial imports and the creation of new consumer products abroad, necessarily also slowed the speed of the substitutionchaining dynamic in Latin America. The production of direct substitutes for imported consumer manufactures led the industrial expansion of this period, with production bottlenecks stimulating an outburst of local inventiveness, that provided the process and product modifications to enable firms to get around the unavailability of imported inputs.[51] The result was intensified use of local resources, including a much higher elasticity of industrial employment per unit of output than prevailed in the Post-War, deeper trickling down of consumer products, and, as indicated earlier, a reversal of the trend toward income concentration. It was with this experience in mind that the overly optimistic ISI theories of the late 1940's were constructed.

Household savings data from the early 1960's for Venezuela and Brazil are a second suggestive piece of evidence. The Venezuelan savings data in Table 8 show a strong tendency for savings ratios of given income levels to drop sharply with greater proximity to the pace-setting consumption centers. Similarly, in Brazil, while 70 percent of the households in Belem saved part of their income in 1961-62, in more affluent and swinging São Paulo the percentage was only 30 percent.[52]

Finally, Table 9 offers poignant evidence on Brazil in the mid-1970's. The family income groups in the table are those whose per capita food consumption in 1974-75 was below the low variant of the FAO-WHO Daily Caloric Requirement. Note that each income class has the same gradients: the percentage spent on food declines and the caloric deficit rises as one moves from rural to towns and cities to the metropoli, while the proportion of families with T-V's and refrigerators rises monotonically as one moves from rural through the two urban locales. No doubt the rural proportions in the last gradient were depressed by lesser access to electricity and greater distance from T-V transmitters; but such complications did not distort the urban part of the durable goods gradient, nor the food expenditure and

164

Table 5.8: Savings Behaviour of Rural and Urban Venezuelan Families in 1962

Location of Families	Monthly Income above which savings were positive (in bolivars)	Families with negative savings rates (percentage)	Overall savings rate of families (percentage)
Rural	400]		
Small Towns	500]	22.0	+ 10.0
All Major			
Cities	2000	67.0	− 10.0
a. Caracas	2000	80.0	− 16.5

Source: "Income Distribution in Selected Major Cities of Latin America and in their Respective Countries", Economic Bulletin for Latin America, Vol. XVIII, Nos. 1 and 2, (New York: United Nations, 1973) p. 43.

Table 5.9: Urban and Rural Family Expenditure on Food and Durable Good Ownership Ratios of Brazilian Families with Nutritional Deficits, By Income Class, 1974-75[a]

Average per capita Expenditure Class in August, 1974 Cruzeiros

2000-6000

A. Food and Nutrition

	% Spent on Food	Caloric Deficit %
1. Metropolitan Families	51.6	30.2
2. Other Urban Families	56.7	26.7
3. Rural Families	64.5	13.6

B. Possession of Durables

	% Families with Auto	T-V	Refrig
1. Metropolitan Families	0.2	10.7	7.9
2. Other Urban Families	0.3	5.7	2.3
3. Rural Families	0.2	0.3	0.7

6001-10,000

A. Food and Nutrition

	% Spent on Food	Caloric Deficit %
1. Metropolitan Families	46.3	20.8
2. Other Urban Families	52.0	14.3
3. Rural Families	60.7	2.3

B. Possession of Durables

	% Families with Auto	T-V	Refrig
1. Metropolitan Families	1.1	33.8	22.5
2. Other Urban Families	0.7	17.3	11.9
3. Rural Families	4.0	6.2	4.8

10,001-14,000

A. Food and Nutrition

	% Spent on Food	Caloric Deficit %
1. Metropolitan Families	41.3	14.5
2. Other Urban Families	47.5	12.2
3. Rural Families	58.1	-3.3

B. Possession of Durables

	% Families with Auto	T-V	Refrig
1. Metropolitan Families	1.8	43.4	30.1
2. Other Urban Families	2.0	12.4	16.3
3. Rural Families	1.5	7.6	5.1

14,001-18,000

A. Food and Nutrition

	% Spent on Food	Caloric Deficit %
1. Metropolitan Families	39.0	12.2
2. Other Urban Families	42.2	6.7
3. Rural Families	49.4	0.0

B. Possession of Durables

	% Families with Auto	T-V	Refrig
1. Metropolitan Families	2.5	57.0	33.9
2. Other Urban Families	3.8	42.3	30.2
3. Rural Families	7.3	81.9	29.0

18,001-22,000

A. Food and Nutrition

	% Spent on Food	Caloric Deficit %
1. Metropolitan Families	36.6	23.3
2. Other Urban Families	39.7	4.5
3. Rural Families	--	--

B. Possession of Durables

	% Families with Auto	T-V	Refrig
1. Metropolitan Families	6.8	70.7	67.8
2. Other Urban Families	10.5	44.5	59.7
3. Rural Families	--	--	--

22,001-26,000

A. Food and Nutrition

	% Spent on Food	Caloric Deficit %
1. Metropolitan Families	39.0	8.9
2. Other Urban Families	38.7	8.9
3. Rural Families	--	--

B. Possession of Durables

	% Families with Auto	T-V	Refrig
1. Metropolitan Families	5.6	80.9	74.4
2. Other Urban Families	8.9	58.7	61.0
3. Rural Families	--	--	--

Table 5.9 (cont'd)

a Caloric deficit is the percentage caloric shortfall from the "Low" FAO-WHO Daily Caloric Requirement.

Source: Computed from World Bank, Brazil: Human Resources Special Report (The World Bank, Washington, DC, 1979) Tables B.1 to B.4, Annex III, Appendix B. Original data from Instituto Brazileiro de Geografia e Estradística, Estudos Nacional da Despesa Familiar, ENDEF, Despesas das Familias: Dados Preliminares (Rio de Janeiro, 1979),

Table 5.10: The Relative Costs of Alternative Zero Caloric Deficit Diets in Brazil at 1974-75 food prices, According to Geographic Location

Geographic Location of Family	Alternative Food Consumption Diets		
	Type I	Type II	Type III
Rural Brazil	100	100	100
Other Urban Locales	177	113	131
Metropolitan Areas	197	145	138

Notes: Diet Types. Type I: Diet with food consumption of Brazilian households who were at the zero caloric deficit level in 1974-75. Type II: The food items actually consumed by the poorest 20 percent of Brazilian families scaled up proportionately to an adequate caloric total. Type III: A calorically adequate diet made up only of cereals, in the proportions actually consumed by deficit families.
The relatives are weighted averages of individual relatives from 22 Brazilian sub-regions.

Source: World Bank, op.cit., Annex III, pp. 66-68.

caloric deficit gradients. Moreover, as indicated
by Table 10, which costs three alternative zero caloric deficit budgets in 1974-75 prices, food prices
also formed a rising gradient as one moved up from
rural to the two urban locales.

Combining the prices with the food expenditure
gradients leads to the astonishing conclusion that
the price elasticity of demand for food of the
undernourished urban families in each income class
was greater than unity. They treated food as a
luxury expenditure! Not surprisingly, despite the
concentration of medical facilities in the cities,
in each of the main three geographic regions of
Brazil, average life expectancy at birth in 1970 was
higher for the rural than for urban components of
the poorest 65 percent of the families.[53]

These results are reinforced by other surveys
for metropolitan São Paulo. These show rising accumulation of household durables accompanied by a
decline of per capita food consumption among the
metropolitan Paulista working classes and a deterioration of housing conditions during the 1960's and
early 1970's.[54] They also show a rise of infant
mortality rates in 1960-73 that reversed the substantial fall of such rates during the 1950's. By
contrast, in the rest of the state of São Paulo infant mortality rose in the 1950's but declined in
the subsequent 15 years.[55]

Generalized, the inverse relation between
household savings rates and proximity to centers of
modern consumerism reported for Venezuela and Brazil
may help explain the anomalies of Table 6 referred
to earlier. Asunción, with the highest income concentration of the four cities was also the most
provincial. Similarly, the Brazilian food-mortality
data probably indicate what underlied the lack of
significant correlation between the relative changes
of per capita income and of the PQLI index in Latin
America during 1950-75.

CONCLUDING REMARKS

This paper has, I trust, demonstrated that consumption should not be treated merely as a passive
consequence of the technological trends, accumulation rates, ownership patterns and the changes in
socio-economic structure that have accompanied
modern economic growth. Differences in what I've
called consumption style, and the cultural forces
that account for these differences, have been active
partial determinants of the varying technological,
structural and output patterns, both in the earlier

168

era of modern economic growth and today. For the economic historian, comparative consumption styles provide an important analytic link between the sociological and economic forces that generated the diverging growth and social welfare patterns of the past. For the humane-minded among the social scientists dealing with economic development problems of today, investigating the socio-economic forces that currently shape consumption styles in the LDC regions is, I believe, an important prerequisite for better understanding the widely different social welfare consequences of contemporary economic growth in the LDCs, and for identifying strategies that could strengthen the disappointingly weak relations between the growth of output and the growth of welfare in such LDC regions as Latin America.

NOTES

1. The Argentine estimates are by the Naciones Unidas, Comisión Económica para América Latina, El Desarrollo Económico de la Argentina (México, D.F., 1959). The Mexican estimates are from Enrique Pérez López, "The National Product of Mexico: 1895-1964" in Mexico's Recent Economic Growth: the Mexican View, Monograph No. 10 of the Institute of Latin American Studies, University of Texas (Austin: University of Texas Press, 1967). The Chilean estimates are by Marto A. Ballesteros and Tom E. Davis, "The Growth of Output and Employment in the Basic Sectors of the Chilean Economy, 1908-1957" Economic Development and Cultural Change Vol. 11, No. 2 (January, 1963).
2. For the Argentine negative growth rate estimate see Aldo Ferrer, The Argentine Economy (Berkeley: University of California Press, 1967) pp. 54-55. For Mexico see Clark W. Reynolds, The Mexican Economy: Twentieth Century Structure and Growth (New Haven: Yale University Press, 1970) Appendix A. For Brazil, Celso Furtado, The Economic Growth of Brazil (Berkeley, University of California Press, 1963) pp. 114-18. For Colombia, Luis Ospina Vásquez, Industria y Protección en Colombia, 1810-1930 (Medellín, 1955) pp. 422-37 and William P. Mc Greevey, An Economic History of Colombia, 1845-1930 (Cambridge University Press, 1971), Chapters 3-4.
3. E.g. Brazil, according to Nathaniel Leff, "Economic Retardation in Nineteenth Century Brazil", Economic History Review Second Series XXV No. 2 (August, 1971). Peru, according to Rosemary Thorp and Geoffrey Bertram, Peru, 1890-1977: Growth and Policy in an Open Economy (New York, Columbia University Press, 1978) Chapters 2-3. Colombia accord-

ing to Ospina Vásquez, loc.cit. and McGreevey, loc. cit.

   4. Ferrer, op.cit. pp. 54-55; Carlos F. Díaz-Alejandro, Essays on the Economic History of the Argentine Republic (New Haven, Yale University Press, 1970) p. 3; Fernando Rosenzweig, "El Desarrollo Económico de México de 1877 a 1911" El Trimestre Económico Vol. 33 (julio-septiembre, 1965) pp. 405-54; Ballesteros and Davis, op.cit. Markos Mamalakos raises Chilean growth of output per head for the entire period 1855-1930 to nearly 2 percent per annum. The Growth and Structure of The Chilean Economy: from Independence to Allende (New Haven: Yale University Press, 1976) pp. 4-9. His estimate, which has Chile growing at a one-third faster rate than Argentina over that period, seems much too high. It is inconsistent with various social indicator comparisons between the two countries as well as with the end year differences in GNP per head.

   5. Unfortunately, on this as on may other quantitative questions concerning Latin America's economic past, conjecture is still the better part of valuation. Pre-World War I investment rations are virtually non-existent, and those that exist, e. g. for Argentina, are quite disputable. In its retrospective construction of Argentine national accounts for 1900-1950 the United Nations, Economic Commission for Latin America, produced a ratio of over 40 percent for 1900-14. Díaz-Alejandro has knocked the figure down to 18 percent by merely revaluing the ECLA investment components in 1937 Argentine prices, instead of the 1950 prices used by ECLA. See Díaz-Alejandro, op.cit. pp. 28-29. Both series, however, drift down during the 1920's. Since Argentina remained among the more rapidly growing group of Latin American countries in the 1920's, it seems plausible to conclude that there was at least a general leveling of investment/GDP ratios in the 1920's.

   Foreigners (exclusive of immigrants) owned 48 percent of the Argentine stock of productive capital in 1913, the ratio falling to 37 percent in 1937. Ibid. pp. 29-30. Foreign ownership of the capital stock probably peaked at lower percentages in the other Latin American countries, but was probably above 30 percent in Porfiriato Mexico, and not much less in Chile, Uruguay and Brazil.

   6. Morris D. Morris, Measuring the Condition of the World's Poor (New York: Pergamon Press, 1979). His choice of the three components for the PQLI was based on three criteria: they are fundamental "output" dimensions of quality of life; the basic sta-

tistics are widely available in the LDCs (albeit of uneven reliability); each of the "qualities" is inherently egalitarian (only one life for the Tsar and for Ivan the mouzhik), so that interpretation of changes of PQLI is not complicated by wealth concentration trends, in contrast to other candidates for quality of life indicators, such as physicians, telephones or motor cars per capita. In other words, the PQLI captures only a limited aspect of the quality of life, but that relatively unambiguously.

7. Computed from ibid. Appendix B, Table 1, Appendix C, Table 1, and GNP per capita growth rates from World Development Report, 1978, Appendix Table 1 and U.S. Agency for International Development, Gross National Product: Growth Rates and Trend Data by Region and Country RC-W-138 (Washington, D.C., July, 1968) Table 1b.

8. The curbing of industrial imports during World War I had merely depressed aggregate industrial output in Argentina, Chile and Mexico; reinforced in Mexico by the disruptions of the Revolution. See United Nations, Economic Commission for Latin America, The Process of Industrial Development in Latin America (New York: the United Nations, 1966) Figure 1, p. 10.

9. Ibid. Figure IV, pp. 23-24.

10. David Felix, "Economic Development: Take-Offs into Unsustained Growth" Social Research, Vol. 2 (June, 1969) Table 3.

11. ECLA, op.cit. pp. 35-45.

12. For Colombia, see Albert Berry and Miguel Urrutía, Income Distribution in Colombia (New Haven: Yale University Press, 1976) and Albert Berry and Ronald Soligo, "The Distribution of Income in Colombia: An Overview" in Berry and Soligo eds. Economic Policy and Income Distribution in Colombia (Boulder, Colo., Westview Press, 1980) pp. 1-45. For Mexico, see David Felix, "Income Distribution Trends in Mexico and the Kuznets Curves" in Richard S. Weinart and Sylvia Hewlett, eds., The Political Economies of Brazil and Mexico, to be published this year by ISHI press. Estimates for the other three mentioned countries, plus single year estimates for a few others are given in Adolfo Figueroa and Richard Weisskoff, "Viewing Social Pyramids: Income Distribution in Latin America" in Robert Ferber, ed., Consumption and Income Distribution in Latin America (Washington, D.C., Organization of American States, 1980) pp. 257-294.

13. On the algebra involved see Sherman Robinson, "A Note on the U Hypothesis Relating Income Inequality and Economic Development" American Eco-

nomic Review, Vol. 66 (June, 1976).

14. Figueroa and Weisskoff, op.cit. Tables 5
and 7: William R. Cline, Potential Effects of Income
Redistribution on Economic Growth (New York, Praeger
1972) p. 113. However, Berry and Urrutía, op.cit.
pp. 64-69 cite evidence of rising inequality in the
Colombian rural sector since the thirties. Evidence
for a similar trend in Mexico since 1940 is cited in
Felix, op.cit.

15. The numbers and the basis for the guesti-
mate of the 1910 Gini are discussed in Felix, "Income Distribution Trends in Mexico", op.cit.

16. A.L. Bowley's estimates of the income
share of the top 5 percent in Britain is 48% in 1880
and 43% in 1913; off the top 17 percent in 1880 it's
58% and for the top twenty percent in 1913 it's
59%. Cited in Simon Kuznets, "Quantitative Aspects
of the Economic Growth of Nations: VIII. Distribution of Income by Size" Economic Development and
Cultural Change Vol. XI No. 2 Part II (January, 1963)
Table 16. Bowley's shares for the top 5 percent of
pre-World War I Britain are higher than those for
the Mexican top 5 percent of post-World War II Mexico. While the share for the top 17 percent in 1880
is about equal to that of the top 17 percent in
Mexico in the mid-1970's.

17. Berry and Soligo, op.cit. pp. 14-17.

18. Non-market land grabbing petered out in
the majority of the Latin American countries by World
War I. It still persists today according to jour-
nalistic reports in such "moderately authoritarian"
countries, (Professor Jeane Kirpatrick's antiseptic
phrase) as Paraguay, Guatemala, Honduras and fron-
tier Brazil.

19. The above pattern during the Mexican Por-
firiato is described in considerable detail in the
following monographs of the 10 volume Historia
Moderna de México series edited by Daniel Cosio
Villegas, México, D.F., Editorial Hermes, 1956-71:
Fernando Rosenzweig, "La Industria" and Luis Cossio
Silva "La Agricultura" in El Porfiriato: La Vida
Económica Vol. 7, and Moises Gonzalez Navarro, La
Vida Social Vol. 4. On Mexican agriculture see also
Friedrich Katz, "Labor Conditions on Haciendas in
Porfirian Mexico: Some Trends and Tendencies" and
John Coatsworth, "Railroads, Landholdings and Agrar-
ian Protest in the early Porfiriato" Hispanic Amer-
ican Historical Review Vol. 54 (February, 1974).
Ospina Vasquez, op.cit. and McGreevey, op.cit. stress
the pattern in their descriptions of 19th century
Colombian economic growth. On falling real wages in
the state of São Paulo during its 1880-1914 coffee

boom, see Leff, op.cit. p. 491. Evidence of falling
real wages of Chilean peones in central Chile, 1870
to 1920 is given in Arnold J. Bauer, Chilean Rural
Society: From the Spanish Conquest to 1930
(Cambridge: Cambridge University Press, 1975) p. 156
Table 31.

Argentina was a partial exception. In the Pam-
pean region Díaz-Alejandro cautiously suggests a
horizontal trend for real wages in the 19th century,
op.cit. pp. 49-42. It is likely, however, that in
Northwest Argentina, where colonial artisan industry
had been important, real wages probably fell in the
19th century, along with artisan employment. In
coastal Peru, Thorp and Bertram suggest that while
real wages fell, 1900-1930, the wage share fell more
in 1920-30, a stagnating export period, than in
1900-20, an expanding export period. Op.cit. pp.
114-140. The difference may be because the coastal
Peruvian exporters were mines, smelters and planta-
tions whose labor was paid in cash rather than with
in-kind usufructs. It was therefore employment,
more than the intensity with which the labor force
was worked, that swung up and down with export production.

20. Mexican data from Felix, op.cit. Table III.
Brazilian data summarized in Figueroa and Weisskoff,
op.cit. Table 1; Colombian data, Berry and Urrutia,
op.cit. p. 114 and Berry and Soligo, op.cit. p. 5.

21. The study is Fundação Instituto Brasileiro
de Geografía e Estatística, Estudos Nacional da
Despesa Familiar (Rio de Janeiro, 1977). The nutri-
tional findings are summarized in The World Bank,
Brazil: Human Resources Special Report (Washington,
D.C., 1979) Annex III.

Note that the study lowered the FAO/WHO requirements about 10 percent because the average
weight and stature of Brazilians was less than the
norms used by FAO/WHO to arrive at its caloric standards. Statistically, as the report recognizes,
this biases downward the nutritional deficiency percentages, since the smaller weight and size of
Brazilians is itself a result of nutritional short-
falls rather than of genetic inheritance. The
average weight and height of the well-fed Brazilian
income groups is at European standard.

22. McGreevey, op.cit. p. 131, Table 18.

23. The hacienda data are from Harry E. Cross,
"Living Standards in Rural Nineteenth Century Mexico: Zacatecas, 1820-80" Journal of Latin American
Studies Vol. 10, No. 1 (May, 1978). The 1968 Mexican data are computed from Banco de México, La Dis-
tribucion del Ingreso en México: Encuesta Sobre los

Ingresos y Gastos de las Familias, 1968 (México, D. F., Fondo de Cultura Económica, 1974) Cuadro IV-2.

24. For the Colombian improvement over 1891, see McGreevey, op.cit., for the leveling of agricultural real wages after 1935, see Berry and Urrutia, op.cit. pp. 68-72, 90-95. On Mexican post-war agricultural trends, see Salomon Eckstein, El Marco Macroeconómico del Problema Agrario Mexicano (México, D.F., Centro de Investigaciones Agrarias, 1968) and Fernando Rosenzweig "Política Agrícola y Generación de Empleo en México" El Trimestre Económico XLII (Oct.-Dec. 1975). For the deterioration of the consumption levels of the Mexican peon during the Porfiriato see items cited in footnote 18.

25. The British ratio is computed from data in B.R. Mitchell and Phyllis Dean, Abstract of British Historical Statistics (Cambridge University Press, 19b2) pp. 8, 60, 366. The ratio tends downward after 1841. The Japanese ratio is computed from Kazushi Ohkawa and Miyohei Shinohara, Patterns of Japanese Economic Development: A Quantitative Appraisal (New Haven: Yale University Press, 1979) p. 131, Table 6.8 and pp. 278-80, Table A-12. The 5.0 Japanese ratio, however, overstates average rural-urban income differences, since Japanese farm families in the 1930's were still substantially supplementing their agricultural incomes with cottage industry earnings.

26. This was the intent of the original study from which Table 3 was taken. The productivity ranges of Bolivia, Paraguay and Ecuador doubtlessly are close to the Central American countries, but their weight in the overall average is offset by the inclusion of Argentina in that average, so that the overall average is representative of the remaining semi-industrialized countries like Brazil, Mexico, Chile, Colombia and Peru.

The precise criteria used in the study to separate Modern from Intermediate and Primitive is not entirely clear. Aníbal Pinto, who directed the study, explains that the primitive activities are those for which no significant technical improvements occurred since the colonial era; that the modern activities contain the factories, agribusiness export establishments and large mining and petroleum extraction and refining; and the intermediates are activities whose labor productivity in each sector clustered near the average V.A. per worker of all the Latin American countries. He also reports that separation was facilitated by the large discontinuities between each group. Aníbal Pinto, "Naturaleza e Implicaciones de la 'Heterogeneidad Estructural' de la América Latina" El Trimestre Económico XXXVII

174

(México, D.F., enero-marzo 1970), pp. 83-100.

27. Kazushi Ohkawa and Henry Rosovsky, Japanese Economic Growth (Stanford University Press, 1973) pp. 81-83, Tables 4.4 and 4.6.

28. On Japan, see Ohkawa and Shinohara, op.cit. Tables 6.8 and A-12. On Mexico, see Keesing, op.cit. Tables 1 and 2.

29. On Japanese real wage trends see Ohkawa and Shinohara, op.cit. Table 13.5, p. 232, and Ohkawa and Rosovsky, op.cit. pp. 82-87. On Mexican rural and urban wage trends, 1895-1910 see El Colegio de México, Esradísticas Económicas del Porfiriato: Fuerza de Trabajo y Actividad Económica por Sectores (México, D.F., Seminario de Historia Moderna, 1965) pp. 147-51.

30. Keesing, op.cit. p. 723.

31. Ohkawa and Rosovsky, op.cit. Tables 4.4 and 4.6.

32. On Japan, Yuichi Shionoya, "Patterns of Industrial Development" in Lawrence Klein and Kazushi Ohkawa, eds. Economic Growth: The Japanese Experience (Homewood, Ill., Richard D. Irwin, 1968) Appendix Tables 3A-4, 3A-5. On Mexico, El Colegio de México, Estadísticas Económicas del Porfiriato: Comercio Exterior de México, 1877-1911 (México, D.F. 1960).

33. D.C.M. Platt, Latin America and British Trade, 1806-1914 (London: Adam and Charles Black, 1972) is a useful accounting of the pattern as viewed from the British side.

34. Thus a British consular report appraising the Mexican market, observed that three-fourths of the population was "utterly indifferent to the needs and aspirations of civilized humanity". G.F.B. Jenner, Report on the Finances of Mexico for 1886, Parliamentary Papers, 1887, LXXXV, p. 20, as cited in Platt, op.cit. p. 117. Constructions of the Mexican economic pyramid in the 1890's by contemporary analysts, using the 1895 census as the base for their construction, came up with similar proportions. See references in Gonzalez Navarro, op.cit. pp. 383-397. Among the Latin American countries the strata were broadened in urban Argentina; less so in rural Argentina, where apart from a uniquely carnivorous diet, the material standard of rural labor was not notably superior to that of the other countries. E.g. See James R. Scobie, Revolution in the Pampas: A Social History of Argentine Wheat, 1860-1910 (Austin, University of Texas Press, 1964) pp. 64-67, for a description of Argentine rural squalor.

35. Meyer, op.cit. Table 6.

36. William Robertson, History of America

(London, 1777) p. 498, cited in McGreevey, op.cit.
p. 344. Similarly, the 19th century Mexican historian, Lucas Aleman, observed that most fine textiles
were produced in colonial Mexico when wars cut off
access to customary European supplies. When peace
and imports resumed Mexican production fell off
sharply. Cited in William P. Glade, The Latin American Economies: A Study of Their Institutional Evolution (New York: American Book Co., 1969) p. 560,
Note 138.
    37. Platt, op.cit. p. 18 (Quotation slightly
rearranged).
    38. Cited in Charles C. Cumberland, Mexico:
The Struggle for Modernity (London, Oxford University Press, 1968) p. 222.
    39. The testimony of Sir Charles and the
others along similar lines is reproduced in Major B.
D. Basu, Ruin of Indian Trade and Industries (Cal-
cutta, Ro Chatterjee, 1935) 3rd Edition, Appendix J.
    40. Albert Feuerwerker, "Handicraft and Manu-
factured Cotton Textiles in China, 1871-1910", Journal of Economic History XXX No. 2 (June, 1970) pp.
338-78. Sixty-one percent of the cotton cloth produced in China in the 1930's was still handicraft,
as was 68 percent of the total value of industrial
output. Ibid. p. 377.
    41. Teijiro Uyeda, The Small Industries of
Japan (Shanghai, 1938) p. 11.
    42. Henry Rosovsky and Kazushi Ohkawa, "The
Indigenous Components of the Modern Japanese Economy" Economic Development and Cultural Change Vol. 9,
(April, 1961) pp. 476-501.
    43. For a review of these studies, see William
R. Cline, "Income Distribution and Economic Develop-
ment: A Survey and Tests for Selected Latin American
Cities" in Ferber, op.cit. pp. 205-49.
    44. Peter Lindert and Jeffrey G. Williamson,
"Three Centuries of American Inequality", Research
in Economic History Vol. 1 (1976) p. 107.
    45. All this is a hasty summary of two contri-
butions of mine to the liberation movement: "The
Technological Factor in Socioeconomic Dualism: Toward an Economy-of-Scale Paradigm for Development
Theory", in Manning Nash, ed., Essays in Economic
Development and Cultural Change in Honor of Bert
Hoselitz (University of Chicago Press, 1977) pp.
180-211, and "De Gustibus Disputandum Est: Changing
Consumer Preferences in Economic Growth" in Explorations in Economic History Vol. 16, No. 3 (July,
1979) pp. 260-96.
    46. The distinction was essentially positive
rather than normative. Necessities were the wage

176

goods, needed to feed, house and reproduce the labor force, hence were necessary for reproducing and/or expanding national output. "Superfluities" played no such productive role. Adam Smith and later classicals gave a pejorative twist to the dichotomy primarily because superfluities represented unproductive use of the social surplus which reduced capital accumulation, with Malthus, of course, dissenting on this point. In the affluent, socially integrated countries of the 20th century, the concept of "wage goods" becomes amorphous, and a more relevant dichotomy may be between private "habitual" goods, and status goods, with that dichotomy operative to a degree in all classes. For further discussion see Felix, "De Gustibus ....", op.cit. pp. 263-78. The older dichotomy was the more relevant for the 19th century, and probably remains so for the 20th century LDCs.

47. For elaboration and citations, see ibid., pp. 284-292.

48. David Felix, "The Dilemma of Import Substitution" in Gustav Papanek, ed., Development Policy: Theory and Practice (Harvard University Press, 1968) pp. 70-72.

49. Richard Weisskoff and Edward Wolff, "Linkages and Leakages: Industrial Trading in an Enclave Economy", Economic Development and Cultural Change Vol. 25 (1977) pp. 607-28.

50. Nathaniel Leff, "Multinational Corporate Pricing Policy in Developing Countries" Journal of International Business Studies (Autumn, 1975); Eileen MacKenzie, "Marketing in Brazil Comes of Age" and "Measuring the Growing Consumer Market" in Brazilian Business Vol. XVII, No. 1 (January, 1977).

51. On the rise of local patenting and the post-war decline in Argentina, see Jorge Katz, Importación de Technología, Aprendizaje Local e Industrialización Dependente (Buenos Aires, Instituto Torcuato Di Tella, 1971) Chapter 9. On a similar fall in Chile see Corporacion de Fomento de la Producción, La Propriedad Industrial en Chile y su Impacto en el Desarrolla Industrial (Santiago, septiembre 1970) mimeo.

52. "Income Distribution in Selected Major Cities ...", op.cit. p. 43.

53. Computed from World Bank, op.cit. Annex 1, Tables C.1 and C.3.

54. Wells, op.cit. pp. 263, 266-67, 269-71.

55. The infant rates are computed from World Bank, op.cit. Annex 1, Table 12.

Chapter 6

CHANGES IN LIFESTYLE IN JAPAN: PATTERN AND STRUCTURE OF MODERN CONSUMPTION

Mine Yasuzawa

Chapter 6

CHANGES IN LIFESTYLE IN JAPAN: PATTERN AND STRUCTURE
OF MODERN CONSUMPTION
Mine Yasuzawa

SOCIAL AND ECONOMIC BACKGROUND TO THE CHANGES IN
LIFESTYLE IN THE NINETEENTH CENTURY

When a nation is confronted with a different civilization, there must arise some confusion in the way
people accept or reject it. Some people might yearn
after the new things introduced from the foreign
civilization, believing them to be superior to their
own, but many would reject them, thinking these
strange things would unsettle their lives. Japan
was confronted by such a new civilization and such
confusion when the country was opened up to the
western world in 1859, after a long period (some two
and a half centuries) of seclusion from the outside
world. But it was not until the end of the Tokoguwa
Dynasty and the beginning of the restoration of the
sovereignty of the Emperor in 1868, that Japan set
out on the road of modernization and industrialization, which eventually meant westernization.
    The administrators of the new government at the
Meiji Restoration, put their efforts into establish-
ing and organizing new political systems and setting
up modern industries based on European models and
America, in order to deal with these countries in
international relations. Thus the dawn of the new
era for Japan as a whole began by taking the new
turn of accepting the things of the western world,
introducing their cultures as well as their scientific knowledge and technology.
    In this chapter, we intend to deal with the
changing lifestyle and consumption of the Japanese
people in social and economic transition, for there
were great differences between East and West. And
there was, of course, some confusion at first in
accepting and adapting innovations from the West.
Isolated as Japan was under the rule of the Tokugawa government, she had already achieved a certain

181

level of social, economic and cultural development
in her own way during the first half of the nineteenth century. This period was characterized by
the expansion of markets and consumer activity even
in rural areas. The peasantry could enjoy some of
the surplus from their farm products with rising
productivity coupled with an almost stable level of
land tax.[1] Also there were coming about better
chances of obtaining cash earnings with so-called
"second jobs", some people engaging in business as
local mercants or in petty trade as craftsmen,others
as village shopkeepers, and many earning wages as
part-time labourers. In the home, women were busy
spinning or weaving to earn cash, besides doing
their work in the fields. Sometimes a small workshop was set up in a village, where a small number
of women were employed in manufacturing cloth. Thus
the self-sufficient economy in rural areas was gradually disappearing at the turn of the nineteenth
century.

Things, previously enjoyed only by town dwell-
ers, made their appearance in rural life. Even town
entertainments, as well as consumer goods, were introduced into rural society. Kabuki plays and folk
dances, performed by the peasantry themselves on
particular occasions, became popular. They still
survive as traditional arts and festivals in each
locality. Making a group pilgrimage to a famous
temple or shrine became another recreation for the
peasantry. Sometimes they spent a great deal of
money from their instalment savings on such a trip.[2]

All these phenomena were the result of market
development in relation to the increase of saleable
products in agriculture and cash earnings from their
second jobs.

The "enlightenment movement", inspired by the
government at the start of the Meiji Restoration,
contributed to the change of lifestyle in favour of
the western way of life through the modernization
and industrialization of the country. It was, of
course, not a rapid change, but came about over a
period of time, by trial and error. The first two
decades after the Meiji Restoration were a somewhat
confusing period spent in adapting the western systems to the feudal society of Japan, which,in every
respect, had to make great efforts to overcome the
difficulties of adaptation. It was a great national
undertaking.

The old social regulations enforced by the
former government of the Tokugawa Dynasty, were all
annulled by the new government. Everyone now had a
free choice of occupation, residence and dress.

Some new regulations, however, were issued by the new government to help people to adapt to a modern society such as that of the western world. For example, men adopted short hairstyles. The Emperor himself had his hair cut short in March 1873, and showed himself in western style clothes in October of the same year, the Empress, in the meantime, adopting the custom of wearing European style dresses.

A flood of imported articles swept on to Japanese market which had not yet been fully organized for distribution. Moreover, the people were not yet used to them. Since those who had been abroad and become familiar with western manners, had shown how to use foreign-made goods, high officials of the government, rich merchants, wealthy farmers and leaders of the new society were beginning to purchase them, at first, as status symbol. Then those goods gradually came into wider circulation throughout the country, for they were recognized as commodities of great use in daily life. It was reported in a newspaper in 1878 that foreign-made goods were on sale even in the countryside and people were willing to purchase them in spite of prices being much higher than in towns and cities.[3] Blankets, umbrellas, mantles, clocks, lamps, cotton and woolen fabric and sugar, etc. were popular items among imported consumer goods. It was said that a British merchant staying in Japan imported umbrellas from England in 1859, but he had to send them back home because the circumstances were not yet favourable for their sale. After the Restoration, demand for imported umbrellas increased so much that five hundred thousand dozen umbrellas were imported in 1872.[4] It was because people found the foreign-made umbrella easier to handle and much lighter to carry than the traditional one made of bamboo sticks and oil-coated paper. Thus various kinds of commodities, which were to improve the living conditions of the Japanese people, were imported in ever increasing quantities, until indigenous industries were established to produce these goods at home to supply the consumers.[5]

Another important factor in the change of lifestyle is to be found in the period of the social mobilization of class strata. The former warrior class was dissolved into multifarious social groups, some becoming high officials of the government, others entering business or financial circles, while many went down in the world. A former local merchant might succeed in entering the very heart of the business centre of the country, while a rich merchant in a city would lose his former social standing on account of his lack of ability to adapt to the new business world. Promising opportunities opened up for those who had an enterprising spirit, during the time of transition which covered the last three decades of the nineteenth century. A great number of people moved into cities and towns from rural areas, some being employed in large, modern factories, while many came to find employment offering better earning prospects[5], for new occupations were created in towns and cities as the result of the reorganization of social institutions. The police force, fire service, post office and railways, as well as administration and education, provided new areas of work. Even the lowest classes were able to find a livelihood as rickshawmen in urban areas until streetcars were introduced, first in Kyoto in 1894 and then in Tokyo in 1903.[6]

A new social mobility enabled people to change their way of life, in so far as they could afford to do so. Most people, especially those in the lower social strata, still kept to their traditional lifestyle, although some changes occurred in the course of economic development. Income differentials between the social classes also affected the level and the course of the changes in lifestyle. The upper classes always took the lead in adopting the new fashions of living, the lower following in due course, as their income increased. By the 1920's, even the working class could enjoy a certain standard of living, as we shall see later.

CHANGES IN LIFESTYLE AND CONSUMPTION IN THE PERIOD OF TRANSITION.

Food

Various kinds of foreign food were introduced after the Meiji Restoration, such as vegetables, fruits and many types of processed food.* These were at

---

* Many foodstuffs people now eat daily have an overseas origin or are derived from seeds of superior quality to the indigenous varieties, introduced ater the Meiji Restoration, such as peas, tomatoes, onions, cabbage, etc., peaches, pears, apples, grapes, etc. Newly introduced foods were bread, biscuits, wine, beer, etc.

first imported, and then the authorities encouraged home production, thus improving the quality and increasing the range of products. A remarkable change in the eating habits of the Japanese was seen in the consumption of meat and pork, which had previously been a religious taboo for Buddhists, although they had already been eating poultry and the flesh of some wild animals such as the wild boar. However, the method of cooking and the manner of serving the new meats remained the same as for traditional Japanese food. They were seasoned with soysauce and sugar, served with cooked rice and eaten with chopsticks. Sugar was one item among imported foods which had a significant effect upon the Japanese palate. As Yanagida Kunio, a famous ethnographer, indicated, food became much sweeter after the Meiji Restoration.[7] Sugar imports increased tremendously throughout the remainder of the nineteenth century. They stood at about 10,248,000 pounds in 1868, but increased to as much as 231,564,000 pounds in 1890.[8]

It must be emphasized, however, that the typical change in the daily food intake was the increasing consumption of traditional food, mainly rice, as a staple food. Rice, of all the cereals, was the one which was held in high esteem by the Japanese, particularly polished rice, which was a luxury. Hitherto they had eaten it in the rural areas only on special occasions. In cooking it, they usually mixed other low-quality cereals, such as millet, and vegetables with a small amount of rice. The first step people took towards improving their diet was to increase the quantity of rice consumed, once the level of rice production had been raised and the area of rice cultivation increased.[9] Increasing rice consumption must have contributed to raising the populations' intake of calories and nutrients as a whole.[10] There was a shift to other kinds of cereals, such as barley, wheat, and rye,

Table 6.1: Shift in per capita consumption of rice, 1868-1914

period	quantity	index(%)
1868-1879	0.70 koku*	100.0
1880-1887	0.80	114.3
1888-1898	0.93	132.9
1899-1914	1.20	145.7

* one koku = 4.96 bushels.

and also to the recently introduced potato. A large part of the source of calories was covered by carbohydrates.[11]

It is well known that the main source of animal protein for the Japanese is fish. But this perishable food was eaten only by people living in areas where it could be delivered immediately. For supply to places outside these areas it was usually salted or dried. Around the turn of the century, a small fishing motorboat was completed in Osaka, which was more advantageous than the large steamboats used before deep-sea fishing became popular. Fish production after 1900 increased remarkably as well as did the number of wholesale markets for perishables (fish and vegetables). The index of the fish yield in the years 1910, 1914,1919 and 1923 indicates a great growth in fish supplies, starting around 1900.*

Meat consumption. As meat was a food for the wealthy and usually served at restaurants or other eating places in large towns, its consumption was generally very low before World War II. Eating out was another phenomenon which became popular in urban life. In cities and towns, where the population was increasing rapidly and modernization was proceeding at a high speed, people would not hesitate to accept new lifestyles. As working outside the home became

---

* The number of wholesale markets for perishables in 1882 and 1907.

Year	Fish market	Vegetables Market	Fish & Vegetables market	Total
1882	242	48	159	449
1907	681	128	230	1,039

Source of data: Nakamura Masaru. "Ichiba ga kataru kindai Nippon" (The history of modern Japan: the Wholesale market), Tokyo, 1980, p. 83.

Annual index of fish yield

Year	1910	1914	1919	1923
Index(%)	100	157	190	223

Source of data: Arisawa Hirome, Chead ed., "Nippon Samgyo Hyakunenshi" (The history of one hundred years of Japanse industry), Tokyo, 1966, p. 190.

the accepted norm, people gradually became accustomed to going out either to work or for recreation. In 1888, the first coffee house was opened in Tokyo and, by 1897, there were as many as 143 coffee houses serving coffee, tea and soft drinks. There were 4,470 lunch-rooms serving traditional menus, 476 high-class restaurants and the same number of public houses serving mainly Sake (Japanese wine). Coffee houses were for the modern set, while lunch-rooms were used by the working class. For the majority, however, these changes came about after 1900, when the level of incomes rose through the successful establishment of modern industries and as the result of general economic growth.[12]

Clothing

The traditional materials for clothing were linen, silk and cotton, of which linen had been in use since ancient times, being as valuable a material as silk. Cotton was introduced into Japan as early as the eighth century, but actual cultivation did not start until the seventeenth century. Cotton growing expanded greatly, as it was found that cotton was a suitable material for everyday clothes. Cotton soon came to popular use among the majority of people, for they were strictly prohibited from using silk. Furthermore, the use of silk, was limited to the warrior class as a luxury. Of course, there were always some who disregarded the regulation, as the rich grew in number among the merchants and the farmers, the growth being particularly rapid in the latter half of the Tokugawa period. When dress regulations were repealed by the Meiji Government, everybody was free to wear what he liked,though silk was still somewhat expensive for the lower classes. When imported cotton fabric (calico) was offered at low prices, it was most willingly accepted by consumers. But, of course, it seemd it might damage traditional textile manufacture. After the establishment of the modern textile industry in the 1880's, increasing imports of raw cotton made it possible for   large, modern factories to produce cotton yarn to meet the demand of the small traditional, cotton industry. They started supplying cotton yarn to small factories as well as individual weavers working at home. Individual households in the rural areas also wove cloth for their own use previous to 1900. As they could now obtain cheap factory-produced yarn, there followed an increase in clothing consumption.
    Imported cotton fabric, as well as what was

produced on large-scale factories at home, differed in width from that woven in the small traditional workshops or individual homes. The former was double-width and not suitable for making kimonos, while the latter was single-width and just right for making traditional Japanese clothes. Thus the modern sector of industry contributed to the survival of the traditional sector by helping it supply consumer goods for the increasing demand of an expanding market. Cotton-growing at home eventually, decreased as imported raw cotton increased its market share by virtue of price which was nearly half that of home-produced raw cotton. An increase in the consumption of cotton clothes went hand in hand with the establishment of the modern cotton textile industry. Moreover, the survival of traditional cotton manufacture was a characteristic feature Japanese economic development.[13]

All this influenced Japanese dress. The per capita consumption of cotton fabric increased remarkably during the forty years following the Meiji Restoration (as shown in Table 2). To meet the increasing demand not only for cotton fabrics but also other materials such as silk and, later, linen, led

Table 6.2: Per capita consumption of cotton fabrics, 1870-1910

Year	Quantity	Ratio of increase every 5th year	Index
1870	1.61 tan*		100.0
75	1.92	19.3%	119.3
80	2.29	19.3	142.2
85	2.31	0.9	143.5
90	3.46	49.8	214.9
95	4.17	20.5	259.0
1900	4.46	7.0	277.0
05	4.73	6.0	293.8
10	5.93	25.3	368.3

* "Tan" is the length of material required for making a Kimono.

Source: Nakamura Takahide, "Zairai Menorimonogyo no Hatten to Suitai" (The Development and the Fall of the Traditional Cotton Industry), in "Essays on Quantitative Economic History, Vol. 2, Tokyo, 1979, p. 221.

to the construction in 1897 of a wooden loom, based on imported modern looms, by Toyota Sokichi of Sizuoka Prefecture, followed by others. Such looms benefited traditional weaving-mills by increasing productivity. They also enabled small-scale enterprises with little capital to equip with modern machinery, because these wooden looms sold at much lower prices than foreign-made machines, - at a quarter, or even an eighth of their price.[14]

The westernization of dress also provides interesting glimpses of the changes in the lifestyle of the Japanese. As already mentioned, the Emperor himself appeared in western dress as early as 1870. Those who had been abroad also allowed themselves to be seen in public in western-style clothing. But the wholesale adoption of western fashions came with the new uniforms for military personnel. The army based theirs on the style of the French army, and the navy on that of the British navy. Other uniforms were adopted to identify occupational groups, such as policemen, mailmen, firemen, etc. High schools and colleges also introduced uniforms for the students. Businessmen, bankers, doctors, teachers and the leaders of the new society, as well as high officials and members of the Diet, began to wear western-style suits. Woolen materials for western-style clothes were largely imports, and their cost was considerable, which discouraged the wide spread of western-style clothes. Another obstacle to the adoption of western dress was that men only wore them in the course of their duties and changed into kimonos at home, to sit on the Tatami mat floor. Besides, women, except for the wives and daughters of high society, continued to wear traditional kimonos.

A woolen industry was first established in 1878 as a government enterprise to supply materials for military and civiliar use. It was taken over later by a private company. It took a certain length of time for the industry to see a favourable period.[15]

The adaptation of imported goods, clothing in this case, to the existing lifestyle provides an example of some interest. Blankets, for example, were used for shawls or overcoats in winter, wrapping them over the shoulder, then folding them into a triangle, a new fashion which increased in popularity. Mantles (or cloaks) and invernesses were worn by men over kimonos. They were very useful going out into the winter cold, for hitherto there was no such garment. Meanwhile, a woman's coat for wearing over a kimono was also designed and came into wide use. Western-style shawls also became fashionable for women, as the level of consumption of clothing rose about 1900. The wearing of caps and hats was accepted fairly early, when men's hair styles became short - usually close-cropped. All these new fashions in clothing, imported at first, were designed to suit the traditional needs of the people and supplied by traditional craftsmen or small-scale factories.

Housing, household equipment and utensils

Housing is the most conservative part of living, for a building lasts a long time, even though most Japanese houses are made of wood. In cities and towns, however, western-style buildings of stone and brick were designed and constructed, at first, by foreign architects, then later by Japanese, educated and trained by them. Government and commercial offices, banks and hotels were built in modern, western style, while the majority of poeple continued to live in small wooden houses. The rich occupied large residences, while the working class usually lived in tenement houses partitioned into many units. In the rural areas, farmers' houses and peasants' cottages kept to traditional styles with thatched roofs. Rooms in Japanese houses are usually separated by sliding doors, and there is no private room for the individual. In the 1920's, particularly after the great earthquake in the Tokyo area, a type of house with a separate, independent western style drawing room became popular among the middle class people. They prefered a lifestyle based on individuality, and a type of house designed for their needs became popular. Kerosene lamps, among all household facilities and utensils (desks, tables, chairs, pans and stoves, etc.), were the first item to be accepted and widely used until electricity and gas-supply began in large cities and towns around 1900.[16] They made rooms much lighter than the former seed-oil lanterns, and evenings turned out to be more important and useful in people's lives. They could now spend their evenings either working or in recreation. Housewives now did their sewing and mending and students could read and do their homework in the evening. Meals could be prepared even after dark. Cooking pans of varying sizes, large and small, also influenced traditional Japanese cookery, for previously only a few types of large pans had been obtainable for cooking meals in Japan. Pans of smaller size were accepted for popular use by small households in urban areas.[17]

The construction of railways and the consequent

development of transportation systems during the Meiji period (1868-1912) facilitated the distribution of commodities throughout the country and helped to expand the market, which consequently stimulated the consumption of new goods and changes in lifestyle.[18] Many kinds of goods were sent from the areas where they were produced to places which could not produce them. After the Tohoku line of the Japan National Railway between Tokyo and Aomori (in the far north of Honshu Island) was opened in 1891, water melons were sent to Sendai, a city on the line, every day in summer, and pork was despatched from Fukushima to Tokyo, so that pig-breeding developed in Fukushima Prefecture. Also cherries grwon in Yamagata and Fukushima suddenly became popular in the markets of more distant areas. After the completion of the Tokaido Line between Tokyo and Kobe in 1890 (this line had already been constructed halfway, as the first line between Tokyo and Yokohama in 1872), glass production in Osaka became very active, as the products could now be transported to the places on the railway line. Thus, by the end of the nineteenth century, all the main railway routes were completed, and facilities for freight distribution as well as passenger traffic increased.

It was after 1900 that changes in lifestyle spread among the mass of the Japanese people the length and breadth of the country. It mus be emphasized that those new types of commodities, imported from abroad in the first instance, were always being improved for popular use, and their production at home made it possible to offer them at lower prices, which eventually led to mass consumption.

HOUSEHOLD CONSUMPTION AFTER 1900

Comparison of household consumption in different areas

Around 1900, the lifestyle of the Japanese was, for the most part, transformed from that of a medieval society to a modern one. People were now using a great variety of commodities, which were being sold in the remotest parts of the country. The supply of consumer goods went on increasing, as society became geared to consumption. At the same time, weaving fabrics at home for making up into garments for own use was declining, and most households in the rural areas were beginning to buy in materials for this purpose.[18]

Naturally, the level of consumption will differ from area to area according to the differing economic conditions obtaining in those areas. Even in the same area, villages have their own characteristics as far as the level of economic development is concerned. Here we can present an example of a district approximately midway along the coast of the Sea of Japan. Three villages, close to each other, show different conditions and characteristics of consumption even in the same area.

Table 6.3: Average household income and expenditure (1901).[19] (Yanagida, Yadago, and Misaki villages in Ishikawa Prefecture)

Village	Yanagida	Yadago	Misaki
No. of households	540	545	340
Monthly income	¥ 17.054	¥ 14.726	¥ 11.515
Total expenditure	15.469	12.354	12.015
	(100.00)*	(100.00)	(100.00)
Items Food	9.053	6.975	8.124
	(58.52)	(56.46)	(67.62)
Clothing	1.075	0.770	1.028
	(6.95)	(6.23)	(8.56)
Housing &	1.049	0.718	0.848
fuel	(6.78)	(5.81)	(7.06)
Other ex-	4.292	3.892	2.015
penditure**	(27.75)	(31.50)	(16.77)

* The figures in brackets are percentages of total expenditure.
** Including education, medical care and health, social activities, transportation, etc.

The inhabitants of these villages, located in a remote part of the country, were mainly engaged in agriculture. However, there are some differences in income or expenditure. In Yanagida village, 89% of the households were engaged in agriculture, but many of them had other sources of income in forestry, sericulture, and as technical craftsmen, which consequently brought in more income than was the case in the other two villages. This village shows the highest level of income and expenditure and exhibits household consumption which is typical for the district. Yadago village has an advantageous location, lying, as it does, close to a port as well as a railway station, and villagers had the opportunity of be hired as workers in nearby towns. The level of consumption was less than that of Yanagida, but they spent a larger proportion of their income on items other than food, clothing, and housing.

192

Besides, they made more savings out of their income. This must have been a new type of lifestyle resulting from the change in circumstances and economic and social development.

Misaki village, with the lowest income level, is typical of the villages which were left behind in the march of progress. A contemporary writer from the village wrote, "The people of this village used to eat little rice, but millet and the leaves of a certain tree and wore only cotton clothes in the Tokugawa period. But, after the Meiji Restoration, they became accustomed to eating more rice and wearing silk clothes on feast days. So the things which elderly people call luxuries have become a part of everyday custom. The village, however, has a standard of living below that of the district".[19] This description gives a picture of the changing lifestyle of the period. It will be seen that the average household economy of Misaki did not balance, expenditure being in excess of income. People suffered from the difficulties of village life.

Here is another example of a village in the north of the Kanto district, of which Tokyo is the centre.[20] Only data for average household expenditure on food, clothing and housing in 1901 are available. It is Kurohone village in Gunma Prefecture, a village which is said to have been very prosperous with sericulture and related manufactures ever since the Tokugawa period. The villagers seem to have enjoyed a much better life than the inhabitants of the three villages mentioned above. Average food expenditure was ¥ 12.251, which shows a much higher level of food consumption than the former three villages. This sum is almost equivalent to the total household expenditure of Yadago and Misaki. But expenditure on clothing and housing show little difference: ¥ 1.549 for clothing and ¥ 0.917 for housing.

With regard to household expenditure on food in Kurohone, about 60% went on rice, 12.6% on vegetables and about 12% on seasonings such as soysauce, miso, salt and sugar. As much as 9% was spent on tea, sake wine, tobacco and cake. It should be realized that the consumption of important nutrients, such as animal protein, was very low: only 3.8% was spent on fish, eggs and milk. No meat was eaten at all. This was the typical Japanese diet in the rural areas before World War II.

The period around 1910 saw Japan almost completely modernized. Industry had reached a sufficient level to compete with developed countries. National income in 1900 was ¥ 6,232 million and rose

Table 6.4: Average household income and expenditure in 1911

Area	Ibo	Onga	Minami-tsuruga	Takoshima
No. of households	17,287	24,576	15,271	318
Monthly income	¥27.127	¥29.827	¥26.740	¥31.012
Total expenditure	26.744	24.800	26.266	25.677
Items: Food	13.927	16.011	19.417	15.813
Clothing	2.397	2.392	1.031	2.665
Housing	3.446	2.185	2.215	2.627
Other expenditure	6.974	4.212	3.603	4.572

Composition of expenditure (percentages)

Area	Ibo	Onga	Minami-tsuruga	Takoshima
Total expenditure	100.00	100.00	100.00	100.00
Items: Food	52.08	64.56	73.92	61.58
Clothing	8.96	9.65	3.93	10.38
Housing	12.89	8.81	8.43	10.23
Other expenditure	26.08	16.98	13.72	17.81

Source: The "Gunze" and "Sonze" of each area (Reports of the survey of each country and village)1903.

to ¥ 7,834 million by 1910: i.e. a rise of 26 points in a decade.

Monthly household income had risen slight to between ¥ 20 and ¥ 30 depending on the economic environment.

Here we are able to compare the household economies of four widely distributed areas: Ibo county, close to Osaka; Onga county, in the north of Kyushu; Minami Tsuruga county, in the far north of Honshu, and Takoshima village in central northern Honshu. From these places we were able to obtain data on household consumption for the year 1911. Each is representative of its area. (See Table 6.4).

The figures of average household income and expenditure in each area would explain the economic context of each area and the level of consumption which each had attained. The highest income level of the four areas is that of Takoshima, whose geographical location does not seem to be favorable. The villagers had long been engaged mainly in fishing and had an enterprising spirit, never missing opportunities for economic development. After the Meiji Restoration, they started sericulture on a large sclae and this became one of the main sources of their large income. Besides, their traditional fishing industry also became very prosperous as the demand for fish increased by virtue of the development of transportation. Production of Somen (dried noodles) was another traditional industry, whose products were shipped to distant areas. All these old and new industries, in spite of their small scale, benefited the village. Onga, next to Takoshima in respect of household income, was a county in which heavy industry was established in 1897, and a relatively large number of households were those of factory workers and labourers. Ibo County is a typical one that had had experience of traditional industry and the distribution of goods through a port in the County, while the main work was agricultural. As it was located close to Osaka, which used to be the largest business centre in Japan before the Meiji Restoration and still held that position at that time, the County had an advantage in starting small-scale light industries, such as soysauce and somen (dired noodles). Lastly, Minamitsuruga is a very different type of agricultural county, though it was later to become well known for its apple orchards.

The differences in expenditure on food and "other expenditure" are relatively large. Two reasons can be found for the high proportion of expenditure on food in Minamitsuruga. One is that the average size of family unit was the largest for the four areas, i.e. 6.9 persons, while the other averages are: 5.3 (Ibo), 4.99 (Onga) and 5.8 (Takoshima). The other reason is possibly the economic backwardness of the area, resulting in "other expenditure" (on medical care, education and social activities, etc.) being the lowest of the four. A typical urbanization of household consumption can be seen in the figures for Onga, while a very high level of household consumption is revealed in the figures for Ibo. In spite of having the highest level of household income, Takoshima and Onga show the least propensity for consumption, leaving a large surplus for savings. This is surely an interesting phenomenon, and a question to study concerning consumption in modern Japan.

Apart from the total of expenditure on food, consumption of each item of food would reveal the eating habits of each locality. Among the four areas, Onga is the most advanced with Ibo next, in respect of the consumption of newly introduced food.

Table 6.5: The Trend of household consumption in specific items: comparison of the four areas (percentages)

Item	Ibo	Onga	Minami-tsuruga	Takoshima
Meat, pork & poultry	100.0	187.5	51.0	5.8
Eggs	100.0	217.4	67.4	182.6
Milk	100.0	161.0	24.4	36.6
Sugar	100.0	53.9*	41.0	78.1
Fruit	100.0	183.6	150.0	74.3
Imported liquor	100.0	90.0	16.0	10.0
Cigarettes**	100.0	587.9	51.7	53.4
Hairdressing	100.0	114.7	62.7	100.0

* Sugar consumption in Onga is rather low, but two-thirds of it is refined sugar of better quality, while only half the sugar consumed in the other areas was refined.
** The Japanese used to smoke shredded tobacco. Cigarettes were introduced from abroad.

CONSUMPTION OF TOKYO WORKING-CLASS HOUSEHOLDS

We next turn to survey material which illustrates the living standard and level of consumption of the working-class population of Tokyo after 1900. Surveys were organized by the Government for the purpose of finding out the living conditions of the people in the lowest strata of society. Surveys in 1911, 1916 and 1921 are available for comparison. The data refer to factory workers as wel as craftsmen and labourers in casual employment.

The 1911 data* were roughly classified in respect of each item of household expenditure. As to food consumption, the largest portion of the sample is a group spending between ¥ 8 and ¥ 10 (55%), and the next, one spending between ¥ 10 and ¥ 15 (28%). These two groups cover 83% of the households in the east end of Old Tokyo. 13% of them spent less than ¥ 5 on food, and only 4% could afford better food and spent over ¥ 15. The average expenditure on food can be estimated at about ¥ 10.

The smallest portion of household expenditure went on clothing. As little as ¥ 1.00 or less was spent on clothes by 80% of households. This goes to show how poor their dress was. In the previous examples, even the lowest spending on clothing exceeded ¥ 1.00. Only 6% of them could afford ¥ 1.00 to ¥ 2.00 for clothing. Besides, there were 11% of households who spent nothing on clothes, wearing, as they did, only garments given to them by relatives or friends. Rent was an essential part of household expenditure, in so far as people had to find shelter somewhere in the town. Most of them lived in small tenement houses, partioned off into three to eight units. The rent paid by 80% of the sample was ¥ 1.00 to ¥ 3.00. 13% of households paid a rent of ¥ 3.00 to ¥ 4.00, 4% less than ¥ 1.00, and the rest (3%) each had a house to themselves, paying rent in excess of ¥ 5.00. Masaoka Shiki, a famous haiku poet of the day, paid ¥ 6.00 in rent around 1900. Takahama Kyoshi, another famous haiki poet, lived in a house rented at ¥ 16.00. The authorities concluded that those living in a tenement house or paying a rent of ¥ 3.00, or less, should be classified as the city poor.

Regarding "other expenditure", more than half the households spent from ¥ 1.00 to ¥ 3.00 (53%),

---

* The survey covered 3,047 households in the quarters where the lowest classes lived.

and a further 42% from ¥ 3.00 to ¥ 8.00. The average spending was ¥ 5.00.

More interesting is a profile of their eating habits and leisure activities. Their meals were, naturally, very frugal: rice, vegetables and fish were eaten only when they had money to spare.

Table 6.6: Composition of meals (excluding rice*)

Vegetables only	52%	Vegetables and pickles	2%
Vegetables and fish	35%	Vegetables and dried food	3%
Vegetables and meat	2%	Other food	6%

* Rice is a staple food for the Japanese. Most of the nutrients came from rice in those days.

Another survey, involving 344 working-class households, was carried out in 1912. Average household income was estimated at ¥ 28.12, and expenditure at Y 26.53. No other data of the households are available in this survey.

Among the hobbies and leisure activities of these 344 working-class families, the most popular was going to Yose (a variety theatre), where they could enjoy traditional entertainment such as music, popular songs, story-telling, etc. 82 persons out of 344 went regularly to Yose, i.e. 24.8% liked this traditional entertainment which they also frequently organized among themselves at home. Going to a playhouse was another popular amusement. 55 persons (16%) said they enjoyed this form of entertainment. Sumo (Japanese wrestling) was also popular, and attended by 7.2% during the Sumo season.

Motion pictures were also becoming popular in Tokyo and 29 persons (8.4%) stated that they liked to go to the cinema. There were a few people (18), whose hobby was reading or painting. Also the same number of people liked Go (a board game) and Shogi (chess). Other hobbies were fishing or Bonsai (dwarf-tree growing). 11.3% of those questioned had no hobbies.

Out of 344 families 238 (69%) took a daily newspaper, as well as weekly or monthly magazines. 30 persons (8.7%) liked reading fiction. Small as the number is, it is very interesting to find 15 persons who liked reading books on natural science.

Half of the heads of the 344 households drank, but smokers constituted only 19% of their number. Poor as they were, they seem to have enjoyed life. Many of those who had come to the city from the rural areas had a certain level of education. They had come full of ambition, only to fail.

During and after World War I, the standard of living gradually rose, although the 1916 figures for the households of factory employees appeared to be almost identical with those for 1912. In 1921, working-class family income increased remarkably. Although the price index for consumer goods rose 11 points in five years, household incomes rose as much as 54 points (43 points in terms of real income), while real expenditure rose 57 points over that of 1916, which shows a great change for the better in the level of consumption of factory workers and craftsmen, and labourers as a whole. These statistics, showing rising affluence, could be taken as evidence that Japanese industrial society was stable and prosperous.

Table 6.7: Income and expenditure of Tokyo working-class households (1916 & 1921)

Item/Year	1916	1921
Household income	¥ 28.51	¥ 72.26
Household expenditure	27.88 (100.0)*	63.74 (100.0)*
Food	11.55 (41.4)	34.86 (54.7)
Clothing	2.09 (7.5)	4.41 (6.9)
Housing	4.90 (17.6)	4.66 (7.3)
Electricity & fuel	1.71 (6.1)	4.39 (6.9)
Other items	6.18 (22.2)	11.48 (18.0)
Extras	1.45 (5.2)	3.94 (6.2)

* Composition of expenditure (in percentages).

Table 6.8: Expenditure on individual foodstuffs

Item/Year	1916	1921
Rice % other cereals	¥ 5.23 (45.3)	¥ 16.91 (48.5)
Meat, pork & poultry	0.48 (4.2)	0.41 (1.2)
Milk and eggs		0.33 (0.9)
Fish	1.07 (9.3)	3.34 (9.6)
Vegetables	1.31 (11.3)	3.27 (9.4)
Seasonings	2.79 (24.1)	2.84 (8.1)
Tea, liquor, tobacco & other delicacies		4.88 (14.0)
Table-ready meals & eating out		2.88 (8.3)
Total	11.55 (100.0)	34.86 (100.0)

A comparison of household expenditure in 1916 and
1921 shows that total expenditure on food in 1921
had increased three times since 1916 whilst the diet
had improved in variety. Spending on clothes also
had more than doubled and the increased consumption
of electricity and fuel suggests that the people
were enjoying more comfortable evenings. Another
feature of food consumption is the increasing expenditure on instant foods and eating-out. The consumption of rice, fish and vegetables increased remarkably, while food from other animal protein
sources showed only a small increase. Spending on
delicacies, such as tea, liquor, cake and tobacco
(cigarettes), comprised a relatively large part of
the expenditure of working-class households.

Table 6.9: Breakdown of "miscellaneous" expenditure
between 1916 and 1921.

Item/Year	1916	1921
Medical care & hygiene	¥ 2.28 (36.9)	¥ 2.44 (21.3)
Education	0.92 (14.9)	3.70 (32.2)
Social activities	0.88 (14.2)	1.24 (10.8)
Hobbies & recreation	0.36 (5.8)	0.68 (5.9)
Other expenses	1.74 (28.2)	3.42 (29.8)
Total	6.18 (100.0)	11.48 (100.0)

Under "miscellaneous" expenditure, the most obvious
change is the increase in spending on childrens'
education. More than four times in money value and
twice as much in percentage terms. These figures
are evidence for the Japanese tendency to attach
much importance to the education of children, when
they have money to spare.

CONCLUSION

Two main factors brought about the change in Japanese lifestyle: firstly, the influence of western
culture, which made a great impact on the Japanese
when that country was opened up to the outer world
with its different civilization, and secondly, the
outcome of economic development following the industrialization of the country after the Meiji Restoration.

In accepting the offerings of western countries,
there arose much confusion, as was to be expected,
but the Japanese adapted them to suit their tra-

ditional way of life. Nevertheless, in the process, changes did inevitably occur in their lifestyle.

Commodities have to be marketed at a price which the consumer can afford and, consequently, in increasing quantities. To meet consumer demands, the traditional sector of Japanese industry made every effort to learn and improve on the technology necessary for manufacturing the new products in quantity. This inevitably led to increased consumption and so the changes in lifestyle of the Japanese people.

NOTES

1. The land tax during the Tokugawa period was very complex and differed from district to district. But the rate, with few exceptions, tended to decrease or stay the same. T.C. Smith gives excellent examples in his article, The Land of the Tokugawa Period, Journal of Asian Studies, Vol. 18. no. 1, 1958.

2. "Tanomishiko" (an instalment savings and mutual financing association) was an organization for mutual aid in the community during the period. Mine Yasuzawa, Bakumatsuki Tamanoson no Tanomoshiko (Studies on the mututal financing system in the Tama rural area in the early 19th century), Journal of Tama no Ayumi, Vol. 12, 1978.

3. Keizo Shibusawa (ed.), Meiji Bunka Shi (The Cultural History of Meiji), Vol. 13, p. 436 (Abbreviated title: M.B.S.).

4. Western umbrellas were soon supplied by indigenous craftsmen, who acquired the skill from a foreign trader in Yokohama , and in the 1890's every home, even those in the remote areas, kept one or two western umbrellas, most of which were produced in Japan, ibid., p. 435.

5. Eva Ehrlich, The Model of Japan's Closing Up: Two-Pole Industrialization, Acta Oeconomica, Vol. 23 (1-2), 1979, pp. 146-9; K. Nakagawa and H. Rosovsky, The Case of the Dying Kimono: The Influence of Changing Fashions on the Development of the Japanese Woolen Industry, Business History Review, Vol. 32, no. 1-2, 1963, p. 80.

6. The urban population increased at a great rate between 1888 and 1913. The share of the total population of Japan (accounted for by towns and cities with a population of over 10,000) was 12.9% in 1888, 17.7% in 1898 and 24.9% in 1913. The number of villages, towns and cities, classified by population :

Population/Year	1888	1898	1908	1913
Less than 10,000	70,272	13,794	12,084	11,887
10,000-50,000	110	213	344	432
50,000-100,000	8	12	19	26
Over 100,000	6	8	10	11

Source of data: MBS, Vol. 11, p. 110.

7. Kunio Yanagida, Meiji Taisho Shi: Sesohen (The History of the Meiji and Taisho Period: a Phase of Life), Tokyo, 1930 (revised edition, 1976), Vol. I, p. 60.

8. Sugar production was already being carried out in the islands of Shikoku and Kyushu during the Tokugawa period, but was not significant. The increasing supply of imported sugar improved the Japanese cuisine as well as increasing the consumption of sweets.

Sugar imports: 1868-1890

Year	Amount	Year	Amount
1868	10,248,352 pounds*	1880	92,769,800 pounds
1869	41,311,425 pounds	1885	141,510,501 pounds
1870	82,974,409 pounds	1890	231,564,223 pounds

* Originally the figures were expressed in Kin (a unit of weight). 1 Kin = 1 1/3 pounds
Source of data: The Shogyo Shiryo, Vol. I, no. 9, Osaka, 1894.

9. Among cereals, wheat and rye increased in production most remarkably. The potato became a popular constituent of daily meals as soon as it was introduced, while the cultivation of sweet potatoes, which had been a traditional food in some areas, also increased.

Production Index of Cereals and Potatoes*

Item/Year	1878-82	1888-92	1898-1902	1908-12
Rice	100.00	130.35	142.50	169.70
Barley	100.00	130.79	162.95	178.39
Wheat	100.00	146.52	198.14	225.48
Rye	100.00	138.44	193.47	204.70
Sweet potatoes	100.00	234.75	254.61	332.62
Potatoes	100.00	511.11	744.44	1,911.11

The increasing ratio of productivity per Tan (= 0.245 acres) was as follows: rice: 116%, barley: 103%, wheat: 132%, rye: 148%, sweet potatoes: 198%, and potatoes: 600%.
* Source of data: MBS, Vol. 11, p. 497.

10. Yasuhiko Yuize, Shokuryo no Keizai Bunseki (Economic Analysis on Food), Tokyo, 1971, p. 13. Over 80% of the calorie intake was derived from

carbohydrates i.e. cereals and potatoes, and about
73% of this total was supplied by cereals alone in
the period of 1909-13.

Calorie Intake: per capita per day (in percentages)

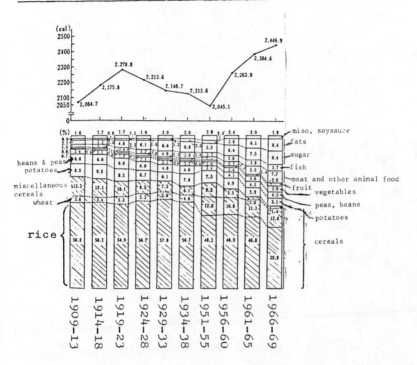

11. Ibid., p. 17. More than half the protein
intake was come from carbohydrates. It was about
57.58% between 1909 and 1918, but decreased to 55%
during the period 1919-23.

Protein Intake per capita per day (in percentages)

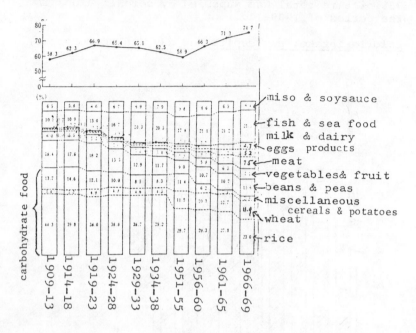

12. W.W. Lockwood (ed.), The State and Economic Enterprise in Japan: Essays in the Political
Economy of Growth, Princeton Univ. Press, 1965 (Japanese edition, Tokyo, 1966, pp. 53-68 and pp. 171-
9).

13. Eva Ehrlich, ibid., pp. 146-8.

14. Hiromi Arisawa (ed.), Nippon Sangyo
Hyakunen Shi (One hundred years of the history of
Japanese Industry), Tokyo, 1966, pp. 131.2.

15. K. Nakagawa and H. Rosovsky, ibid., pp.
72-4.

16. Keizo Shibusawa (ed.), MBS, Vol. 12, pp.
322-32. The construction of a gas supply system was
begun in Yokohama as early as 1872 to provide gas
to the foreign concession, and, in Tokyo, in 1874,
for street lighting. It was, however, after 1900,
particularly around 1910-19, that the domestic consumption of gas for lighting, heating and cooking
increased. By 1911, there were 44 towns and cities
with gas-supply systems. Electricity came much

later. The Tokyo Electric Company was established in 1886 and started to supply electricity the following year. It was after 1900, -as with gas- that domestic consumption of electricity showed a marked increase. In Tokyo, in 1904, electric lamps exceeded gas lamps in number. The two sources of energy began to be used for different purposes; gas mainly for fuel, and electricity primarily for lighting and power.

17. Kunio Yanagida, ibid., Vol. I, pp. 62-3. Masatomo Yamaguch, Zusetsu Daidokoro Dogu no Rekishi (The Illustrated History of Kitchen Utensils), Tokyo, 1978, pp. 83-90.

18. Kiyoko Segawa, Nihonjin no I-Shoku-Jyu (Food, Clothing and Housing of the Japanese People), Tokyo, 1964, pp. 132-5.

19. Ishikawa Kenshi Shiryo, The Historical Records and Materials of Ishikawa Prefecture, Ishikawa Prefecture, 1978, Vol. 5, p. 125.

20. Keizo Shibusawa (ed.), MBS, ibid., Vol. 12, p. 195.

STATISTICAL SOURCES

Household consumption after 1900

1. Ishikawa Kenshi Shiryo (Historical records and materials of Ishikawa Prefecture), Ishikawaken, 1978.

2. Hyogoken Ibo Gunze narabini Chosonze (the Reports of the Intensive Survey of Ibo County, and also Towns and Villages in the County, of Hyogo Prefecture), Hyogoken Ibogun, 1908.

3. Onga Gunze (the Reports of the Intensive Survey of Onga County of Fukuoka Prefecture), Ongagun, 1912, (Revised edition, Chihoshi Kenkyu Kyogikai, Tokyo, 1979).

4. Minamitsuruga Gunze (the Reports of the Intensive Survey of Minamitsuruga County of Aomori Prefecture), Minamitsurugagun, 1911, (Revised edition, Meicho Shuppan, Tokyo, 1975.

Consumption of Tokyo working-class households

1. Saimin Chosa Tokeihyo (Statistical tables of the conditions of the working-class in Tokyo), Naimusho, Vol. I, 1912, Vol. II, 1912, Vol. III, 1921, (Revised edition, Keio shobo, Tokyo, 1971).

Chapter 7

CONVENTION, FASHION AND CONSUMPTION : ASPECTS OF
BRITISH EXPERIENCE SINCE 1750

Walter Minchinton

Chapter 7

CONVENTION, FASHION AND CONSUMPTION : ASPECTS OF
BRITISH EXPERIENCE SINCE 1750
Walter Minchinton

Current prestige, tradition, authority, fashion,
respectability often supplement or displace the play
of individual taste, good or bad, in moulding a
class and family (and, one should perhaps add, a
regional or national) standard of consumption.

John Hobson

Although Adam Smith argued that 'consumption is the
sole end and purpose of all production', it is with
production and distribution rather than consumption
that economists and economic historians have been
largely concerned.[1] And when demand has been discussed, it has been largely on the assumption that
the consumer was an economic man. The theory and
measurement of consumer behaviour was developed
during the nineteenth century on the basis of the
concept of marginal utility. It came to be held
that the consumer derives a positive satisfaction or
utility from the purchase of a commodity but that
the additional satisfaction which he derived from
purchases of further units of the same commodity
would decline as his purchases increased. With a
given amount of money to spend, therefore, a consumer would distribute his expenditure among commodities so as to maximise the total satisfaction or
utility that he got from all his purchases. The
advantage of this rather crude model of consumer
behaviour, which has undergone considerable refinement at the hands of modern mathematical economists,
was that by extracting the main economic variables
- income and price - from the remaining influences
it enabled discussion to become more sophisticated.
But, as critics have pointed out, the model assumes
a rational person bent on scrupulously maximising
his satisfaction in a rather mechanistic way whereas
individual behaviour in the real world was rather

different. Individual preferences, social pressures, customs, habits and fashion need to be taken into account.

Such a view had a respectable pedigree. Adam Smith defined as necessaries 'not only the kind of commodities that are indispensably necessary for the support of life, but whatever the custom of the country renders it indecent for creditable people even of the lowest order to be without ... Under necessaries', he went on, 'I include not only those things which nature but those things which the established rules of decency have rendered necessary to the lowest order of people'.[2] Thus Adam Smith certainly took account of other factors affecting the pattern of consumption apart from the economic. In the course of the nineteenth century there was some desultory discussion of such matters. Writing in 1834, John Rae discussed the propensity among men to attain a factitious superiority over one another. This may be termed vanity, and is gratified by the evident possession of things which others have not the means of acquiring. It calls for the possession of commodities of which the consumption is conspicuous, and which cost much labour, though not better qualified, or but little better qualified, to supply real wants.[3] On this notion Bagehot commented in his *Economic Studies* (1880) but is was Thornstein Veblen, who in arguing that the consumption of the wealthy classes was aimed particularly at demonstrating status rather than satisfying basic needs, took up Rae's suggestion and gave the terms 'conspicuous consumption','conspicuous leisure' and 'pecuniary emulation', phrases which vividly summed up particular kinds of behaviour, wider currency.[4]

Although such problems apparently escaped the attention of Alfred Marshall, following John Rae, a number of economists including Henry Cunynghame, Alfred Pigou, and John Meade have tried to keep such issues alive in the mainstream of economic discussion. They have commented on situations where the utility functions of one individual contains, as variables, the variety of goods consumed by other persons; they have discussed inter-personal effects on demand and have paid some attention to external economies and diseconomies of consumption, to cases where the market demand curve is not just the lateral summation of individual demand curves. Bringing some of the threads of the discussion together Harry Leibenstein has distinguished three types of external effects on utility:[5]

1. The bandwagon effect: the extent to which the demand for a commodity is *increased* due to the fact that others are also consuming the same commodity. It represents the desire of people to purchase a commodity in order to get into the swim of things: in order to conform with the people with whom they would wish to be associated: in order to be fashionable or stylish: or, in order to appear to be 'one of the boys'. And social taboos, to the extent that they affect consumption, are, in a sense, bandwagon effects in reverse gear.

2. The snob effect: the extent to which the demand for a consumers' good is decreased owing to the fact that others are also consuming the same commodity (or that others are increasing their consumption of the same commodity). This represents the desire of people to be exclusive; to be different; and to dissociate themselves from the 'common herd'.

3. The Veblen effect: the phenomenon of conspicuous consumption. But whereas Veblen implied by this phrase the proclivity of some to make their level of income obvious by ostentatious purchases, Leibenstein defines this effect as a discussion of the extent to which the demand for a consumers' good is increased because it bears a higher rather than a lower price.

   Sometimes economists have commented in other terms in which demand for a cheap article is low because its price suggests that it is an 'inferior good' and every street salesman will tell of instances in which his sales have increased when he has raised rather than lowered the price of some articles he has had for sale. The difference between the 'snob effect' and the 'Veblen effect' therefore is that the former is a function of the consumption of others, the latter is a function of price.

Two other kinds of non-functional demand are noted by Leibenstein. The first is *speculative demand* where people will often 'lay in' a supply of a commodity because they expect its price to rise: in earlier times such behaviour would have been described as 'engrossing'. The second is

irrational demand which consists of purchases that
are neither planned nor calculated but are due to
sudden urges, whims etc. and serves no rational
purpose but that of satisfying sudden whims and
desires.[6] As supermarkets recognize, it is not an
insignificant element in the pattern of demand.
They are wont to display certain types of articles
in a strategic position in their stores, counting on
spur of the moment decisions to buy at the point of
sale.[7]

Such then is some of the theoretical background
to a discussion of the social elements which help to
determine patterns of consumption to which we will
have the opportunity to make reference in the discussion which follows. For convenience, our consideration of such matters will be divided into two
parts. First we shall examine the long-run social
factors which play on demand. As a shorthand they
may be summed up in the terms 'convention' or 'custom'. They are not immutable but on the whole,
while changing, do so slowly. The force of custom
or convention exercises a conservative or restrain-
ing influence on consumption. The other part of our
discussion will concern the short-run social factors
which influence the basket of goods and services
which people demand. While not entirely satisfactory, this aspect of the discussion can be summed up
by the word 'fashion'.

CONVENTION AND CUSTOM

A rule of conduct on what may or may not be done by
members of a given group or commodity.

Before the industrial period many activities
and modes of behaviour in Britain, as elsewhere,
were subject to custom. Of the various elements
which combined to exercise a social influence on
consumption, one of the most powerful was religion
which served as the cement of many societies.
Though its influence continued to weaken in some respects with urbanisation and industrialization,
religion still was an important force in Britain in
the eighteenth and nineteenth centuries. In industrializing Britain, it was the influence of non-
conformity which was of prime importance though some
influences survived of the older Puritan sects and
of the established church.

The operation of the non-conformist social
ethic can best be seen by looking at one regional
society in Britain where the influence of the established church, of the older Puritan sects and,
for that matter, of the Roman Catholic church was

unimportant, that is Wales and particularly rural west Wales. The influence of non-conformity can be seen in a number of directions. Perhaps most vividly in terms of Sunday observance.

Though times are changing, the term 'continental Sunday' still carries an aura of riotous and licentious behaviour. Unlike European countries across the Channel, a strict sabbatarianism reigned in Wales in the nineteenth century and still, to some extent, does today. On Sunday the great majority of adults attended the church or chapel while the children went to Sunday school. In addition, Sunday saw a slowing down of the tempo of life, the reading of religious books in the home, the use of the parlour in the afternoon (often the occasion of a family gathering), and a general effort to make behaviour conform to a rigid idea of what was proper. This usually meant the suppression of many weekday activities.[8] In west Wales, it was still an exception, for example, to see anyone drawing water from a public tap or pump on Sunday, this was always done on Saturday evening. And the arrival of piped water in villages in west Wales in the 1930's posed a problem. Should the use of the tap in the kitchen be restricted by the same rule that governed the use of the public pump which, incidentally, was even locked on the Sabbath if it was privately owned. In most cases what was not seen in public was deemed not to hurt convention (or conscience) and common sense prevailed. Thus many of the formal aspects of behaviour by which much store was set were merely conventional. They added up to 'respectability'.

And then there was the common attitude towards buying a Sunday newspaper. It too was considered to be against the accepted code of behaviour, and there was much criticism as late as 1960 of those who bought papers from a van which appeared on the square at mid-day. "I don't buy Sunday papers on principle" was a common and emphatic reaction to this. But most significant was the attitude of those who did buy them, some surreptitiously having them bought for them by someone who cared less about public opinion, others admitting to buying them almost guiltily: "We take a Sunday paper, unfortunately, but I don't suppose we should." Other answers to the question of whether or not a Sunday paper was taken were these: "We take a Sunday newspaper - unfortunately! I remember a time when we dared not." "I read it after tea, so that it doesn't interfere with Sunday school".

Similarly when the wireless arrived, listening

was restricted to programmes in keeping with the day. There was no whistling on Sunday, no playing with a ball even in private and no reading of anything except sacred literature. Children were forbidden to play games. Clothes were not hung out on the line to dry - it would show others that work had been done that ought not to have been. And it was wrong to go to the beach, though one could walk to the edge before and after the services always providing one was dressed in 'Sunday clothes' which meant for men wearing a suit and for women a hat and appropriately sombre clothes.

Observance of the Sabbath more seriously meant not working on Sundays. "I'm not religious by any means", said one person, "but the least we can do is not to break the Sabbath. We've been praying for fair weather to take in the crops, yet if we had it next Sunday, some people would be out working on the hay. We deserve rain because it is sinful to work on the Sabbath". Only one farm gathered hay on a subsequent Sunday and someone pointed out they were Unitarians. But one farmer on a fine Sunday night after weeks of rain, took his men out into the fields a few minutes after midnight in order to get in the hay: he would not dream of breaking the Sabbath.

Similarly herring fishermen at Aberporth in Cardigan Bay used to come down to the beach just before twelve on Sunday night to wait there until midnight before launching the boats to take out and set the nets.

But as well as Sunday observance and temperance, the chapel also often had a hold over its congregation on weekdays when choir meetings, bible classes and other activities were held. And the influence of the chapels was thrown against the theatres both because plays were considered to be immoral and because theatres were held to be the resort of prostitutes. Some denominations, notably the Society of Friends, the Quakers, came out openly in favour of modest dress, they were against fashionable clothing. But can they be said to have entirely avoided conspicuous consumption? Even if clothes were sombre, would not the point about standing be made discreetly but nonetheless clearly by fineness of cloth, by style and cut, by quality and newness?[9]

Thus formal religion was a fundamental factor in the lives of the people and its institutions were universally recognised. But its influence was not confined to the church or chapel, religion was a pervasive element which penetrated all aspects of

life of the community. Respect was given to a
person not for his wealth but for the position he
occupied in the chapel. To be an elder, to be entitled to occupy the big seat in the chapel,
brought prestige perhaps only equalled by success
at an eisteddfod - an annual competitive festival
of the arts - for performance in the arts or for
writing poetry. And this respect was not confined
to the chapel; it was a decisive factor in the as-
sessment of the status of an individual in the community.

Such an attitude was important as far as economic activity was concerned. As I have described
elsewhere, the tinplate area of west Wales was
egalitarian in temper. [10] The rationale of capitalism had not been fully accepted and the unre-
strained pursuit of profit was not generally recognised as the end of human endeavour. West Wales
was not in any true sense an acquisitive society.
In such a context therefore the tinplate maker had
little incentive to pursue wealth aggressively.
With a modest sum it was comparatively easy to become a prominent member of local society and to
enjoy a comfortable standard of living. Moreover,
the fiat of the chapel was inimical to conspicuous
consumption and a deterrent to competitive emulation. Life was lived in a goldfish bowl and social
pressures towards conformity were so great that it
was very difficult for a deviant individual to
diverge from the commonly-accepted norms of expenditure.

Though houses were small and families were not,
the front parlour was not in general use. In some
cases, this was the room where the family met on
Sundays; in others the front parlour was used only
for special occasions such as weddings and funerals.
When death occurred in the family, the deceased
would be placed in a coffin which would occupy the
front parlour, which was something of a shrine.
Here too were on display, once the camera had been
invented, photographs of weddings and christening
parties.

And non-conformity was also influential as far
as the consumption of alcoholic beverages were concerned. In the early nineteenth century when it
was said that the shortest way out of Manchester
was by drink, standards of living were rising slowly (or in some cases falling) and drunkenness was a
severe problem. While the prospect of rising
living standards helped effectively to blunt the
necessity for such oblivion, religious organizations played a considerable role in the temperance

movement, in urging people to abstain from drink,
in propaganda for teetotalism.[11] From the pulpit
the ideal placed before the congregation was not
temperance but total abstinence. The chapel associated itself further with the aim of teetotalism
through youth organisations such as the Band of
Hope and through Rechabite meetings in the chapel.

For the lower orders of society in other parts
of Britain the Salvation Army after its formation
attempted to grapple with the drink problem. And
the activities of such campaigners secured the
limitations of the hours of public houses and their
closure on Sundays. For agricultural workers, such
agitation also led eventually to the abolition by
the Act of 1886 of cider truck, the ending of a
situation in which farm workers, particularly at
harvest time, were entitled to payment in kind
rather than in money.[12]

And emphasis on temperance was allied with an
espousal of thrift not only by religious bodies.
Samuel Smiles, the secular prophet of the Victorian
age, argued in favour of self-help and thrift. The
object of his book entitled *Thrift*,[13] he asserted,
was 'to induce men to employ their means for worthy
purposes and not to waste them upon selfish indul-
gences'. He argued in favour of appropriate institutions such as co-operative societies, friendly
societies and savings banks to provide a home for
the savings of the thrifty. As growth got under
way in the nineteenth century and advancement became possible the perceptive worker saw that thrift
provided a route to improvement and the 'self-made
man' became an object of esteem. A secular doc-
trine of wealth became allied with a Puritan one of
restrained expenditure.

The architecture of religion deserves a pass-
ing comment. As non-conformity gained adherents in
the nineteenth century, larger places of worship
were required and so chapels became not only bigger
but more ostentatious. An element of rivalry between different denominations led to some competitive emulation by conspicuous expenditure. To take
one example Bethesda chapel in Morriston in the
Swansea valley, an enormous chapel, came to be
known as the cathedral of non-conformity. In the
Anglican church it was the liturgical movement
which led to a change in the form of churches. The
well-lit Georgian box with its side galleries was
replaced by the neo-Gothic church with chancel,
nave and aisles, stained glass and a dim religious
light. The sacraments replaced the reading and
preaching of the word as the central acts of Angli-

can worship.

By the nineteenth century the influence of religion on food was less pervasive. In previous times Roman Catholicism and the established church had argued for the consumption of fish on Fridays - indeed the Elizabethan government, intent on making the fisheries a nursery for seamen, had enacted additional fish days, but such concerns had not found great favour with non-conformists. And the Lenten fast, as much an economic necessity as a religious observance at a time when the winter supplies of meat were running out, came to be looked on as a Popish practice, resolution being weakened by the changed supply position and the availability of meat both from home supplies and from imports.

Because non-Christian religions were of small importance in nineteenth century England, their precepts with regard to food production or consumption were not of general importance, however significant they may have been for their own members, as with the Jews.

Of all human activities, eating is highly affected by social influences. Men and women living in societies do not, as Magnus Pyke has written, ingest nutrients, they consume foods. More than this, they eat meals.[14] So what is eaten, when it is eaten and how it is eaten is socially controlled. In their discussion of the food of the poor in the nineteenth century, Jack Drummond and Anne Wilbraham asserted 'that the diet of farm hands in some parts of Scotland and the far north of England had not changed for centuries. They still lived principally on oatmeal, milk and vegetable broths. This was due', they continue, 'in no small measure, to the survival of the primitive system of providing the men working on the estate with food as part payment of their wages!'.[15]

Then in common with many westernised societies, an aversion, equivalent to a taboo, existed against eating the flesh of dogs or rats or of eating insects. There was a general consensus about unacceptable foods. But Britain differed from continental Europe in refusing to eat horseflesh. In 1867 when the price of meat rose because of a cattle epidemic, there was a serious attempt to introduce chevaline as its sponsors called horseflesh, to the British public, but the campaign was not successful.[16] More recently, in the Second World War, although margarine made from whale oil is widely eaten, there was a resistance to eating whale meat.

217

Regional variations in diet, particularly, the division between North and South in England, together with the greater readiness of the South, as compared with the North, to experiment, are obviously the consequence of a number of factors, such as climate and social class. The North is more working class, its members less mobile and the family of greater importance. All this offers resistance to change.[17] Northerners, it is said, tend to be harsher and more puritanical. The North thus favours stiffer brushes, coarser suitings, harsher surfaces. Northerners, American presidents please note, tend to be chewers of sweets, Southerners, suckers. Yet not all their views about food, or for that matter, other issues, are self-evident. A survey in 1945 found that coalminers in Durham ate, on average, only 0.2 oz of cheese a day while coalminers in South Wales ate 1.8 - 1.9 oz a day, that is nine times as much or more. When asked to explain their aversion to cheese, Durham miners claimed it was 'binding'. But when some Durham miners were transferred to work in South Wales, they soon came to eat cheese without either complaint or ill-effect. The compulsion of custom, reinforced in Durham by family bonds, was loosened when the group was split up and the bonds of familiar inter-relationship was broken.[18]

Yet there was a change in modern Britain. The per capita consumption of alcohol declined, the intake of tea and coffee increased. With rising incomes more cocoa, and sugar were also purchased. But tea became a drink of mass consumption while coffee remained an upper-class drink. And while the historical process whereby fish and chips became associated seems to be obscured and certainly complicated, it has been suggested that the high proportion of women and girls employed in the Lancashire cotton industry, leading to a dearth of domestic labour, resulted in the adoption of fish and chips as a ready-made meal.[19]

Further, as a result of the changing pattern of economic activity, the growing importance of industry and trade compared with agriculture, there were changes both in the composition and timing of meals. One notable change in the course of the nineteenth century was the growth in popularity amongst the upper-classes of what has come to be known as the 'English breakfast'. Instead of the eighteenth century breakfast of cold meat, cheese and beer, the majority of the well-to-do adopted the three or four course meal of porridge, fish, bacon and eggs, toast and marmalade which maintained

its popularity until recently when notions of
dieting led to the so-called 'continental breakfast'
gaining in favour.[20] In few areas of human behaviour do the early conditioning of customary use and
inbred tradition exert so subtle an effect on the
mind as in the case of meals.

Not only the content of meals but their timing
was determined by custom. Here, too, there was
change. In the late eighteenth century rich and
fashionable people ate their dinner at 5 or 6
o'clock but in the nineteenth century 7 o'clock was
the more usual hour. It was this change that led
to the disappearance of the old 'supper' and to the
custom of eating luncheon in the middle of the day.
In the early part of the nineteenth century luncheon was often quite a light repast, perhaps nothing more than a glass of wine and a biscuit, but it
gradually took the more elaborate form common in
the mid-twentieth century. The late evening 'supper' of the eighteenth century was replaced by tea
or coffee and cakes, with possibly cold punch or
light wine for the men, served at about 9.30 pm or
10.00 pm.[21] Thus the timetable of meals had a
sexist component. It also had a class component.
Such a timing and terminology applied to the upper
and middle classes: the working class took dinner
in the middle of the day and then at 5.30 pm or
6.00 pm took high tea.

Convention also applied to dress. Until recently it was commonly accepted that there should
be a clear difference made between the dress of men
and women, of boys and girls. Although subject to
fashion,[22] dress also had a class component: that
of males gave some indication of their breeding and
occupation, that of women provided a vehicle both
to indicate class and display wealth. There was
clothing which was socially regarded as appropriate
for each occasion. To deviate was to risk ostra-
cism and to be derided as Bohemian.

Convention or custom also influenced the way
in which people spent their time. The old aristocratic landowning society had a high leisure preference. To fill their waking moments a highly
ritualised round of visits, entertainments and
functions was accepted and pursued. Sport was subject to the restraints of convention and had its
hierarchy of prestige. Para-military pursuits such
as hunting, shooting and fishing were the preserve
of the landowner. For the working classes the
pattern of such leisure as was available was equally socially determined. There was a sequence of
folk festivals which persisted with some vigour in

the face of industrialisation while new practices
developed. Paternal employers came to organise
works outings while religous organisations, friendly societies and the like arranged special functions for their members. The timetable of sport in
England was also influenced by custom. Because
cricket was a summer sport, football came to be
played through the winter, even though the weather
sometimes became too inclement for even the
hardiest spirits.

And in death as in life there were conventions
to be obeyed. The funeral provided an occasion to
establish individual identities often denied in
life. The English term 'funeral rites' lacks the
sonorous sound of the French 'pompes funèbres' but
funerals served as an opportunity for a display of
wealth and standing. The funeral baked meats often
provided an occasion for a considerable celebration.
Lavish preparations were made even in non-conformist
west Wales to feed the guests, both relations and
friends. Tablets in church of chapel were replaced by tombstones where display became more or-
nate and ostentatious. The bandwagon rolled as
pecuniary emulation sought conspicuous display.

Throughout society the conventional use of
living space tended to be rigidly determined. In
the upper reaches of society, rooms were provided
in houses for many activities. The gentlemen
withdrew from dinner to the withdrawing or drawing
room to enjoy the ritual of port and cigarettes
after dinner. Attached to bedrooms, there were
dressing rooms. For the children, there was a nursery. And so on. The builders' magazines and
architects' journals provided details of the appropriate conventional arrangements. The kitchen
was at some distance from the dining room so that
dinners could be isolated from the noise, smell and
heat of the kitchen but suffer from having to eat
food which had to be reheated. Convention rather
than convenience thus determined the allocation of
social space within a house. Down the social scale,
too, the use of living space, as indicated earlier
in our discussion of west Wales, was also highly
ritualised.

Such influences were also not without their
effect on the nature of business buildings also.
In a century where every decade was punctuated by
a financial crisis which led to a considerable
number of bankruptcies, architecture was employed
to bolster public confidence. Banks built themselves solid and impressive premises in an attempt,
sometimes mistaken, to imply that their concerns

were 'safe as houses'. Lesser concerns adorned their shopfronts with the phrase 'Established in 1867' or some such date to suggest that they were not fly-by-night traders. Another aid to custom was the legend that the firm were 'By appointment' butchers, bakers and candlestickmakers to Queen Victoria or some other member of the royal family. Not price or quality were the reasons for seeking custom, but the appeal was th snobbery.

Or to take another example. In 1866 the lord of the manor of Seaton, Devon, Sir Charles Trevelyan, decided to commission the construction of a bridge across a fairly narrow river, the Axe, near the point it enters the sea. His architect produced plans for a single-span bridge in concrete but these were turned down by the Board of Trade who considered the proposal too daring. Instead a three-span bridge, now the oldest surviving concrete bridge in England was built. And, in order that those crossing it would not be alarmed by the fact that they were crossing a bridge, constructed in a revolutionary and untried material, the concrete was patterned to simulate construction from stone blocks.[23]

Within English society, it has been argued, social groups could respond in different ways to similar situations. It has been suggested that the novels of Antony Trollope show two kinds of Herefordshire families: the county and aristocratic families forming a closed and stable group and the fringe world trying to break into what they regard as privileged circles. Though both groups had the same consumption norms, they differed in the economies which their poorer members made. Whereas county widows and impoverished squires did not disguise their stringencies: those attempting to climb socially were intent on preserving a private show while economising in private. The one group used marriage to reinforce its position, the other attempted to use marriage as a means of self-advancement.[24] Thus it was not wealth but social position which determined patterns of expenditure.

Though convention was conservative it was not immutable. The changing patterns of economic activity, the shifting requirements of labour had their effect on patterns of behaviour. And they were aided in England by the fluidity of English society, but the ease with which the middle class could rise and marry into the aristocracy and artisans into the bourgeoisie. This provided suitable conditions in which social emulation, which it has been argued provided part of the motive power for

English industrialisation, could flourish.

The changes in the structure of industry, in the products it produced or whose imports it made possible, the growing incomes which were generated were all important in making the material changes possible. But important too for changes in consumption was the attitude of mind. The Puritan was typically associated with a wish to limit expenditure on material desires and we have already seen how such strictures at the hands of non-conformists were effective in west Wales. The religious commonly took a vow of poverty. Such attitudes seemed appropriate when output was growing slowly but when with industrialisation the speed of growth not only quickened but appeared to be sustained and cumulative, then the old precepts of poverty ceased to appeal. The quickening pace of technological change began to provide glimpses of abundance which made dreams of affluence possible. To reinforce the material desires, philosophers and economists came to expound a hedonistic calculus rather than asceticism and helped to undermine the restraints of custom and convention. Thus seeds of an acquisitive society were soon to germinate and flourish. But all was not lost, the power of custom and convention was not entirely destroyed and some restraint was still exercised on the pace of change.

FASHION

> As good to be out of the world as out of
> the fashion.
>
> Colley Cibber

While custom and convention are concerned with long-run stability in the nature of needs to be statisfied, fashion is concerned with short-run order. Fashion implies a continuing pattern of change in which certain social forms enjoy temporary acceptance and respectability only to be replaced by others more abreast of the times. But, though favouring change, fashion is not anarchic. Fashion provides for an orderly march from the immediate past to the proximate future. It is a reflection of a common sensitivity and taste.[25] Fashion then is the epiphenomenon of convention, the disciplining force of consumer choices in the face of an expanding market of alternative goods.[26] But that which is fashionable is not always highly regarded because it is of greater utility or superior merit. Instead it is a response to the direction of taste. The most obvious aspect of consump-

Table 7.1: Distribution of wealth among people of 25 and over England and Wales, 1911-13

Amount of capital	No.of persons	% of all persons	Amount capital £millions	% of all capital	Average holding
Above £25.000	32,000	0.2	2,685	41.3	84,000
£10.000-25.000	57,000	0.3	930	14.3	16,300
£5.000-10.000	81,500	0.4	635	9.8	7,800
£1.000-5.000	426,000	2.3	1,030	15.8	2,400
£100-1.000	1,766,000	9.4	670	10.3	380
Below £100	16,382,500	87.4	550	8.5	34
Total	18,745,000	100.0	6,500	100.0	350

Source: Mark Abrams, The condition of the British people, 1911-4, (Gollancz, 1946), p. 110.

period between 1750 and 1914 Paris was the centre of upper-class fashion and the high-born and well-to-do in other countries did their best to emulate the French in style, colour and fabric. In the main the pace was set by the aristocracy and conventional consumption was often formed by imitation of the class above. But the display of the aristocracy came to be challenged if not emulated by the rising wealth of the industrialists. Though sometimes pejoratively desribed as 'the nouveaux riches', their purchasing power formed the basis of their competitive emulation. Nor was the fashionable traffic all in one direction. Some fashions in clothes were taken over from the lower orders. Amongst women, prostitutes and mistresses were commonly said to be the most fashionably dressed and were sometimes innovators of fashion. This spread of fashion was aided not only by personal contact between mistress and maid and by the demonstration effect but also by the increased circulation and number of fashion magazines and by the invention of the paper pattern which enabled the home dressmaker to run up clothes in the latest fashion.[27] In the fashionable world of clothing a number of trends were apparent. First, where men's clothing was concerned the business clothes of one generation tended to be replaced by the leisure clothes of a subsequent generation. The top hat and the morning suit for the business man gave way to the lounge suit. Fabrics too became lighter in colour and lighter in weight. Details of apparel also altered, the size and shape of lapels and pockets, the cut

of the sleeve, the number of buttons on the cuff.
Coats were sometimes single-breasted, sometimes
double-breasted. The cut of the trousers also
varied. And such was the pursuit of fashion by
some that it was said that when on one occasion
Edward VII's valet pressed the king's trousers in
error at the side rather than front and back, other
men at court copied. The size, shape and colour
of the tie varied, as did the colour and cut of the
shirt. The shape and character of the collar
changed. So one could go on and list the variations
in male attire, which perhaps deserve more sustained treatment than they have so far received.
    Female fashion has been more fully discussed.
What women wore, it has been argued, had very
little to do with practicality. The choice of
clothes was determined not so much by the need to
keep warm or in the impulse of modesty. The nineteenth century began with a return to nature and
the Greeks. After 1815 there was, it is said, a
shift to prudery and romanticism. By the 1840's
the popular image of woman had changed and she was
now seen as wife and mother with demure self-ef-
facement. Then in the 1860's came the age of the
crinoline, most inappropriate for travelling in railway compartments, but the first great triumph, so
it has been said, of the machine age - the application to female costume of all those principles of
steel construction employed in the Menai Bridge and
the Crystal Palace. Woman became an unapproachable
goddess. By the 1870's the acceptable female shape
changed again. The main component was the bustle
with the contrast of a narrow waist produced by
tight lacing. This was followed by the pre-
Raphaelite phase with the concept of woman as
mysteriously medieval. At the end of the century
practical influences had some effect on fashion with
women riding bicycles and taking part in more active
sports. Such variations could be explored to the
present day. In recent times perhaps one of the
most marked twists of fashion has been towards a
unisex fashion. Through the media deliberate attempts have been made in the early 1980's to extend
the fashion market to the pre-teenagers. As a
result it is said that the sales of 28 inch bras,
high heels for tots and make-up for the under-11s
are soaring.[28]
    Though account has sometimes however to be
taken of practicality the choice of clothes has
tended to be less determined by the need to keep
warm and be protected from the elements or to safe-
guard health than by impulses of modesty, and the

wish to demonstrate wealth, status or sexual appeal.

Changes in fashion clearly had considerable influence on the demand for particular products. Viticulture, sericulture, horticulture in its more refined products, and the management of ostrich farms - this comment was written in 1893 - are liable to be affected by changes in fashion. The fur-trapper's fortunes also are not exempt. Decline in demand for finer furs often reduces the Hudson's Bay Companies' dividends. In the crinoline days, Bradford dress goods from English wools were in great demand, but when ladies preferred clinging fabrics (cashmeres etc.) the advantage went to the soft goods of France.[29] The corset created a demand for whalebone stiffeners, the crinoline for steel hoops. Between the wars the corset declined and the bra became fashionable. And when women took to wearing trousers different types of foundation garments were required. So the fortunes of industry and commerce were very much affected by the spin of fashion's wheel.

The attempt to remain in the fashion was an endless pursuit. It has been suggested that a timetable for a particular dress or costume might be:[30]

Indecent	10 years before its time			
Shameless	5 "	"	"	"
Outré or daring	1 "	"	"	"
Smart	-			
Dowdy	1 year after its time			
Hideous	10 "	"	"	"
Ridiculous	20 "	"	"	"
Amusing	30 "	"	"	"
Quaint	50 "	"	"	"
Charming	70 "	"	"	"
Romantic	100 "	"	"	"
Beautiful	150 "	"	"	"

Although most obvious in the case of clothes, the rule of fashion ran more widely though the timescale might differ. People, and women especially, change their clothes more easily than they change their style of interior decoration and much more quickly than they change their architecture. In such matters there tends to be a gap in taste of a generation or so. In the 1970's and 1980's we appreciate the nineteenth century architectural achievements but in the 1920's Kenneth (now Lord) Clark recalls that Victorian neo-Gothic was 'a kind of architecture which everyone agreed was worthless'. Taste in the arts, in music. painting,

sculpture, the theatre and dance also ebbs and
flows. After their deaths composers and painters
often undergo a period of neglect, sometimes, but
not inevitably to return to favour when the critical
perspective has changed. With furniture and houses
the amount of expenditure involved and the degree of
permanence were factors which affected the pace of
fashionable change. The purchase of luxury items
and furniture, while it owed something to function,
was considerably influenced by matters of fashion
and taste. A reflection of fashion as much as of
inflation 'do-it-yourself' house decoration has
recently enjoyed a vogue.

Children's games were also subject to fashion,
popular for a period and then dropped. Who now
remembers the yo-yo? And the skateboard enjoyed a
popularity more transient than some British local
authorities recognised with their specially-built
skateboard arenas, now a costly and embarrassing
irrelevance. Sports, too, enjoy their vogue.
Amongst some concerned about physical health,
jogging became an acceptable pursuit. And, as the
capital investment has been possible, squash has
gained in popularity. But golf, a plebian activity
in Scotland, remains stubbornly a middle and upper
class activity in England. Support for indoor
sports has also waxed and waned. A generation ago,
billiard halls and snooker halls closed as they lost
esteem, with billiards being regarded as a more
respectable sport than snooker. But, of recent
years, television has made snooker, with its range
of coloured balls more photogenic than the black
and white of billiards, a cult game which now has a
following both as a participant and as a spectator
sport. But television with its accessibility and
constantly changing programmes has severely affected
the cinema. The large auditorium with its Wurlitzer
organ, and its queues for seats on Saturday nights
is almost as extinct as the pterodactyl, having been
replaced by a series of small auditoriums with a
choice of programmes. With mechanical gaming
machines, fashion also takes its toll and 'space
invaders' will soon be threatened by the new wave
of machines or perhaps will be abandoned as other
outlets for skill and chance emerge.

The later twentieth century has seen the range
of fashion extended and a shift in leadership. In
the affluent society a greater proportion of the
population had sufficient income to enable them to
jump on the whirligig of fashion. And a new youth
culture developed which set the pace. These were
predominantly in the 16-26 age group, relatively

well-paid but with little in the way of financial
obligations to family or property. Ostensibly in
some respects the adoption of casual wear they did
not escape the discipline of fashion. 'Dressing
down' rather than 'dressing up' became the rule of
fashion. Quickly it had to be not just jeans but
faded jeans, scruffy jeans, branded jeans, designer
jeans and so on. The mods and rockers, the punks,
established their own modes of dress, hairstyles,
forms of facial make-up. In the market for consumer durables, such as transistors and motorcycles,
teenage demand has been significant. In fashion
terms, the teenage world has been particularly
volatile, because it has been more affluent, 'free'
of the restraints of family and opposing the older
generation. The speed of change has been facilitated by the ephemeral transient nature of the
teenage generation. Class identification has to
some exente been replaced by identification by age-
group. The pursuit of fashion has become a game
played by a larger section of the population.
    In the spread of fashion since 1945 four fac-
tors have been of importance. First, there was
generally a rise in incomes and a development of
social provisions which gave rise to two catch-
phrases 'the affluent society' and 'the Welfare
State' which established a safety net beneath all
but the most unfortunate and the very poor. Then
there has been a trend towards a smaller family
size. The recognition that parents had more disposable income enabled a market for perambulators,
'nursery' equipment, children's clothes to be ex-
ploited.
    Thirdly, advertising became more purposeful
and professional as it increased its range through
the press, with colour supplements for newspapers,
magazines dealing with women and other specialist
groups and most influentially through television
advertising largely pitched at the affluent 16-26
generation, an acceptable unisex drink. The cinema
and the theatre also played their part in establish-
ing new lifestyles.
    Fourth were the developments in marketing.
Hire purchase and deferred payment arrangements
facilitated the acquisition of consumer durables
while the marketing of goods was aided by the
growth of mail order houses with their seductive
catalogues penetrating the home and by supermarkets
with a wider range of goods invitingly on display.
    Yet advertising and marketing are not all-
powerful: while undoubtedly there have been spectacular promotional successes there have also been

failures. While there is an extensive market for
women's cosmetics and toiletries, the market for
male toiletries appears to be stubbornly limited.
There are, too, would-be fashions which fail to
gain acceptance. Though there is some confusion in
the literature about this, the term 'fad' ought
usefully to be restricted to describe such forms of
behaviour which do not receive universal or continuous acceptance but are taken up only by a
portion of a group. So for health foods, the
espousal of alternative power technologies, the
ecology movement and the reaction against the norms
of the consumer society, of which Belgium provides
examples in this volume, have remained the 'fads'
of a few rather than the 'fashion' of the majority.

NOTES

1. The literature on demand in economic history is still comparatively limited but see Eliza-
beth Gilboy, 'Demand as a factor in the industrial
revolution', Facts and factors in economic history:
articles by former students of Edwin Francis Gay
(Cambridge, Mass., Harvard U.P., 1932), pp.620-39;
Joel Mokyr, 'Demand vs supply in the industrial
revolution', Journal of Economic History, XXXVII
(1977), pp. 981-1007; Eric L. Jones,'The fashion
manipulators: consumer tastes and British Industries, 1660-1800' in Louis P. Cain and Paul J.
Uselding (ed.), Business enterprise and economic
change: essays in honor of Harold F. Williamson
(Kent, State U.P., 1973), pp. 198-226 and Walter
Minchinton, 'Patterns and structure of demand' in
Carlo Cipolla (ed.), The Fontana economic history
of Europe: the sixteenth and seventeenth centuries
(Collins, 1974), pp. 83-176 and 'Patterns of demand,
1750-1914' in Carlo Cipolla (ed.), The Fontana economic history of Europe: the industrial revolution
(Collins, 1973), pp. 77-186.
2. An inquiry into the nature and causes of
the wealth of nations (Cannan ed.Methuen, 1961),II,
pp. 388-40.
3. The sociological theory of capital, being
a complete reprint of the new principles of political economy, 1834 (New York, MacMillan, 1905),
Appendix I, Of luxury, pp. 245-276.
4. In his The theory of the leisure class, an
economic study of institutions (MacMillan, 1899).
5. 'Bandwagon, snob and Veblen effects in the
theory of consumers' demand', Quarterly Journal of
Economists, LXIV (1950), pp. 183-207.

6. All this foregoing assumes that income is a parameter and does not vary.

7. In aggregate of course 'impulse' purchases may not fluctuate greatly.

8. The following account draws on the accounts of 'Aberporth' by David Jenkins and Emrys Jones on 'Tregaron' in Elwyn Davies and Alwyn D. Rees, Welsh rural communities (Cardiff, University of Wales Press, 1962), pp. 1-60, 67-109 and Alwyn D. Rees, Life in a Welsh countryside: a social study of Llanfihangel yng Ngwynfa (Cardiff, University of Wales Press, 1951) passim.

9. I owe this point to Dr. John Rule.

10. 'The tinplate maker and technical change' Explorations in Entrepreneurial History VI (1947), pp. 1-11.

11. On this point see A.E. Dingle, 'Drink and working class standards in modern Britain, 1870-1914' in Derek Oddy and Derek Miller, The making of the modern British diet (Croom Helm, 1976), pp.131-2.

12. See my 'The British cider industry since 1870', National Westminster Bank Quarterly Review, November, 1975, p. 162.

13. Murray, 1880, p.vi. The passage continued 'Many enemies have to be encountered in accomplishing this object. There are idleness, thoughtlessness, vanity, vice, intemperance. The last is the worst enemy of all. Numerous cases are cited in the course of the following book, which show that one of the best methods of abating the Curse of Drink, is to induce old and young to practise the virtue of Thrift'.

14. Food and Society (Murray, 1968), p. 67.

15. The Englishman's food: five centuries of English diet (Cape, new ed., 1957), p. 329.

16. The Englishman's food, p. 308.

17. See David Allen, 'Regional variations in food habits' in Oddy and Miller, The making of the modern British diet, pp. 135-47.

18. Pyke, Food and Society, p. 43.

19. William H. Chaloner, 'Trends in fish consumption' in Theodore C. Barker, John McKenzie and John Yudkin, (ed.), Our changing fare: two hundred years of British food habits (MacGibbon & Kee, 1966), p. 110.

20. The Englishman's food, p. 335.

21. Pyke, Food and Society, p. 37. Writing in 1967 he continued: Few Englishwomen trained to use all their intellectual faculties at Oxford University stop to question the truth of what they assert with such authority to their husbands and

children, that a hot breakfast of porridge, bacon
and eggs is essential for proper nutrition regardless of the evidence of the millions outside England who subsist without these items in the morning.

22. See below, pp.222 seq.
23. Walter Minchinton, Devon at work (David &
Charles, 1974), p. 74.
24. This paragraph derives from Mary Douglas
and Baron Isherwood, The world of goods: towards an
anthropology of consumption (Penguin, 1978), pp.
84-5.
25. See Herbert G. Blumer, 'Fashion', International encyclopedia of the social sciences (Mac-
Millan Company and The Free Press, 1968).
26. I'm grateful to Professor Van Holthoon
for helping to clarify my discussion in this point.
27. On these questions see Caroline A. Foley,
'Fashion', Economic Journal III (19893), pp. 458-
74; James Laver, Taste and fashion from the French
Revolution to the present day (Harrap, new ed.,
1945) and Quentin Bell, On human finery (Hogarth
Press, new ed., 1976).
28. See Minchinton, 'Patterns of demand',
Fontana Economic History of Europe, III, p. 96-9.
29. Patricia Jones, 'Hypocrisy and the
nymphet trade', Sunday Times, 3 May 1981, 36.
30. Foley, 'Fashion', pp. 470-2.
31. Laver, Taste and fashion, p. 202.

In revising this paper for publication I have been
grateful for comments from Brian Clapp, Stephen
Fisher, John Rule and the members of the pre-
conference seminar held at Groningen, May 1981.

Chapter 8

FOOD CONSUMPTION IN GERMANY SINCE THE BEGINNING OF INDUSTRIALISATION: A QUANTITATIVE LONGITUDINAL APPROACH
Hans J. Teuteberg

Chapter 8

FOOD CONSUMPTION IN GERMANY SINCE THE BEGINNING OF
INDUSTRIALISATION: A QUANTITATIVE LONGITUDINAL
APPROACH
Hans J. Teuteberg

The description of the consumption of the main foodstuffs in Germany since the middle of the nineteenth
century, that is, since the beginning of industrialisation, meets with several barriers. First of all,
a comprehensive history of nutrition and changing
food habits is lacking. Therefore we are left with
preliminary works of several disciplines and particular studies which deal only with regions, time
periods, or categories of foodstuffs.[1] Another obstacle is that primarily production, trade, and
preparation of victuals are discussed, while the
sector of consumption gets short treatment. Among
other things this has to do with the fact that food
and meals have left relatively few traces in history
in comparison with other historical events. Because
we lack sources, it is rather difficult to recon-
struct broad coherent patterns. Above all, most
historians looked upon daily eating and drinking as
an object which was not worth an academic engagement.
So we can tell today only in vague outline how consumption of foodstuffs had developed in the past and
which structural changes occurred. Research on a
quantitative basis is especially lacking.[2] Given
the expanding computer work in economic and social
history it seems high time now to gather all statistics of food consumption and related material. Of
course, many doubts and gaps remain which can only
be cleared by new research in future. Before we
come to the figures of food consumption and their
interpretation, some remarks seem necessary about
the general changes of our nutritional system in the
last two hundred years. For purposes of simplifi-
cation we can discern four different stages:[3]

Pre-industrial stage. Until the late 18th century in
Germany as in modern developing countries, the dominant food habits were characterized by a high per-

Chart: The vicious circle of malnutrition in pre-industrial society

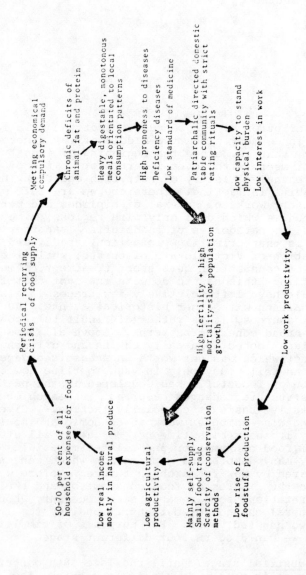

centage of vegetable foodstuffs, mostly in a form of pap or broth. There was a lack of animal fat and protein and therefore of essential amino-acids. As our chart "The Vicious Circle of Malnutrition in Pre-Industrial Society" demonstrates, we can see a chronic deficiency of calories as well vitamins and trace elements. Bulky difficult to digest and monotonous meals fitted to local consumption patterns were the rule, and crises of subsistence or supply returned periodically. The chronic undernourishment of at least two thirds of the German population made them prone to deficiency diseases and illnesses which could not be controlled and combated because medical standards were too low. The results were a high rate of mortality and a low labour productivity because of diminished physical vigor. The relative slow increase in net agrarian production in the centuries before industrialisation had to do on the one hand with the economy of pure subsistence in the framework of "the whole house" (O.Brunner), the lack of possibilities for conserving and transporting victuals over longer distances, and irrational farming methods, and on the other hand with the relatively low ability to stand physical burdens as a result of poor nutrition. The vicious circle of undernourishment in other words destroyed all efforts for a significant improvement of the living standard. In contrast to our modern "affluent society" foodstuffs were evaluated from the standpoint of energy and satiation; taste, digestion, appearance, smell and colour were put in the background and rather neglected.

Transition stage. Between the late 18th and the early 19th century a gradual change resulting from the spread of home industry could be seen in the traditional meal system of rural families. Those parts of the agrarian population released from the older system of food provision enlarged their palette of nutrition with the help of the new cash in hand. As Günter Wiegelmann recently demonstrated with maps, the crucial changes of our meal system were not initiated merely by urbanisation and industrialisation after the middle of the 19th century. The "proto-industrialisation" (Frank Mendels) in the countryside was in general more important for this alteration. It seems obvious that zones of early industrial concentration are correlated with the appearance of food and meal innovations: potatoes, beet sugar, chicory coffee, and spirits began to be incorporated into daily menus of the "working classes" after 1800. New regional mobility, the

possibility of early marriages and the infiltration
of the new medium, cash money, in all sectors of
daily life, altered deeply the manners of fare too.
Although the agrarian home workers, small peasants,
tenants and day-labourers kept mainly to their old
meal monotony, to a certain amount of self-sufficiency and to the hierarchy of prestige and need
formed by the rules of their village-life, they became more and more susceptible to the nutritional
patterns of the urban and civic middle classes. In
this stage, however, great oscillations between
scarce and sufficient provisions certainly remained.
Waves of high food prices and diseases persisted.
50 to 80 percent of the small incomes of the households had to be spent, on the average, for nutrition:
therefore only compulsory needs could be satisfied.

Stage of "Nutritional Revolution". The definitive
conquering of the caloric deficit was achieved within a few decades after 1850 by rationalisation of
agriculture, trade, transport, and conservation
techniques, to which the rising nutritional sciences
gave decisive impulses. In spite of the huge con-
current increase of population, food supply per
capita improved. The decreasing food expenditures
in the household budgets signalled the final break-
out from the "Malthusian trap" (Carlo Cipolla).
Animal fat and protein were replacing carbohydrates
in respect to nutrition balance, but there still remained a deficit in vitamins and minerals, as far
one can see. On the whole there was a trend toward
products which were more digestable and tasteful and
which have more calories. As seems to be typical for
industrialisation substitutes for luxurious food and
drink were used by the lower classes for reason of
price. The consumption of meat, animal fat, and
eggs, but also of fresh vegetables, fruits and sugar
increased while the consumption of rye-bread, legumes and potatoes decreased. Serious supply crises
were of less concern at this stage. With growing
urbanisation the food supply became more and more
dependent on distant markets. Therefore new difficulties of adapting to changing market patterns
arose. The lack of market surveys, the animosity
against innovations, and the limited knowledge of
scientific nutrition rules were the main reasons why
people clung to traditional agrarian eating and
drinking habits. Further potential improvements in
the diet were therefore prevented. Food expenses
are regulated after Ernst Engel's famous law: The
lower the income, the larger the proportion of total
income expended on foodstuffs, and vice versa.

236

Stage of affluence. After recovering from World War II, all income groups in Western Germany were able to afford a nutritionally adequate diet. Instead of satisfying a compulsory need, people were able to choose their foodstuffs more or less free from economic constraints. By 1974, only 29 percent of all expenses by a two-person household of pensioners were spent for food. Above a certain income range, the German households were nearly price inelastic when buying foodstuffs. On the other hand there are noticeable new tastes, differences of prestige and new claims of quality which can be defined as new social pressures. A completely autonomous choice of food does not exist. There are growing demands to refine agrarian products, establish an aesthetic and hygienic packaging, for fresh products year around and for a maximum of frozen preservation. Conservatism of taste and meal monotony have not disappeared completely. Pre-industrial differences between feast-meal and weekday food, and in regional kitchen habits are still well recognizable. The tendency to rationalize kitchen work and to shift domestic service from the housewife to external institutions correlates with the growth of the canning and beverage industry. There is, furthermore, a spectacular tendency to change from the patriachic table community, which celebrates traditional eating rituals, to the anonymous, unconventional, outdoor-feeding. Because of the rigid school and working schedules which are not very well adapted to our natural biological rhythm, the domestic table community is nowadays in West Germany in a danger of loosing its function as a centre for socal communication in the family. But the dominant pattern on the whole is the "good housewife" of the 19th century middle-classes. So the food supply in the affluent society has been assured, but there are still old patterns of disfunction. The major problem is not to fight hunger but overweight. This could be called the "new social question".

After this introductory overview of changing nutritional patterns through the period of industrialisation, we now focus our attention more closely on the main topic: the changes in rates of absolute consumption of various foodstuffs. Early statisticians used net agricultural production as a point of departure for estimating food consumption. One simply took the amount of foodstuffs produced in a country, added the food imports, subtracted the exports, and then placed the resulting total in relationship to the population at the time. Where such information was lacking, it had to be determined by estimating procedures and extrapolation.

There has long been a consensus that such per-capita estimates are very inexact, and that numerous ambiguities and possibilities for error seriously reduce the value of such data. Before the founding of the German Reich in 1871, only the larger German states possessed "Statistical Bureaus", and the serial data they produced are of widely varying quality. The gaps become more numerous and the figures more questionable, the further one goes back into the 19th century. In the 18th century one can only rely on chance findings, mostly data of a regional or local nature. As a general conclusion, because of the varying quality and coverage of the statistical material, the various quantitative estimates for the period before the mid 1800's can hardly be compared with one another, and allow safe generalization only about a few selected problems.

Historians of nutrition have another serious problem with which they must wrestle: no distiction was made in per-capita consumption between private, public, agricultural or "industrial" uses. Thus complicated estimating procedures had to be applied to separate the amount of grain that was used for baking bread and other household consumption from the other part of the crop that was used regularly and in large amounts as livestock feed, for next year's seed, and for alcohol production, not to speak of rodent damage and other losses. With consumption ratios gained from more differentiated regional or local data, one could arrive at percentages to apply at the state or national level. An additional source of error is that the amount of land in cultivation was rather imprecisely determined prior to the time of the first general land surveys, so that one comes up with widely varying estimates of the ratio between cropland and wasteland or fallow. Similar contradictions arose from the calculation of yields per unit of land, because for a long time information on the amount sowed and harvested remained very imprecise. Thus the basis upon which a "normal harvest" was calculated varied widely.

Just as problematic was the fact that the "Statistical Bureaus" could not determine the livestock holdings very precisely. To avoid taxes, farmers often failed to report all their cattle. There were also great differences of opinion as to the average slaughter weight of livestock and the amount of waste involved in meat production.

By the mid 19th century, the degree of rationalization and intensivization of agriculture varied widely from region to region in Germany, as Viebahn's statistics show, so that calculations of net agricultural productivity also vary widely. The greatest divergences can be found in calculations of yearly milk production per cow. The various types of fodder crops, improved breeding, quality of pasture, and the fact that cattle were still used as draft animals in many areas, could result in widely varying milk production.

In Germany there is the additional problem that the internal consistency of time-series data is disrupted by several major boundary changes. Statisticians have established the principle that figures should always be based on the territorial status at the time. As a result, the data from 1850 to 1975 are based on five not entirely identical territorial units; in addition, the atypical periods of the two world wars and their immediate aftermath are omitted. Most problematic, however, are the limitations of per-capita statistics: all diferences of age and sex, of occupation and income, and also regional, religious, and cultural variation, are blended together in an arithmetic average.

Thus one should not read too much into such per-capita data, since consumption figures were arrived at rather indirectly from statistics of agriculture, trade, and population. These annual figures can only reflect certain trends of development, and must be supplemented by other calculations. The following factors appear to have influenced the per-capita rates of foodstuff consumption:

1. the social structure, i.e. population growth, age structure and occupation;
2. income and price structure (inequality of income, price elasticity);
3. yearly economic trends (harvests);
4. technical progress and mechanization (increased net productivity, better methods of preservation, improvements in transportation and communication);
5. the spread of information about the science of nutrition;
6. matters of taste, preference and prejudice;
7. the development of the living standard in general, for example desire for conspicuous consumption.

For all the caution warranted in using per-capita figures, it is still important to examine their general trends. One important advantage is

that they are easy to calculate and provide a basis
for quick comparison on a national or international
basis. The following figures provide an initial
survey of the per-capita consumption of various
foodstuffs on a yearly basis from 1850 to 1975.
From 1880 on, the basis for these calculations was
the Statistical Yearbook of the German Reich and its
successor for the Federal Republic, and from 1957 on
the special Statistical Yearbook on nutrition, agriculture, and forestry. Additional information was
drawn from other works, for example the periodical
"Wirtschaft und Statistik", Walter G. Hoffmann's
standard work on the growth of the German economy
since the mid-nineteenth century (1965), the inter-
pretive investigations by D. Grupe and D. Petzina,
and the reporters of the German Society for Nutrition.[4] Following are some observations and comments
on the time-series data on 22 categories of foodstuffs:[5]

Bread and Flour (Chart 1).[6] It is immediately apparent that the consumption of such staples was much
higher in the 19th century than it is today. Bread
and porridges, along with the potato, constituted
the real nutritional backbone of ordinary Germans.
They were not, as in the present, supplements to the
main dish; they were, day in and day out, the main
dish. Peaks of consumption were reached between
1878-79 and 1893-1913. This is a reflection of
falling Germain grain prices with the competition of
overseas imports, and the resulting protective tariffs, leading to sharp price increases and the substitution of other articles for bread and potatoes.
The yearly fluctuations resulting from varying harvests became less and less significant; the supply
of bread had become practically independent of local
climatic influences. Though the mid 18th century
still witnessed bread riots, skyrocketing prices,
and speculations as a result of harvest failures, a
century later these could be compensated by the surpluses of overseas producers. With increasing
rationalization and intensification of agriculture,
a broader range of crops resulted, so that the consumer had more possibilities of substitution.
    In the course of the last century the Germans
changed their preferences from rye bread to wheat
bread. From the data it is apparent that the consumption of rye, after an initial increase, began to
stagnate at the hight of industrialization around
1880, and has decreased sharply especially in the
postwar period. By 1975 it was only one-fourth of
what it had been in 1850. In contrast, wheat con-

Chart 1: Consumption of rye and wheat (flour and bread) per head/kg and year,1850-1975

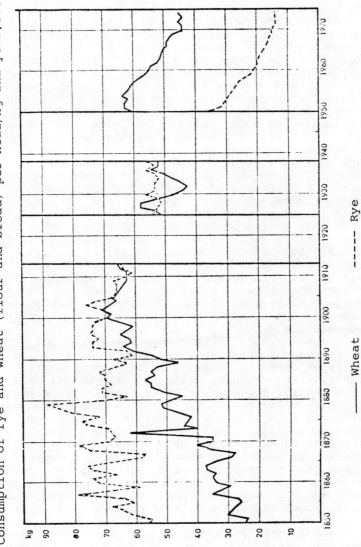

—— Wheat   ----- Rye

sumption shows a long period of steady growth,
reaching a plateau that only began to decline with
the affluent society around 1955. It is less apparent today that the Germans are a nation of wheatbread eaters, because so may mixed flours are used.
A similar trend can be observed in all industrial
nations: with increasing standards of living, more
white breads are consumed, reflecting the social
preference for wheat over rye. Nutritional psychol-
ogists have suggested that this is related to the
higher gluten content of wheat, which bakes lighter
and is thus more tasty. Black bread formerly contained a higher proportion of water and crude fiber.
The result was moldy, slimy bread with water streaks
under the crust. In spite of Justus Liebig's early
investigations, most people remained ignorant of the
fact that whole-grain bread had a higher nutritional
value. Thus rye remained the most commom grain only
until the beginning of the 20th century, though it
must be remembered that a large proportion was consumed in forms other than bread.

Other grains besides wheat and rye thus
played only a marginal role. Barley was used especially for brewing and distilling, as a coffee
substitute, and in soups. As real coffee became
affordable, this showed a decline. Oats ('Hafer')
had the advantage of a high fat content, but oatmeal
spoils quickly and develops a bitter taste when left
standing, and in addition it bore the stigma of the
poorhouse.

Rice ('Reis') , with less protein but more
starch than other grains, was originally eaten primarily as dessert, cooked with milk and flavored
with raisins or plums. With the development of instant pudding desserts, rice was demoted to a part
of the everyday meal. By 1900 rice consumption was
six times that of a half century previously, encouraged by falling prices from cheaper transportation and the development of mechanized milling processes. Polished rice came into use in soups and as
a side dish to meats and fish. The only reminder of
its former high social position is rice pudding with
sugar and cinnamon. Current rice consumption fluc-
tuates widely around the level of 1890.

Potatoes (Chart 2) [7]. Formerly eaten more but valued
less than grains, the "apple of the earth" had
reached Europe from South America already in the
16th century, but was long regarded as fit only for
livestock or paupers. It was not yet known that
this nightshade relative contained important amino
acids and high levels of Vitamin C and Potasssium.

242

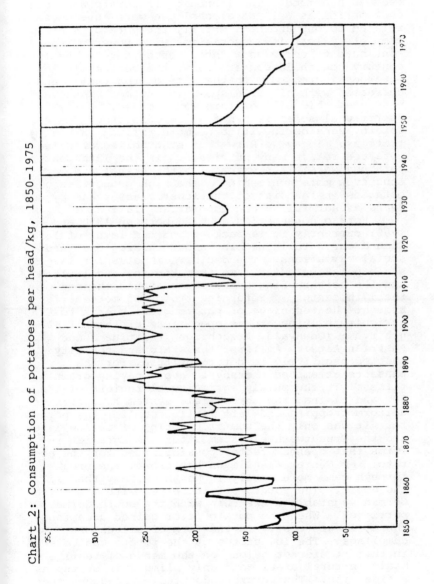

Chart 2: Consumption of potatoes per head/kg, 1850-1975

After repeated attempts in the 18th century, the potato found a permanent place of German menus during the great agricultural crisis at the beginning of the 19th century, when the low grain prices led farmers to the realization that this lowly root crop could be distilled into alcohol and the wastes used as hog feed. The increases in potato and pork consumption as well as alcohol use were thus closely related to one another. Still, the potato never completely lost its association with poverty, and continued to serve as a "bread substitute". As 19th century household budgets show, the consumption of potatoes increased with the size of the family and decreased with higher disposable income. Whenever possible, this bill of fare was avoided. Early nutritional scientists had a low opinion of the potato, considering it to be more filling than nutritious. Today we know that even boiled or fried potatoes retain many nutrients. In the 19th century potatoes were often eaten with the skins, and were thus even more nourishing. The high proportion of potatoes in the diet of the lower classes was by no means as harmful as contemporaries claimed.

Potato consumption doubled between 1850 and 1900; currently it is back around the level of 1855. Such a curve tells nothing about the regional and social variations. The decisive impetus for large-scale potato growing came from England and Ireland and the neighbouring Netherlands around the end of the 17th century. Returning troops of mercenaries brought the technique of potato growing back to the agriculturally underdeveloped areas of the Mittelgebirge : (Odenwald, Erzgebirge, Palatinate and Austrian Alps). At first the state and nobility reacted negatively to potato culture, for the peasants attempted thereby to avoid paying grain tithes. In the purely agricultural regions of the lowland plains, the three-field system necessitated uniform cropping and left little room for the potato. It was only the summer planting of fallow lands and the Fruchtwechselsystem after the agrarian reforms that opened greater possibilities for the potato. As Günter Wiegelmann has shown, the breakthrough came more easily in North Germany than in the South. The potato fit in better with the north German vegetable stews than with the south German porridges. When the potato later gained acceptance there, it was mostly in the form of salads or dumplings. The low status of the potato can be seen in that it did not belong on the menue of festive meals in rural areas, and only climbed in status as a side dish. The potato undoubtedly broadened the

nutritional spectrum in Europe a great deal. Like
rice in the developing countries of the present, it
was able to keep pace with the nutritional needs of
a rapidly growing population. The familiar population explosion of the 19th century correlates
noticeably with the spread of the potato in Germany.

Legumes, Vegetables, and Fruits (Chart 3)[8]. The
consumption of legumes, which goes back to the
Germanic tribes, declined sharply with the beginning of industrialization. The long cooking time
required for peas and beans, their poor digestabi-
lity, and their low position on scales of taste and
prestige are the main reasons. In North Germany
dried grey peas was the main fare, in South Germany
"horse" or "sow" beans, and in all regions, but especially in the Southwest, yellow peas and lentils.
Between 1805 and 1815 in Prussia, three times as
much land was planted with legumes as with potatoes.
Already by 1862 these proportions were reversed,
with three times as much land devoted to potatoes.
This rapid downward trend continued on into the
20th century. Consumption dropped from over 20
kilogram per person in 1850 to less than one kilogram in 1975, barely 4 percent of the earlier rate.
Legumes are no longer the staple they once were,
probably because meats have replaced them as a
protein source; the only place they still persist
is as an ingredient for stews.

A comparison with other vegetables (Chart 4)
suggests that also here a substitution process has
taken place. Like fresh fruit, fresh vegetables
were until the late 19th century a luxury of the
upper classes. Such vegetables were not very filling, and their nutritional value had not yet been
recognized. A decisive factor was also the price,
which was much higher than for dried peas and beans.
Because of the high water content, vegetables could
not be very well stored or transported and were
only available in season. According to Viebahn's
statistics from around 1850, vegetable consumption
was mainly restricted to the cabbage family,
carrots, onions, and cucumbers, with many of the
present day varieties either unknown or rare luxuries.

Regional peculiarities played an important
role. Bavarians loved their sauerkraut and turnips,
but turned up their noses at carrots and green
beans. In North Germany cabbage greens were especially popular, one of the few vegetables also
available in winter. Nowhere in the country was
there much love for spinach; besides its strange

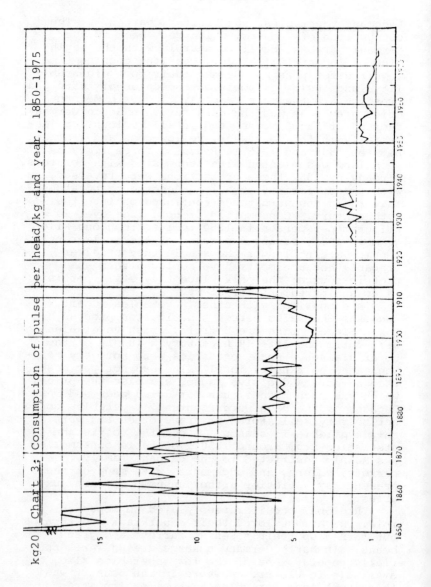

Chart 3: Consumption of pulse per head/kg and year, 1850-1975

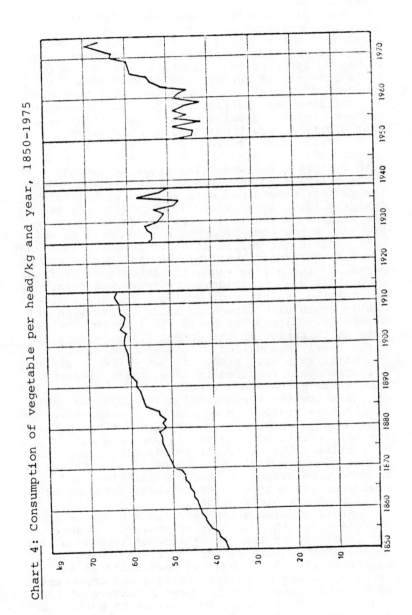

Chart 4: Consumption of vegetable per head/kg and year, 1850–1975

smell, taste, and appearance, it also spoiled easily. Sauerkraut was popular everywhere - its stereotype as the German national dish has some basis in fact.

Agricultural statistics demonstrate that large scale production of vegetables and fruits only began during the last half of the previous century. Alongside the older production for home use there sprung up large-scale, industrial production of a whole spectrum of garden vegetables. With the progress of urbanization, more and more people were cut off from self-sufficiency, so that vegetable peddlers found a growing market, and truck farmers on the city's edge flourished and prospered. But large scale truck farming is a relatively recent phenomenon; according to statistics from the mid 19th century there were wide areas of Germany with nothing more than home production. By the end of the century demand had even reached such levels that the first large-scale imports were registered. The figures on vegetable consumption are very imprecise, since home production is so hard to estimate. Given the difficulties of preservation, many products were only available on the local weekly markets. For a long time, the importance of fresh vegetables was overshadowed by preserved forms such as pickling, salting, or drying. The canning industry began with expensive luxury items such as asparagus. Already by World War I there were 32 canning factories in the German Reich, with a combined yearly production of one million cans. But not until 1916 were producers subjected to state inspection and required to label their products with trade marks and net weights.

The low fruit consumption (Chart 5) had many of the same reasons as vegetables. With water content as high as 85 percent and low fat and protein content, fruits spoiled easily and were not very attractive. The extremely low levels through the Bismarckian Era include a degree of uncertainty as to home production. Apples, pears, plums and cherries were mostly eaten in dried form and as an ingredient for other dishes.

Fruit growing often remained a hobby or a showpiece for the nobility or religious orders. Not until the beginnings of scientific agriculture in the 18th century did fruit growing reach a higher level. Only then did horticultural societies begin the selective breeding and improvement of orchard trees which had been a feature of Roman times, developing varieties adapted to particular soils and climates. Rural clergymen played an im-

248

Chart 5: Consumption of fruits and citrus fruits (tropical fruits) per head/kg and year, 1850-1975

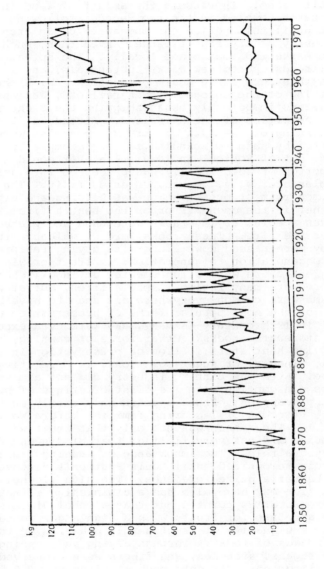

portant role here. The three nursery, introduced to Germany by the Scottish gardener James Booth, had gained such popularity by 1850 that commercial nurseries could hardly keep up with the demand for fruit trees. In Prussia the amount of land in orchards doubled in the two decades following 1878. Not until this period can one speak of an orchard industry of any significance. Even then, much of the marketing took place locally. The spread of railroads opened new market potentials, and made possible more large scale production. With the opening of the Cologne-Minden railroad, Westphalian peasants immediately began shipping their cherries to the cities of the Rhineland. Already at the beginning of the 19th century green apples were exported by ship to Scandinavia, for example 20.000 tons out of Rostock in 1820. Whatever could not be exported or sold locally was processed into juice, applesauce, wine, cognac, or dried fruit. The most common form of preservation was slicing and drying, either in the open air or on the hearth fire. Often special drying racks were used and placed over the fire. These racks were so valuable that they were passed down along with drying recipies from generation to generation; in fruit-growing regions there were often special drying-kitchens. There were many regional specialities, but stewed plums were common everywhere and seem to have been one of the most popular forms of preservation of all in 19th century Germany, and were even exported in stoneware crocks. Other forms of canning, involving heat sterilization or preservation in alcohol, vinegar, or sugar solutions, were relatively rare. Even the canning industry did not aim at mass consumption with its first offerings of peaches and pineapples. Fruit appears only rarely in the account books of labouring families before World War I. The reason was not only that fruit was expensive and not very filling; fear of disease also played a role. The importance of washing fruit was hardly recognized until Louis Pasteur's discovery of bacteria gained credence. The high alcohol consumption may have also had a diminishing effect: contemporaries pointed out that alcohol diminished the appetite for fruits with a high sugar content.

The quality of fruit hardly measured up to the standards of today. Through drying and canning, the sugars, starches, and fibers were preserved, but important nutrients such as vitamins C, B_1, B_2, carotene, and niacin were lost. Needless to say, it was not until the end of the 19th century that fresh fruit came to play an important part in the common

German diet. The growing market for fruit juice and carbonated beverages certainly played a role here. Even more rapid was the increasing availability of citrus fruits; at the turn of the century practically reserved for the upper classes, they now belong to the common bill of fare. Around 1900 the yearly consumption of citrus fruits was only 2 kilogram per person, as compared to 43 kilograms of domestic fruit; today the respective figures are 22 and 80 kilos. The growing consumption of citrus fruits has been the most spectacular of any of the branches of foodstuffs during this period. The reasons are obvious: tropical fruit not only has a high prestige value, it also tastes good and looks appetizing, and fills in the seasonal gaps left by domestic fruit production (Chart 5).

<u>Honey, Molasses and Sugar</u>[9]. There are large studies on the cultural history of sugar, but we know less about the foundation and development of the sugar industry, and our information on real sugar consumption is meagre. The first comprehensive research gave hints that the expensive colonial sugar did not figure largely in the diet of the working classes for centuries. If a sweetener was used at all, it was usually honey. The production of beet sugar, which had been invented in the 18th century and introduced during the Napoleon wars, remained unimportant for economical reasons at first; the quality was still rather bad. However, the price of beet sugar began to decrease rapidly when the German sugar manufacturers received tax privileges as in France, and the sugar concentration of the beets began to rise, when cultivation, tillage and transport methods improved. But the poor classes turned first to molasses, because this was a rather cheap by-product of sugar manufacturing. In the lower Rhineland, where the first mills for beet sugar were established under the reign of Napoleon, the dark brown "Rübenkraut" played an important role. It was 60 percent cheaper than the cane sugar. Between 1865 and 1880 the Prussian Rhine area produced 1500 to 2200 tons molasses per year and exported a great deal. In these decades molasses was a main foodstuff beside bread for the plain people. This has been overlooked in most histories of sugar (Chart 6).

With the increase of net wages this intervening period of molasses ended. A glance to the statistics shows that at that time the triumphal march of the beet sugar really began. Consumption rose in the whole 19th century by ten times. If we

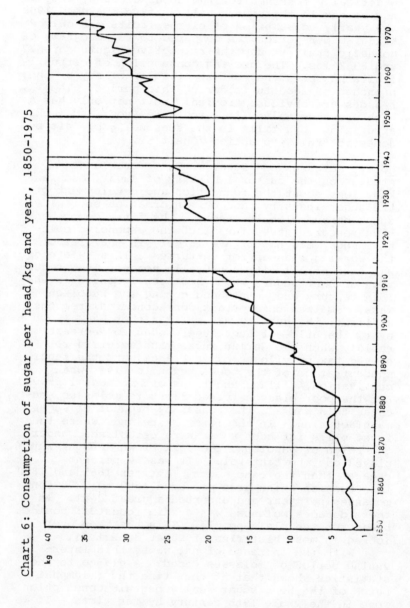

Chart 6: Consumption of sugar per head/kg and year, 1850–1975

neglect honey and the tiny amounts of fructose, milk sugar, and maltose in the grain, the 18th century was still a time nearly without sugar. The preparations of marmalades, jelly, sweet pastry, cakes etc. were nearly impossible for the lower classes. Furthermore, there was no sweetening of coffee, milk or soups. By 1900 the situation had changed totally: As budgets from worker families demonstrate, there was practically no household without sugar. In contrast to many other victuals the sugar price continued declining. The new beet product was a welcome offset to the traditional caloric deficit. Daily meals became more tasteful. The reasons for the growing demand are easy to determine: Sugar could be preserved almost indefinitely; instead of the old "hat-sugar", which could be cut into bits only with some difficulty there was now candy, lump and powder sugar. All this increased the possibilities for using this product. The beet sugar became, last but not least, more and more similar to the refined and superior ranked cane sugar.

Meat[10]. Contrary to former theories we can see in the 19th century a nearly continuous increase of meat consumption, which became really remarkable, only since 1850 (Chart 7). By 1900, people in Germany ate nearly twice as much meat as fifty years earlier. In 1911 the German Reich already consumed as much meat as the Federal Republic in 1955/56. Both worldwars and the subsequent periods of dearth show only a temporary decline. The upper and the middle classes always consumed relatively more meat, but the sharp rise of consumption can be explained only by mass-consumption. The upper and middle classes could have never alone caused this large rise. The increase of the meat consumption between 1850 and 1975 by three and a half times is correlated with a remarkable shift from beef and mutton to pork (as shown in Charts 8 and 9). The consumption of pork rose from 6.6 kg per person and year 1850/55 to 25.5 kg in 1900/13, that is a quadrupling. The proportion of pork within the total meat consumption was enlarged from 35 to 60 percent. During the same period beef only doubled. Mutton and veal was decreasing (Charts 10,11). The preference for pork can be explained as follows: It has more calories than other sorts of meat, it can be prepared quicker and is more useable, especially as bacon and sausages, swineshave relatively little bone and can be used to the last remains. Furthermore they can be fattened rather quick by kitchen

253

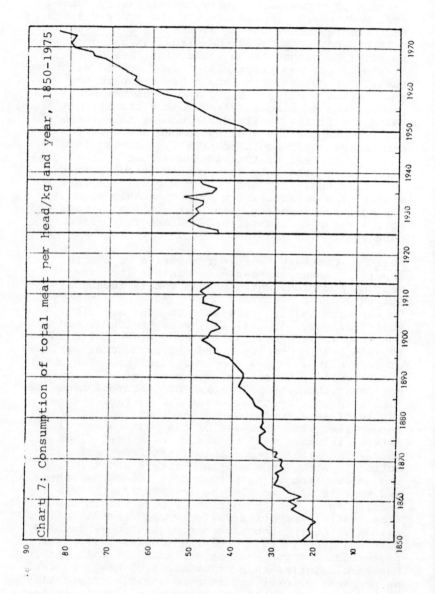

Chart 7: Consumption of total meat per head/kg and year, 1850-1975

Chart 8: Consumption of beef per head/kg and year, 1850-1975

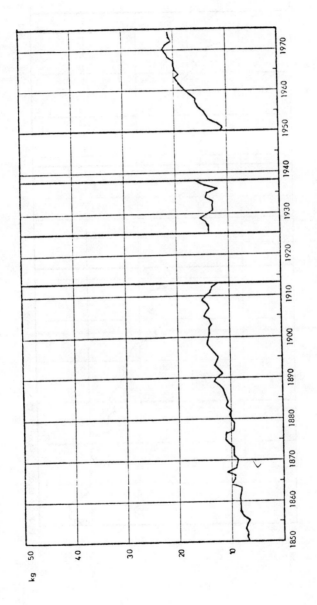

Chart 9: Consumption of pork per head/kg and year, 1850-1975

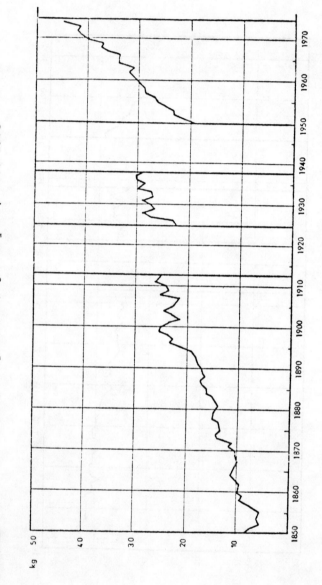

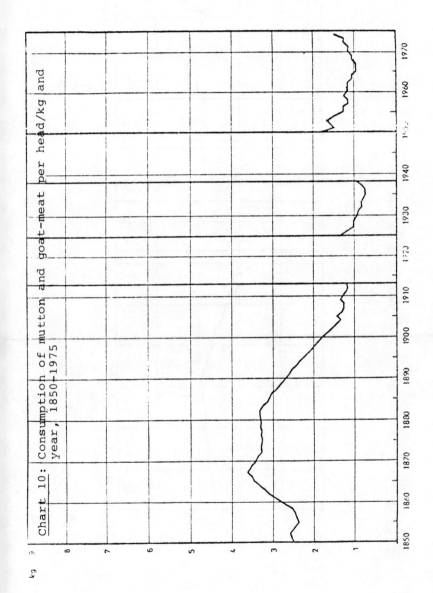

Chart 10: Consumption of mutton and goat-meat per head/kg and year, 1850-1975

257

Chart 11: Consumption of veal per head/kg and year, 1850-1975

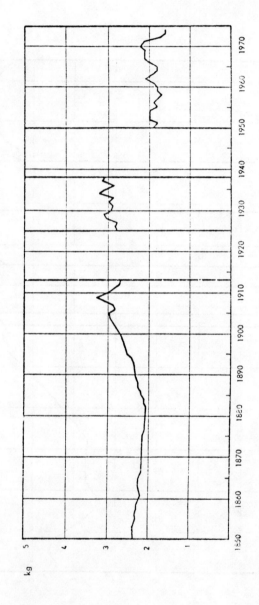

scraps only. Altogether there is no slaughter animal which is more practical.

Contrary to a former hypothesis, we can now see from the statistics that the inhabitants of the 19th century towns consumed more meat in general than those in the countryside. The lower classes could certainly afford only parts of meat with inferior value. In household budgets from the turn of the century, meat from "Cheap Meat-Departments" is sometimes mentioned. This sort of meat had an old tradition in Germany: In the middle ages at many places there were "Kuttelhöfe", "Metzgen" or "Freibänke" (butcher's stalls) for the poor. After the erection of special slaughter houses by town magistrates from the 1860's on, it was not allowed to sell meat of inferior value that was not hygienic. All this sort of meat had to be cooked before sale. The "Cheap Meat-Departments" of the towns were relics from former times and diminished gradually. Absolutely new in the field of meat provision were the horse butchers who gained a foothold with their shops in the big cities. After the meat inspection act these shops had to be kept separate from the slaughter houses, because the horse butchers were glue cookers too. In 1926 there were in the German Reich 126,295 horse butchers shops, but their sales remained small. More interesting is the consumption of offal products ; the sharp increase began after the World War II.

How large the proportion of sausages in total meat consumption was,can't be determined by statistics, because sausages were not sold by weight but only in small pieces of 10, 20 or 30 pennies. Without doubt the consumption centered around hard sausages. The boiled, cooked and fried forms as well as ground raw meat played a minor role. All sorts of sausages were mixed with flour and phosphate as well as with parts of plants, especially with garlics and onions, in order to better the appearance and flavour. Naturally, there were many occasions for adulteration. Often the sausages were full of water and from "dubious origin". Sausage production could not be regulated as effectively as slaughtering. But sausages were very popular and in demand because they could be bought in such small pieces and needed no preparation before eating. The emergence of special sausage manufactures and the triumphal march of the sausages canned and boiled (Frankfurter Würstchen), demonstrates that a larger demand must have emerged very early. Meat extracts, beef cubes and prefabricated beef-teas as well as beef sauces belong

to the 20th century. Game remained a typical food
for upper classes in narrow limits which cannot be
measured. Revolutionary was the sharp increase of
poultry consumption (Chart 12). The "cockerel wave"
which correlates with mechanisation and centralisa-
tion of production as well with deep freezing and
new marketing methods belong to the most recent
times. As in the case of sugar, rapid decreases in
costs of production correlated with a sharp rise in
demand for this former luxury.

Fish.[11] Despite its high nutritional value there
was never a large consumption in earlier times, if
we overlook the sea coast population. Because of
the difficulties in transport and storing, fish was
consumed mainly dried, salted, pickled and smoked.
Fresh sea food did not conquer larger interior markets until the railway age began. In 1909 there
were more than 400 canning factories preserving the
cheap herring. From foreign countries 3,500 tons
canned fish were imported in 1913, mostly sardines
in oil. When an import duty on foreign fish was
cancelled in 1928/29, import of preserved fish rose
to some extent. Herrings and sprats in oil and
tomato sauce Norwegian style gained a ready market,
while the traditional fish smokery declined. The
large increase of fish consumption between 1930 and
1940 is remarkable, but then the consumption curve
went down again(Chart 13).Fish always was a fall-
back or surrogate for meat: both consumption trends
have to be compared. Rather large waste, fear for
poisoning, and a low social image are probably the
reasons why fish consumption had remained rather
small in Germany since 1850. River fish was like
game: an expensive and therefore luxurious product.
The same is true of crustaceans and shellfish.

Milk and Milk Products (Chart 14).[12] In contrast
to sugar, spirits, coffee and spices, milk never
passed through a spectacular introductory phase.
It remained all the time a "natural" foodstuff and
remedy which was consumed like water. Because of
the difficulties of preserving before the age of
modern techniques, milk had to be processed immediately, but no special skills were needed. There
were no special crafts involved in milk production,
because all processing occurred in the field of
traditional house-keeping and husbandry. The retail
milk trade was also very small and on a local basis
only. No taxes could be raised here. So the production of milk cannot be measured in statistical
categories before 1910.

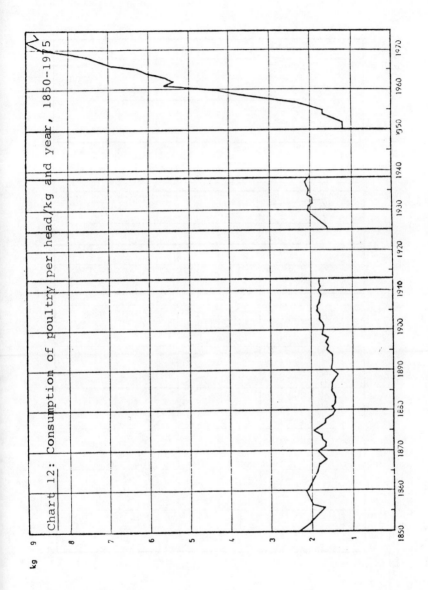

Chart 12: Consumption of poultry per head/kg and year, 1850-1975

Chart 13: Consumption of fish (fresh weight) per head/kg and year, 1850-1975

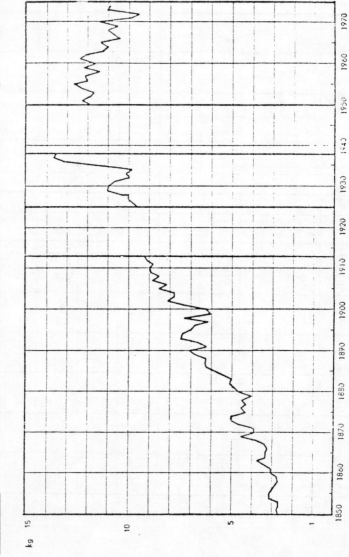

Chart 14: Consumption of milk and milk products per head/kg and year, 1850-1975

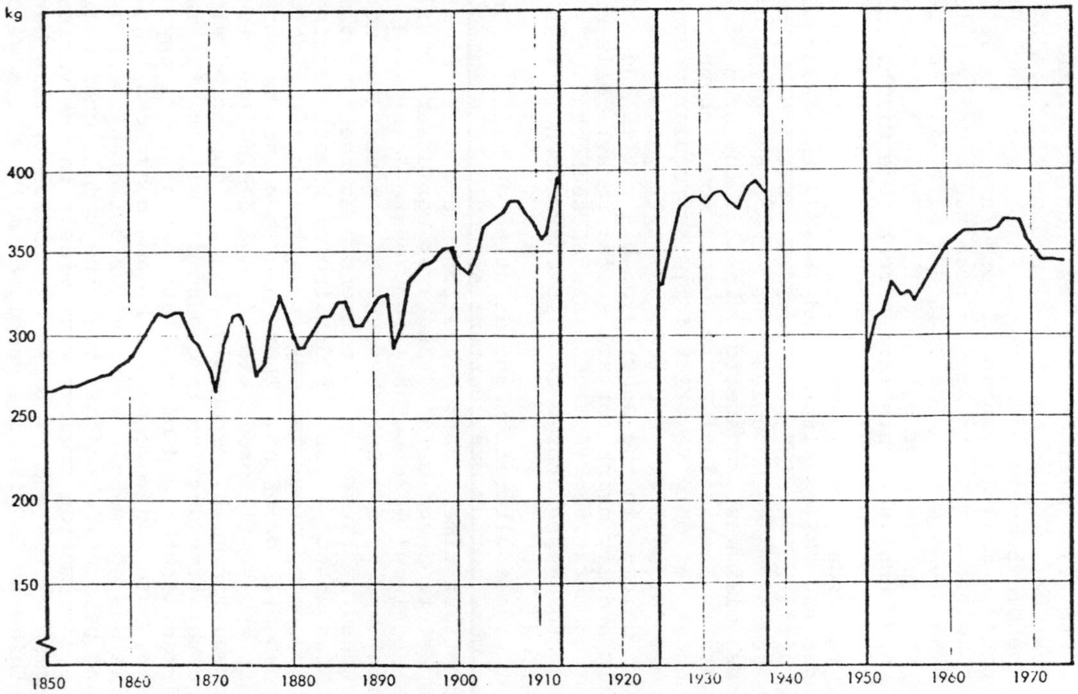

263

The efforts to quantify milk for drinking per capita and year has lead to different and dubious results. We are only sure that the greater part of the milk was processed into cream, butter and cheese. Only a small portion was consumed in fresh or fluid form (whole milk, skimmed milk, sour milk and buttermilk). A minor part was used for fattening livestock. In the reports of medical doctors and in household budgets of worker's families in the 19th century, milk is mentioned very rarely. In 1870/71 the German armies in France received a daily ration of 750 grams meat or bacon and a half litre of beer or wine per soldier but no milk. In 1871 Benno von Martiny published his famous book "Die Milch, ihr Wesen und ihre Bewertung",which marks te beginning of the modern "milk age" in Germany. Shortly afterwards the "Milchzeitung" and in 1874 the "Milchwirtschaftliche Verein" were founded. With the help of these new mass-communications, the consumption of fresh milk was propagated. In 1860 the head of the Prussian Statistical Board, Georg von Viebahn, noted that as yet only few rich families regularly consumed coffee milk or cream. Fifteen years later, hugh dairies in the suburbs of big cities had made milk a daily drink for all social ranks. Milk market cooperatives ("Milchabsatzgenossenschaften") and the cream-separator were also introduced in this period.

The adulteration and diluting of milk, which had gone on for many centuries, could be stemmed for the first time. Pasteurization and cooling of milk were introduced before the First World War. "Milk sanitoriums" were established, where "certified milk" was sold. But the average consumer was not reached by these new inventions. At the same time we can detect a certain decline of breast feeding, which among other factors is linked to the rise of fresh milk drinking. There are some indications that whole milk production lagged behind the rise in demand for milk. Probably this was connected with the relative decline in demand for milk cattle in Germany at the end of the 19th century. In any case, more and more people became convinced that milk was not merely a drink for children, sick and aged persons, which had been the traditional belief. The consumption figures vary widely in the various German states and regions, but obviously this has nothing to do with the supply of milk. Thus we can not measure the trends in consumption of butter, cheese and evaporated milk, because the time series from 1910 onwards are rather short and not comparable with the other data on food consumption.

Remarkable is the increase of oleo-margarine, edible oil and slaughter fat (Chart 15 and 16).

Because of the large extent of home production, data on the consumption of eggs are rather sketchy, but there is little doubt about the general increase per capita since the introduction of "chicken farming" after the last war (Chart 17). In 1850 a person consumed perhaps one egg per week on average as compared to 5.5 nowadays (including industrial purposes). The average size of an egg increased from 50 to 60 grams.

Animal and vegetable foodstuffs in general. The summary comparison of animal and vegetable foodstuffs from 1850 to 1975 shows that througout the 19th century, as in all previous centuries of the pre-industrial period, vegetable nutrients continued to form the backbone of the common German diet. It was not until 1912 that animal products gained a clear lead. Though in previous years they occasionally reached the level of vegetable products, these were more short-term reactions resulting from harvest failures and price fluctuations. It should be noted that after the end of both the First and Second World War there was a sharp but short-term drop in meat consumption, which quickly climbed back to normal levels, however, as soon as accustomed living standards were restored, and the gap between the two consumption curves continued to widen (Chart 18).

Industrialization brought with it a change from predominately vegetable to primarily animal foodstuffs, in other words, from bulky, hard to digest, unappetizing staples to lighter, more easily digestable, more tasty, high energy foods. In nutritional terms this meant a switch from vegetable to animal proteins and from carbohydrates to fats. This revolutionary change in century-long patterns of nutrition is well demonstrated by statistics of agricultural production: Around 1800, for example, over three fourth of Prussian production fell in the vegetable category, and only one fourth in the animal; in the present-day Federal Republic this ratio is nearly reversed.

What factors help explain these remarkable shifts in our nutritional habits? First of all, there is the natural tendency to prefer foods which are more tasty, easily digestable, rich in energy, and easy to prepare. In the place of monotonous, poorly prepared foods, mostly dictated by local custom, we now have more refined, more appetizing, more satisfying, and more varied foods and bever-

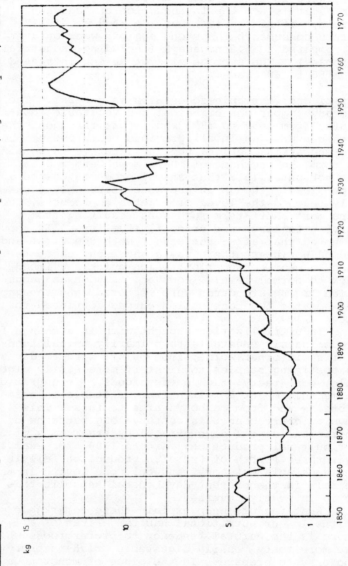

Chart 15: Consumption of edible oil and margarine per head/kg and year, 1850-1975

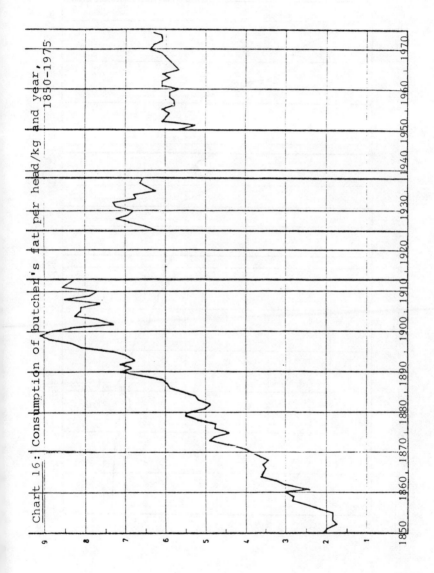

Chart 16: Consumption of butcher's fat per head/kg and year, 1850-1975

Chart 17: Consumption of eggs per head/kg and year, 1850–1975 (1 egg=50 g)

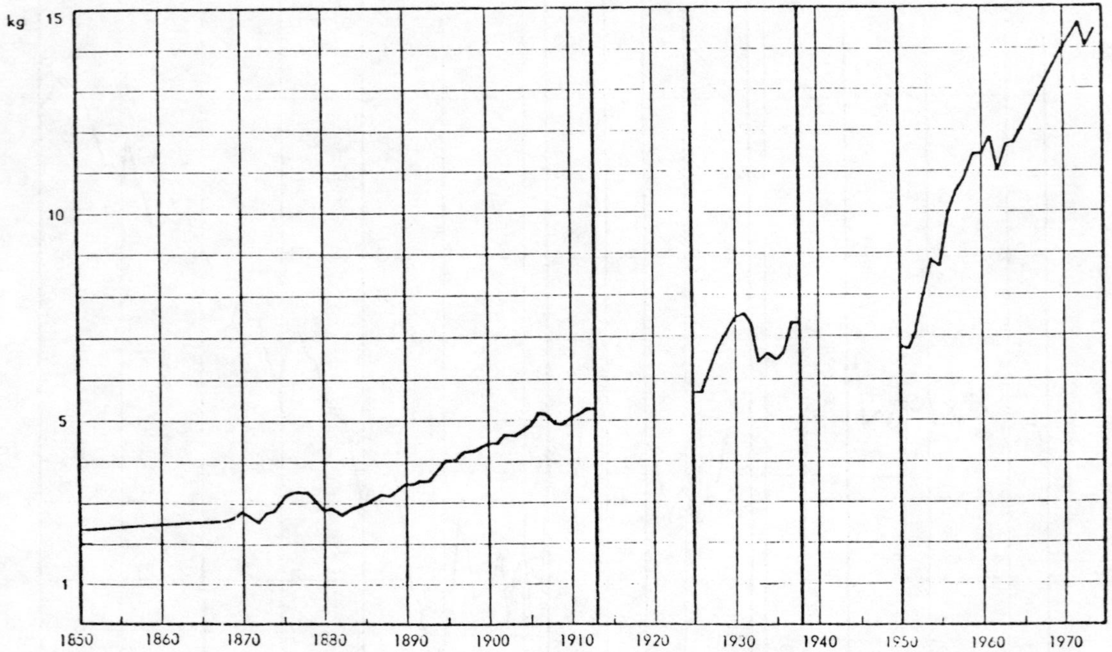

Chart 18: Consumption of vegetable and animal products per head/kg and year, 1850–1975

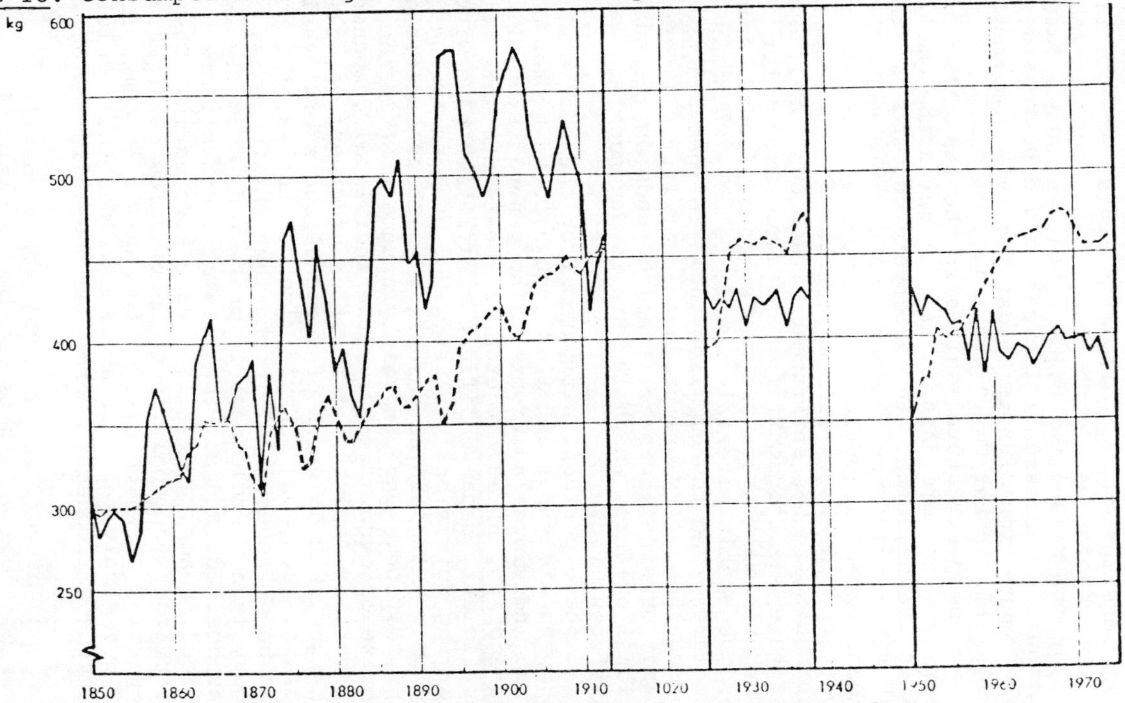

—— vegetable products   ---- animal products

269

ages. The lower classes have always attempted to
imitate the conspicuous consumption of the upper
classes, at first quantitatively with substitutes
and later also qualitatively. In all the industrial
nations of Europe the same process can be observed:
The consumption of meats, fats, eggs and especially
fresh vegetables, fresh fruits, and sugar increases
while the demand for bread, potatoes, and legumes
gradually decreases ("Increasing and Decreasing
in Consumption of Main Foodstuffs 1975 compared
with 1850 in Per Cent" Chart 19).

These structural shifts in the last 125 years
appear even more drastic if one charts the changes
in proteins, fats, and carbohydrates, and especially vitamins, trace elements and caloric value. The
human animal is obviously omnivorous, and can
satisfy his energy from a wide variety of sources,
depending on his environment , and can easily substitute one foodstuff for another. Except for
mother's milk there are no "natural" foods. Animal
and vegetable materials become so only when man
declares them to be, mixes them, refines and pre-
pares them. Any one product is of little importance or significance; it all depends on the nutritional balance, which in turn is dependent on many
different factors.

These per capita figures from the past are
unfortunately not detailed enough to be broken down
into individual nutrients. The general statistical
categories, bread, vegetables, meat, etc. are not
sufficient, because different varieties have widely
varying nutritional values. Not even an average
caloric value can be calculated without additional
information. One can safely assume that in the
course of over a century, the individual components
of certain foodstuff categories underwent major
changes, not to speak of regional and social variations. Just one example: look at the way the hog
has been "redesigned" in the last thirty years.
Today lean, muscle meat is preferred; formerly fat
was desired, and all the less attractive parts
- feed, heads, and tails - were also eaten. The
nutritional composition of meat varies considerably
depending on which part of the animal it comes from.
If one simply takes an average value, the resulting
figures will obscure more than they illuminate.

Any historical investigation of nutrition that
does not deal with this problem is misleading and
worthless for scholars. It appears that the only
valid way to arrive at an equivalent of our modern
nutritional units would be to comb through all

Chart 19: Increase and Decrease in Consumption of Main Foodstuffs in 1975 compared with 1850 in per cent

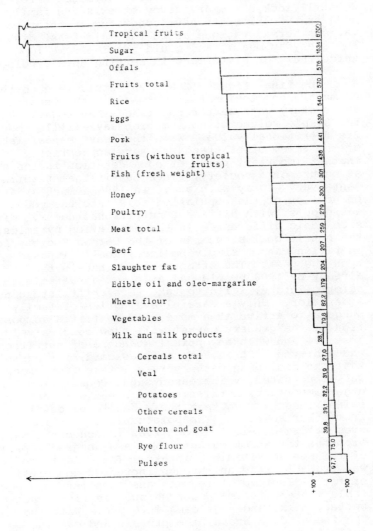

Tropical fruits	8700
Sugar	1034
Offals	576
Fruits total	570
Rice	540
Eggs	539
Pork	441
Fruits (without tropical fruits)	436
Fish (fresh weight)	301
Honey	300
Poultry	279
Meat total	259
Beef	207
Slaughter fat	204
Edible oil and oleo-margarine	179
Wheat flour	82.2
Vegetables	79.8
Milk and milk products	28.7
Cereals total	27.0
Veal	31.9
Potatoes	32.2
Other cereals	39.1
Mutton and goat	39.8
Rye flour	75.0
Pulses	97.7

+ 100   0   - 100

existing family budgets to find out which varieties
make up such categories as pork, beef, or bread.
Of course variation by time, region, and social
class would also have to be taken into consideration. As a control one could use attempts by contemporaries to calculate nutritional equivalents of
foods, although these certainly contained errors.
We still lack a summary study of existing family
budgets. Folklorists have conducted inventories of
various German regions as to the main feast dishes
and everyday meals, and could provide some important
guidelines for historians in setting up a typology.

The final figure (Chart 20) could lead to the
premature conclusion that Germans at the turn of
the century were better nourished than today. But
the simple volume of consumption says little about
its nutritional value. With the heavy manual labour
of the time, other standards were appropriate.
Another important point of consideration is the age
structure of a society, since nutritional requirements vary widely with age. In 1900 a much greater
proportion of the population fell into the younger
age groups, with different nutritional needs. With
such basic differences in the population pyramids,
the nutritional standards of the German Society for
Nutrition cannot simply be incritically imposed
upon the past. The often repeated thesis that
already by 1900 people had attained a sufficient
caloric intake, fails to take this shift into consideration. Only a careful evaluation of family
budgets to arrive at a more differentiated composition of the grocery basket will show conclusively
just how and when an optimal standard of nutrition
was achieved. It is generally assumed, for example,
that the declining carbohydrate intake from bread
was compensated by increased sugar consumption. But
other importants nutrients from bread were not contained in sugar, so that these had to be obtained
from other sources. The potato, like rice in
present day developing countries, rescued the masses
from the threat of malnutrition and assured a part
of the needed Vitamin C intake. The caloric deficit
was probably made up through increased consumption
of fats. Instead of legumes ans suppliers of vegetable protein, animal sources such as fish, cheese,
butter, milk, and eggs came into use. With the
decline of dark bread, the protein and calcium
deficit was made up from milk and cheese, and increased pork consumption took care of Vitamin B_1.
But all these substitution trends were subject to
limitations of a social and regional nature in nu-

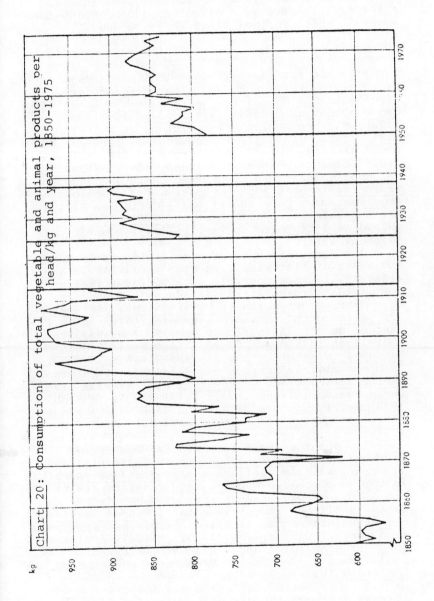

Chart 20: Consumption of total vegetable and animal products per head/kg and year, 1850-1975

273

tritional patterns. Thus many of the conclusions
drawn from these time trends remain speculative or
hypothetical. But is is hoped that this initial
attempt will serve as a stimulus, and point up the
areas in which further research is needed.

NOTES

1. See for the methodological problems of a
history of nutrition Hans J. Teuteberg/Günter
Wiegelmann,Der Wandel der Nahrungsgewohnheiten unter
dem Einfluss der Industrialisierung (Göttingen
1972); Maurice Aymard, "The History of Nutrition
and Economic History", The Journal of European Economic History, Vol. 2 (1972) pp. 201-218; Nils-
Arvid Bringéus/Günter Wiegelmann (eds.), Ethnological Food Research in Europe and USA. Reports from
the First International Symposium for Ethnological
Food Research, Lund August 1970 (Göttingen 1971);
Maria Dembińska, L'alimentation - sujet des recherches dans l'histoire de la civilisation matérielle
(Warshaw 1974).
2. First attempts at quantifying in German
and Austrian historical research are: Wilhelm Abel,
Massenarmut und Hungerkrisen im vorindustriellen
Europa (Hamburg-Berlin 1974); Hans J. Teuteberg,
"Die Nahrung der sozialen Unterschichten im späten
19. Jahrhundert", Edith Heischkel-Artelt (ed.), Er-
nährung und Ernährungslehre des 19. Jahrhunderts
(Göttingen 1976) pp. 202-287; Teuteberg/Wiegelmann,
Nahrungsgewohnheiten pp. 94-198; Roman Sandgruber,
"Nahrungsmittelverbrauch und Essgewohnheiten vom 16.
Jahrhundert bis zur Gegenwart", Beiträge zur historischen Sozialkunde, Vol. 8 (Vienna Jan.-March
1978) No. 1, pp. 11-22; Gertrud Helling, Nahrungs-
mittelproduktion und Weltaussenhandel (Berlin-East
1977).
3. See for these four stages: Teuteberg/
Wiegelmann, Nahrungsgewohnheiten pp. 236, 133 and
312 seq.; Wilhelm Abel, Massenarmut und Hungerkrisen
im vorindustriellen Deutschland (Göttingen 1972);
Rudolf Braun, Die Veränderung der Lebensformen in
einem ländlichen Industriegebiet (Zürcher Oberland)
vor 1800 (Winterthur 1960); Willi Wirths, Ernährung
Ernährungssituation, Vol. 2, Datenlage zur Versor-
gung der Erdbevölkerung (Paderborn 1978); Otto
Neuloh/Hans J. Teuteberg, Ernährungsfehlverhalten im
Wohlstand (Paderborn 1979).
4. Statistisches Reichsamt (ed.), Statistisches Jahrbuch für das Deutsche Reich (Berlin
1880 seq.); Statistisches Reichsamt (ed.), Viertel-
jahrshefte zur Statistik des Deutschen Reiches

(Berlin 1873 seq.); Statistisches Bundesamt (ed.),
Bevölkerung und Wirtschaft 1872-1972 (Wiesbaden
1972); Bundesministerium für Ernährung, Landwirtschaft und Forsten (ed.), Statistisches Jahrbuch
für Ernährung, Landwirtschaft und Forsten (Berlin
1957 seq.); Walther G. Hoffmann, Das Wachstum der
deutschen Wirtschaft seit der Mitte des 19. Jahrhunderts (Berlin-Heidelberg-New York 1965); D.
Grupe, "Die Nahrungsmittelversorgung Deutschlands
seit 1915", Agrarwirtschaft, Vol. 1975 (special no.
3-4); Dietmar Petzina, "Materialien zum sozialen
und wirtschaftlichen Wandel seit dem Ende des 19.
Jahrhunderts", Vierteljahreshefte für Zeitgeschich-
te, Vol. 17 (1969), No. 3, pp. 308-338; Deutsche
Gesellschaft für Ernährung (ed.), Ernährungsbe-
richt, 4 Vols. (Frankfurt a. M. 1969-1980).
    5. The time-series data, which are the basis
for the following charts, are published in Hans J.
Teuteberg, "Der Verzehr von Nahrungsmitteln in
Deutschland pro Kopf und Jahr seit Beginn der Industrialisierung (1850-1975)", Archiv für Sozial-
geschichte, Vol. 19 (1981), pp. 344-349.
    6. See Hans J. Teuteberg, "Die Rolle von Brot
und Kartoffeln in der historischen Entwicklung der
Nahrungsgewohnheiten", Ernährungs-Umschau, Vol. 26
(1979), No. 5, pp. 149-154; Fred Binder, Die Brot-
nahrung. Auswahl-Bibliographie zu ihrer Geschichte
und Bedeutung (Ulm 1973).
    7. Wilhelm R. Fues, Die Geschichte der Kar-
toffel (Berlin 1940); Recliffe N. Salaman, The
History and Social Influence of the Potato (London
1949); W. Völksen, Auf den Spuren der Kartoffen in
Literatur und Kunst (Hamburg 1964); Adam Maurio,
Geschichte der Pflanzennahrung (Berlin 1927); M.
Morineau, "La pomme de terre au XVIIIe siècle", Annales tome 25 (1970), pp. 1767-1785; Hans J. Teuteberg, "Zur sozialgeschichtlichen Bedeutung der Kar-
toffel und ihrer Eingliederung in die deutsche
Volkskost"; Niilo Valonen/Juhan U.E. Lehtonen
(eds.), Ethnologische Nahrungsforschung - Ethnolo-
gical Food Research (Helsinki 1975), pp. 237-265.
    8. L. Reinhardt, Kulturgeschichte der Nutz-
pflanzen (München 1911); Teuteberg, "Nahrung der
sozialen Unterschichten", pp. 255-264; Maurizio,
Pflanzennahrung; W. Lauche, Deutsche Pomologie, 6
Vols. (Berlin 1882-1883).
    9. See Edmund von Lippmann, Geschichte des
Zuckers (Leipzig 1890); Verein deutscher Zucker-
Industrie (ed.), 100 Jahre der Deutschen Zucker-
Industrie 1850-1950 (Berlin 1950); Hans J. Teuteberg, "Zuckerwirtschaft und Zuckerkonsum im histo-
rischen Rückblick", Zucker Vol. 27 (1974), No. 9,

PP. 484-488; Franz Lerner, Aber nur die Biene findet Süssigkeit. Kleine Kulturgeschichte des Honigs (Düsseldorf 1963); Josef Zentis, Die rheinische Rübenkrauterzeugung (Phil. Diss. Cologne 1922); Ernst Engel, "Zur statistischen Ermittlung der Consumtion pro Kopf der Bevölkerung im Preussischen Staate", Zeitschrift des Kgl. Preussischen Statistischen Bureaus, Vol. 4 (1864), pp. 2128-135; Ernst Glanz, "Die Statistik des Zuckers im Deutschen Reiche seit der Einführung der Zuckersteuer (Leipzig 1900).

    10. See for meat consumption Gustav Schmoller, "Die historische Entwicklung des Fleischconsums sowie der Viehpreise in Deutschland", Zeitschrift für die gesamte Staatswissenschaft, Vol. 27 (1871), pp. 284-362; Rudolf Martin, "Der Fleischverbrauch im Mittelalter und in der Gegenwart", Preussische Jahrbücher, Vol. 82 (1895), pp. 308-342; Joseph B. Esslen, Die Fleischversorgung des Deutschen Reiches (Berlin 1912); Wolfgang Wittig, "Die deutsche Fleischversorgung in Vergangenheit, Gegenwart und Zukunft. Die Entwicklung der Fleischversorgung in den letzten 150 Jahren", Der Tierzüchter, Vol. 6 (1954), No. 18, pp. 451-454; Huckert, "Zur Geschichte und Statistik des Fleischkonsums in Deutschland", Zeitschrift für Sozialwissenschaft, Vol. 3 (1900), p. 109 seq.; Hans Feierabend, Die volkswirtschaftlichen Bedingungen und die Entwicklung des Fleischverbrauchs in Deutschland seit Beginn des Weltkrieges (Berlin 1928); Hans J. Teuteberg, "Variations in Meat Consumption in Germany", Ethnologia Scandinavica, ed. Nils Arvid Bringéus (Lund 1971), pp. 131-141; Wilhelm Abel, Wandlungen des deutschen Fleischverbrauchs und der Fleischversorgung in Deutschland seit dem ausgehenden Mittelalter, Berichte über Landwirtschaft, new.ser. Vol. 22 (1938), pp. 411 seq.

    11. The literature about fish consumption in Germany is less than meagre. There is only one comprehensive study: Günter Wiegelmann/Annette Mauss, "Fischversorgung und Fischspeisen im 19. und 20. Jahrhundert: Versuch einer quantitativen Analyse", Bela Gunda (ed.), The Fishing-Culture of the World (Budapest, forthcoming). See by comparison H. Chaloner, Trends in Fish consumption in Great Britain, 1700 to 1850, in: T.C. Barker, et.al., Our Changing Fare: Two Hundred Years of British Food Habits (London 1964), pp. 94-114.

    12. Benno von Martiny, Die Milch, ihr Wesen und ihre Verwertung, 2 Vols. (Danzig 1871); Paul Sommerfeld, Handbuch der Milchwirtschaft, 4th edition (Berlin 1898); F. Stohmann, Die Milch- und

Molkereiprodukte (Braunschweig 1898); C. Meinert, "Die Milchversorgung von Hamburg und Nachbarstädten" and A. Oeser, "Die Milchversorgung von zehn Städten der Provinz Westfalen", Schriften des Vereins für Sozialpolitik, Vol. 140, part 2 (München-Leipzig 1914); Wilhelm Fleischmann, Art.: "Milch und Milchprodukte", Handwörterbuch der Staatswissenschaften, 3rd. edition (Jena 1910), pp. 699 seq.; Jürgen Bücker, Die deutsche Milchwirtschaft im Wandel der Zeit (Hildesheim 1974); Ulrich Neuhaus, Des Lebens weisse Quellen (Das Buch von der Milch) (Berlin 1944); Johannes Riedel, "Die Milchwirtschaft", Handbücher der Wirtschaftskunde Deutschlands, Vol. 3 (Leipzig 1904); Hans J. Teuteberg, Anfänge des modernen Milchzeitalters in Deutschland, Alexander Fenton/Trefor Owen (eds.), Ethnological Food Research - Third International Conference 22. - 27. August 1977, Cardiff, Wales (forthcoming).

Chapter 9

CONCLUSION

Henri Baudet and Henk van der Meulen

A number of commentators were invited to the
Groningen Conference for each paper to be presented.
Each took the lead in the discussions relevant to
his field of specialization. *Peter Klein* (Rotter-
dam) and *Paul Klep* (Nijmegen) commented on the
Belgian contribution; *Patricia van den Eeckhout*
(Brussels) and *Jos Delbeke* (Louvain) were allocated
the Dutch paper. Maurice Aymard was unfortunately
unable to be present at the Conference so that commentaries on his contributions remained in abeyance.
The Japanese paper was provided with a commentary
by *Leonard Blussé* (Leyden) and *Angus Maddison*
(Groningen); the discussion of Latin America problems was initiated by *Gé Prince* (Groningen), *Jan
Willem Drukker* (Groningen) and *François Souty*
(Groningen/Paris). The British contribution was
discussed by *Frits van Holthoon* (Groningen) and
Richard Griffiths (Amsterdam). Finally, the edi-
tors of this volume acted as commentators for the
German contribution.

There is insufficient space in this volume to
reprint in extenso all the commentaries, or to re-
capitulate the six lively and often incisive discussions which followed the commentaries. A number
of theoretical problems, which arose in the course
of the debates, have already been dealt with by us
in the Introduction. We, therefore, restrict ourselves to three central themes: the standard of
living debate, the (macro-)economic basis of the
historical investigation of consumption and, finally, a number of suggestions for a revised formulation of questions and possible further research in
our field.

Paul Klep and Richard Griffiths brought the
discussion most decidedly round to the standard of
living debate, which, whether or not 'in disguise',
would have returned to the ambit of the specialists

in the history of consumption and, consequently, to the Groningen Conference too. Klep mentioned one or two features of that debate, which he was finding again in most of the papers, namely:

- treating real incomes (or even physical consumption) as a measure of prosperity;
- a predominantly (macro-)economic approach to consumption;
- a great deal of attention paid particularly to the working class;
- putting the emphasis on the material conditions of the working class.

Here we could add that the time limits of the research always lie within the period of industrialization.

With such a formulation of the (old) standard of living debate, it can indeed be said that there was some talk in Groningen of reopening it. In this connexion, we would emphasize that, as far as we are concerned, there is not a single objection to reopening the debate. History is frequently nothing more than seeing old questions in a new light. And this brings us to a second observation: 'Die Lage der arbeitenden Klasse' was studied with a view to weighing up the good and the bad that the process of industrialization had brought to society and, particularly, the workers. This was debated in the 19th century and, for the second time, again after the Second World War. The history of consumption, as we now study it, looks at the same process, for the most part, in the period of industrialization, but with a *different* objective and, for that reason, with a number of *different* methods of approach. For these, we refer to much that has already been said in the Introduction. There still remains the very question whether the nostalgia which echoes through the paper contributed by Peter Scholliers and Chris Vandenbroeke, when they talk about the Ancien Régime, and the same nostalgia which probably inspired Paul Klep to refer back to the old debate, does not proceed from a new aspect too, namely leisure preference. Critics of the industrial period, writing in the 19th century and later, whatever their political plumage, will certainly not have seen the presumed preference for leisure (which, incidentally, is open to question) as one of the virtues of the old society.

Inquiries into relations between consumption and business cycles, into the influence of political changes on consumption and, consequently, also

on the material culture of a society, inquiries
into economic backgrounds to (consumer) behaviour
are again new questions addressed to old material,
among other things. Every contribution to this
volume bears witness to this fact.

In this connexion, we also spoke of new
methods. By new methods, we mean not only the attitude and procedures of the cliometrists, but also
the more general tendency to make use of the theoretical arsenal of modern (macro-)economics. More
is meant here than Hartwell's analysis, referred to
by Paul Klep. And besides macro-economics (theories of distribution, growth and business cycles),
the historical investigation of consumption is, at
present, giving way to micro-economics (consumer
behaviour) and psycho-economics (in the area of
behaviour theories too). The beginnings of this
- and more - are to be found in these Conference
papers.

As the second point of our concluding remarks, we
should like to devote a few thoughts to the (macro-)
economic basis of research into consumption. The
contribution of David Felix and the observations of
his commentators offer a good opportunity for this.
Firstly, Felix explicitly goes into distribution of
income, besides economic growth, as a basic vari-
able. The studies of the 'developed' world mostly
proceed implicitly from a certain levelling in the
distribution of income as the result of industrialization and economic growth. Social emancipation
and the introduction of mass consumption go hand in
hand, so to speak. In our opinion, there is a
reason to challenge much in this area; if the data
affords significant possibilities, both European
and U.S. history of consumption would have to
devote greater and more incisive attention to income distribution. However this may be, the great
similarity of incomes in most Latin American countries presents us with specific problems.

Secondly, David Felix is concerned with 'interrelations'. The addition sum of individual
decisions - by whatever factors they may be biased -
has considerable consequences for the development
of the Latin American economies. Felix, for
example, refers to the propensity to 'conspicuous'
consumption of goods *not* produced in South America.
It is almost superfluous to say that the reciproci-
ty factor in relationships does not apply exclu-
sively to less developed countries either.

Problems which have recently occupied our own
attention in this context, i.e. theoretical eco-

nomic backgrounds, are of a micro-economic nature. An old question, which crops up again and again, is: What part is played by prices and, above all, by (relative) changes in prices in the shifts in the consumption pattern? The income elasticities which we have used in our contribution give no satisfactory answer to this question. We must work towards a system of price, income *and* substitution elasticities, with which many behavioural aspects too - again - must be involved in the research.

The third point, suggestions for further research, is relevant to this last observation. We shall *not* offer any programme here for future 'Research into the History of Consumption', but merely a few points, which have emerged from the discussions.

- Much research will have to be directed to improving the data stock, both quantitatively (the amount of data) and qualitatively (particularly the reliability of data). Research, such as Maurice Aymard's and Hans Teuteberg's, which, in itself, indicates a step in this direction, illustrates this point most clearly.
- With more and better data, it will also be possible (and necessary, as was rightly pointed out in various commentaries) to direct 'European' research to problems of income distribution and economic structure. Initiatives in this direction, to be found in the contributions of Scholliers and Vandenbroeke, Baudet and Van der Meulen and, to a certain extent, Minchinton, call for deeper and more detailed examination. As already said, David Felix's paper makes suggestions in this direction.
- In this connexion (distribution), the demand for more and better budgetary data, preferably from as many classes as possible, representing different levels of prosperity, is also important. Data from these budgets can certainly still be found for the recent past. We ourselves hope to stay working, inter alia, in this field in the future.
- A last suggestion with regard to economic backgrounds needs to be made too, particularly in connexion with our own work. We expect thatmore recent data, or very much improved older material, will make a theoretical link possible between (statistical) cross-sections and dynamic time series, and

so bring problems to do with distribution
and growth nearer to solution too.
- A more general point is the call for the
  integration of economic and social (socio-
  psychological) aspects into the research
  into consumption. In this respect, the
  Groningen Conference can be seen most certainly as a model for future ones.
- Finally, research into the problems of the
  lesser developed countries can, in our
  opinion, be useful in the study of (historical) consumer behaviour. The consumption patterns in countries where industrial
  development is beginning to get under weigh,
  can be compared to data derived from our
  own recent past. That the comparison
  should not be made rashly is evident from
  the contributions by David Felix and Mine
  Yasuzawa. Striking differences between
  'Western' and 'non-Western' reactions to
  industrialization and modernization: in
  economic structure, in distribution pattern,
  in cultural background, are precisely a
  stimulus - we have already said it before -
  to new (or different) reseach 'in our own
  field'.

Not only the discussions and conclusions which we
have drawn from them here, but also, of course, the
high quality, without exception, of all the contributions, substantiate the claim that it was an in-
spiring conference.